Sermons for the Christian Year

Sermons for the Christian Year

JOHN KEBLE

Selected and introduced by

Maria Poggi Johnson

WILLIAM B. EERDMANS PUBLISHING COMPANY
GRAND RAPIDS, MICHIGAN / CAMBRIDGE, U.K.

Wm. B. Eerdmans Publishing Co.
255 Jefferson Ave. S.E., Grand Rapids, Michigan 49503 /
P.O. Box 163, Cambridge CB3 9PU U.K.

Printed in the United States of America

09 08 07 06 05 04   7 6 5 4 3 2 1

Library of Congress Cataloging-in-Publication Data

Keble, John, 1792–1866.
Sermons for the Christian year / John Keble ; selected and introduced by
Maria Poggi Johnson.
p.   cm.
Includes bibliographical references.
ISBN 0-8028-2299-1 (alk. paper)
1. Church of England — Sermons. 2. Church year sermons.
3. Sermons, English — 19th century.
I. Johnson, Maria Poggi.   II. Title.

BX5133.K4S44   2004
252'.6 — dc22
2004047851

www.eerdmans.com

Contents

Contents

Foreword

Henry Parry Liddon once said of John Keble that "no-one ever lifted so many to heaven without mentioning it"[1] — an indication of Keble's character, and no less of the character of his Christian life and pastoral practice. John Keble's deep Christian faith was a religion of the heart, but not of a heart worn upon the sleeve. The notes of reverence, reticence, and reserve are characteristic of Keble, yet in no way diminishing the strength of his principles. In him priest, pastor, and poet were blended together. As Newman famously said, it was impossible to paint a man who would not sit for his portrait. Yet Newman, who had shrunk from meeting Keble when as a shy young man he was elected a fellow of Oriel, recognized in Keble an exemplar of holiness. From Keble in particular Newman learnt much of the Fathers, the seventeenth-century Anglican divines, and a sacramental understanding of the church and of Christian life. Conservative, shaped by the old High Church tradition of his father, yet touched by the same Romanticism as Wordsworth and Coleridge, Keble had a keen mind, formed by traditional classical studies, as his still significant *Lectures on Poetry* bears witness.

His contemporaries chiefly noted his holiness, expressed in a deeply attractive character. The novelist Charlotte Yonge, so intimately linked with Keble's Hampshire ministry at Hursley and Otterbourne, noted his

1. Sermon preached at the opening of Keble College Chapel, 1876.

"beamy eyes," which are evident in George Richmond's portrait of him, Richmond himself saying that Keble had one of the most remarkable faces he had ever seen *for one who had eyes to see*. Walter Lock, one of Keble's biographers, wrote of his "clear, brilliant penetrating eyes of dark brown," which "lit up quickly with bright merriment or kindled into fire in a moment of indignation." Sir John Coleridge wrote of "eyes full of play, intelligence and emotion," which followed you while you spoke and lit up when he answered you.[2]

The village pastoral ministry of his Gloucestershire childhood and first curacy at Eastleach bore fruit in the thirty years he served at Hursley, where he restored the church and offered a pattern of parochial ministry that expressed an Anglican ideal. Although Keble's advice and spiritual guidance were frequently sought, Pusey was not alone in blaming the Church for allowing Keble to remain the parish priest of a small and obscure benefice, though there is no hint that Keble would have wished for anything else.

What is most remembered about John Keble are his 1833 Assize Sermon in Oxford on "National Apostasy," which Newman reckoned as the beginning of the Oxford Movement, and his collection of devotional verse entitled *The Christian Year*, of which some poems have become well known as hymns. Keble's preaching has been much less well known, despite the collecting and publishing of his sermons after his death in 1866. His friend and biographer, Sir John Coleridge, wrote that Keble

> was not what is commonly called an eloquent reader or preacher; his voice was not powerful nor his ear perfect for harmony of sound; nor had he in the popular sense great gifts of delivery; but in spite of all this you could not but be impressed deeply by his reading and preaching. When he read, you saw that he felt, and he made you feel, that he was the ordained servant of God. . . . When he preached, it was with an affectionate, almost plaintive earnestness, which was very moving. . . . Like one of the old Fathers he seemed to have caught by continual and devout study, somewhat of the idiom and manner of Scripture.[3]

2. Quotations from W. Thorn Warren, ed., *Kebleland* (Winchester & London, 1900), pp. 1ff.; J. T. Coleridge, *A Memoir of the Rev. John Keble, M.A., Late Vicar of Hursley*, 4th ed. (Oxford & London, 1874), p. 565.

3. Coleridge, *A Memoir of the Rev. John Keble*, pp. 566-67.

Shortly after his death, the landlord of the local inn at Hursley was asked whether he thought Keble was a great preacher. He replied, "Well, I don't know what a great preacher is, but he always made us understand him."[4]

In assembling this collection of Keble's sermons Maria Poggi Johnson has been concerned to illustrate Keble's teaching on the great themes of the Christian liturgical year. There are echoes in these sermons of the style, rhythm, and theological emphasis of the great seventeenth-century bishop and theologian Lancelot Andrewes, whom Keble so much admired, though Keble's preaching has none of the elaborate conceits of Andrewes's exposition of his texts. Both Keble and Andrewes are characteristic in their excitement at Mary Magdalene's running after Jesus, because she is "full of love."

Keble seeks to lead his people in the sanctification of time, following the Fathers in using typology as the key to the Christian understanding of God's providential action in history. His sermons are both moral and sacramental, concerned to inculcate the habits of devotion that underpin the life of grace. His ecclesiology is both baptismal and eucharistic, avoiding the false antithesis between the two that is sometimes found today. There is a simplicity of language in these sermons through which Keble strives to connect with the very ordinary trades and patterns of life that his congregation pursued. The women at the tomb on Easter morning are plain and ordinary, yet called to deliver the overwhelming news of the Resurrection. The Blessed Virgin is an example of "deep reverence — a trembling, aweful sense of the presence and power of God." The depth of blue of the sky on Christmas morning is a sign not merely of the transcendence of God, but of the immensity of his love, which is even more wonderfully concentrated in the Child of Bethlehem. Common meals and meetings are to be sanctified by the Feast of the Eucharist. In Baptism there is an awe and wonder in the "conjoining of the Name of God and the name of the child." In being called by the Divine Name we are made partakers of the divine nature — a reminder of the importance of *theosis*, deification, in Tractarian theology.

In this judicious selection from Keble's sermons we have been given, as Maria Poggi Johnson says, an insight into "one of the great and formative minds of the Oxford Movement at its pastoral work, interpreting and communicating the movement's central ideas and principles" to the ordi-

4. Warren, ed., *Kebleland*, pp. 3-4.

nary folk of a Victorian Hampshire village. When Keble's *Sermons, Occasional and Parochial* were published in 1868, a quotation from Bishop Butler, so much admired by Keble, was placed opposite the contents page. It warned the reader not to expect any connection between the sermons "than that uniformity of thought and design which will always be found in the writings of the same person, when he writes with simplicity."[5] It is that "uniformity of thought and design" that we find in these sermons of John Keble, a "uniformity of thought and design" from which we can still profit as pointing us to Christian truth and the way of holiness.

THE RT. REVD. DR. GEOFFREY ROWELL
Bishop of Gibraltar in Europe and
Emeritus Fellow of Keble College, Oxford

---

5. Bishop Butler, Preface to Sermons, in John Keble, *Sermons, Occasional and Parochial* (Oxford & London, 1868), frontispiece.

Acknowledgments

I am indebted to many people for their intellectual, spiritual, personal, and practical support and encouragement, from my first encounter with the Oxford Movement onwards. Deserving of special mention are: my parents, Gian and Pat Poggi; A. O. J. Cockshut; Fr. D. Stuart Dunnan; Fr. Philip Ursell; Dan Westberg; Larry Bouchard; my colleagues in the Department of Theology at the University of Scranton; the Rt. Revd. Dr. Rowell; Catherine Butler; Bill Eerdmans and Jenny Hoffman. Very particular thanks are due to my husband Glen Johnson, and also to Bruce Robinson.

To Present Every Man Perfect in Christ: Keble, Hursley, and the Parochial Sermons

··

John Keble is most frequently introduced into accounts of Victorian religion, not as the dedicated country parson who preached the sermons in this book, but as the man who delivered the sermon on "National Apostasy" that heralded the start of the Oxford Movement. Although it rather preceded than instigated the *Tracts for the Times*, it is not inappropriate that the 1833 Assize Sermon be regarded as a milestone. John Henry Newman, the greatest figure of the movement's greatest years, himself "considered and kept the day" as the beginning of the movement, and Edward Bouverie Pusey, by whose name the High Church revival came to be popularly known after Newman's secession, called it, perhaps more accurately, an "era" in the movement.[1] However, the man whom Newman regarded as the "true and primary author" of the Tractarian movement was later to remark that he regarded his years with Newman and Pusey at the hub of English intellectual life as "a sort of parenthesis in my life."[2]

As parentheses go, it was a long and remarkably distinguished one, and very much of a piece with the narrative that it interrupted. At the time when he delivered his attack on the "fashionable liberality" and impa-

---

1. John Henry Newman, *Apologia Pro Vita Sua* (1864; repr. New York: Random House, 1950), p. 63.

2. Newman, *Apologia*, p. 46. *The Autobiography of Isaac Williams*, ed. George Prevost (London: Longmans, Green and Co., 1892), p. 118.

tience to be "rid of . . . moral restraint"[3] that characterized English society and politics in the 1830s, Keble was universally acknowledged to be one of the greatest minds and most influential personalities in Oxford. Coming to the university at the age of fourteen, he attained the second double first in its history and continued to accumulate prizes and honors. In 1811 he became a fellow at Oriel, then the most intellectually prestigious of the colleges. There at the age of nineteen he found himself thrown into the company of the brilliant, sophisticated and often abrasive philosophers known as the "Noetics." The devout and conservative Keble had little in common with the liberal and speculative minds of Richard Whately and Edward Copleston, but, despite his isolation from the central stream of intellectual life in the college, he was admired for his intellectual attainments and revered for the almost legendary sweetness and holiness of his character. It was not until the early 1820s, by which time he had become a tutor at Oriel, that he met the men who would form a party to rival the Noetics for ascendancy within the college and surpass them in broader influence. As Keble's friendship and alliance with Hurrell Froude, Edward Bouverie Pusey and John Henry Newman grew, these men became a recognized force within the college and university, making common cause in their opposition to what they saw as a growing liberal hegemony.

In their implacable and often irritable opposition to the forces of progress (as much as he was renowned for the gentleness of his nature, Keble could be astonishingly intolerant of those who disagreed with him) the Oriel colleagues and the broader circle that coalesced around them in the early 1830s were inspired by their devotion to the tradition of the English Church and the Universal Church. With his friends, Keble looked beyond what they saw as the barrenness of the eighteenth century and the chilly glare of the Enlightenment to the somber glories of the Anglican divines, William Laud, Jeremy Taylor, Richard Hooker and Thomas Ken, whom he had learned to revere from his father, and in the study of whom he had immersed himself as an undergraduate. Throughout his life Keble would recommend the works of Taylor, Lancelot Andrewes and John Kettlewell to those who came to him for spiritual guidance.[4] Keble had a special love for

3. John Keble, *Sermons Academical and Occasional* (Oxford: John Henry Parker, 1847), pp. 138, 132.

4. Geoffrey Rowell, *The Vision Glorious: Themes and Personalities of the Catholic Revival in Anglicanism* (Oxford: Oxford University Press, 1983), p. 22.

Hooker, whose works he edited, prefacing them with the remark that Hooker spoke directly to the plight of the modern Church, as

> a kind of warning voice from antiquity, a treasure of primitive, cath-
> olic maxims and sentiments, seasonably provided for this Church, at
> a time when she was, humanly speaking, in a fair way to fall as low
> towards rationalism, as the lowest of the protestant congregations
> are now fallen. Bold must he be who should affirm, that great as was
> then her need of such a defender, it at all exceeded her peril from the
> same quarter at the present moment.[5]

In much the same spirit as Keble undertook his edition of Hooker did he join with Pusey and Newman to edit *The Library of the Fathers*, a series of translations from the patristic literature that had fallen into considerable disregard over the preceding century. By displaying the genius of the primitive Church to their own age, they hoped to recall their ailing Church to her divine roots and to the catholic and sacramental theological vision for want of which she was falling an easy prey to the incursions of secularism, liberalism and infidelity. They also relied heavily on Bishop Joseph Butler for the philosophical language and tools to articulate the vision of universal sacramental reality that they learned from the Fathers.

The Tractarians' immediate and urgent struggle for dominance within the Church of England and against the spread of secularism in English society was a lost cause. But over the course of the century, despite the disaster of Newman's conversion to Rome and despite intense controversies and battles, the influence of the Tractarians, Puseyites or Anglo-Catholics, as they were variously called, did indeed revitalize the sacramental, liturgical, religious and theological life of the Church of England and played a vital role in the evangelism of the new industrial centers, thus strengthening the presence of the Church in the next century. The respect that Keble commanded throughout the country was an invaluable factor in the movement's persistence in the face of varied and fierce opposition. The "parenthesis" that his years at the center of the nation's intellectual and religious life marked for Keble ended, however, nine years before the defection of Newman, and long before the riots and the court cases that accom-

---

5. John Keble, ed., *The Works of Mr. Richard Hooker* (1831; repr. New York: Appleton and Co., 1845), vol. 1, p. lii.

panied the second phase of the Anglo-Catholic revival. In 1836, Keble, to use the words of Newman, "turned from the admiration which haunted his steps, and sought for a better and holier satisfaction in pastoral work in the country."[6] He accepted from a former pupil, Sir William Heathcote, a living at Hursley, near Winchester, where he remained until his death in 1866.

Keble did not altogether withdraw from public life when he left Oxford. His fame as the author of *The Christian Year* alone would have been enough to prevent him from retreating utterly into a life of pastoral anonymity, and his many friendships with prominent religious and intellectual leaders kept him involved, often more actively than he would have liked, in the pressing political, educational and ecclesiastical questions of the day. The depth of his certitudes made him a moral anchor for the Oxford Movement through many turbulent years: as Pusey's biographer Liddon remarked, "when all else had been said and done, people would wait and see what came from Hursley before they made up their minds as to the path of duty."[7] But, although Keble's voice continued to be heard and respected in the great world of Victorian religion after 1836, his principal involvement was with the little world of his parish and the circle of friends who gathered around the vicarage. In leaving Oxford for the care of a rural parish, Keble was returning to his roots. He was the son of a rural pastor, the vicar of Coln St. Aldwyn's near Fairford in Gloucestershire. Family tradition, temperament and religious training were unusually hard to distinguish in Keble's character, and dutiful fidelity to the tradition he had received from his father remained among his highest priorities throughout his life; although he far surpassed the elder John Keble in depth and understanding, the warmest commendation he knew how to give to any religious statement was to say, "Yes, that is exactly what my father taught me."[8]

Keble had already served a term as curate at Hursley, and having found there a most congenial atmosphere was delighted to return. Relations between the vicar and the squire were more than cordial: Keble's views on the proper order and relations of parish life agreed excellently with Heath-

6. Newman, *Apologia*, p. 17.
7. Quoted in Georgina Battiscombe, *John Keble: A Study in Limitations* (New York: Alfred A. Knopf, 1963), p. xvi.
8. Battiscombe, *John Keble*, p. 11.

cote's. Although notable in his devotion to the humblest of his parishioners and in his concern for the humblest of their needs, Keble's hereditary Toryism did not flag in the face of rural poverty and the hardships of the "hungry forties": the age-old hierarchies of rural life were, in his view, part of the providential order of creation. Heathcote, likewise, was a thorough conservative who was regarded by his tenants as an excellent landlord. Thanks in large part to his influence, the parish had been relatively unaffected by the rural unrest attending the vote on the Reform Bill. The local gentry formed a genuine community that was congenial in the extreme to Keble and Charlotte Clarke, the bride whom he brought to his new home and with whom he would have a happy, although childless marriage. The Moberlys, family of the new headmaster at Winchester, and the Yonges from nearby Otterbourne were cut to the same pattern of pious traditionalism. William Yonge's daughter Charlotte, whom Keble prepared for confirmation, was to become Keble's devoted disciple and one of the most popular novelists of the century.

These kindred spirits were, of course, not typical of Keble's parishioners, most of whom were tradesmen and laborers who had fallen into habits of religious and moral laxity under Sir William Heathcote's less dedicated and admirable predecessors. In point of religious understanding and interest they had less in common with the eager Charlotte Yonge than with the Hursley parishioner of the previous generation who, on being asked the meaning of "predestination," responded confidently that it was "some'at about the innards of a pig."[9] Among the descendants of this man Keble passed the rest of his days. To many, including Pusey, it seemed a shocking waste of talent that "through human mismanagement . . . the writer of 'the Christian Year' should, for the chief part of his life, preach to a peasant flock, of average mental capacity."[10] Although Keble might not have fundamentally disagreed with Pusey's description of his "peasant flock," his practice as pastor certainly did not reflect Pusey's disdainful assessment of them and their value. As firmly as he believed in and insisted on the traditional hierarchies of parish society, Keble had nothing in common with the notorious fox-hunting parson of the previous century, who

9. Yonge, *John Keble's Parishes: A History of Hursley and Otterbourne* (London: Macmillan, 1898), p. 88.

10. Keble, *Village Sermons on the Baptismal Service* (Oxford: James Parker, 1868), from the Notice by Pusey, p. iii.

looked on his situation as a pleasant and untaxing opportunity to lead the life of a country gentleman. Keble dedicated himself to the humble souls of his parish with the same commitment and energy he had devoted to the young intellectuals entrusted to him by the Oxford tutorial system.[11] As Charlotte Yonge enthusiastically wrote,

> the vicar was the personal minister to each individual of his flock — teaching in the school, catechizing in the church, most carefully preparing for Confirmation, watching over the homes, and, however otherwise busied, always at the beck and call of everyone in the parish.[12]

Keble's parochial work had the traditional savor of George Herbert's model of the country parson. It also had the fresh taste of the Oxford Movement. Charlotte Yonge commented that "the new state of things was soon felt,"[13] and the sympathetic Heathcote had to caution his new vicar against startling his conservative flock with what looked to them like new ideas and practices, however deeply those "innovations" were rooted in ancient Christian tradition.[14] Keble quickly reinstituted the long neglected tradition of daily services, and he increased the frequency of Eucharistic celebration initially to monthly and later to weekly.[15] He saw it as an essential part of his pastoral vocation personally to oversee the spiritual development of his flock, and he was deeply committed to the work of preparing the youth of the parish for confirmation. As Georgina Battiscombe puts it,

> the villagers of Hursley grew familiar with the sight of a lantern bobbing down lanes and across field paths late at night when wise peo-

---

11. Keble in fact wished that some of the "peasants" of Hursley would have the opportunity, if appropriately gifted, to join the privileged sons of gentry and aristocracy at the university. In his 1839 Crewian Oration he suggested that, by its inaccessibility to the poor, modern Oxford was betraying its roots. See Stephen Prickett, "Church and University in the Life of John Keble," in *The English Religious Tradition and the Genius of Anglicanism*, ed. Geoffrey Rowell (Nashville: Abingdon, 1992), pp. 204-6.

12. Yonge, *John Keble's Parishes*, p. 140.

13. Yonge, *John Keble's Parishes*, p. 99.

14. See Battiscombe, *John Keble*, p. 180.

15. Frequent communion, although not unknown in the previous century, was an exception, and it came to be an often controversial hallmark of Tractarian practice.

ple were comfortably resting by the fireside. The Vicar had gone out to visit and instruct some farm hand in his own home, some lad who could not come to the ordinary confirmation classes because his work kept him in the fields or with the beasts from dawn to dusk.[16]

The work of the pastor may have extended into cottage kitchens at night, but the center of the parish remained the church itself. Keble was far removed from the Gothicizing enthusiasm for church architecture that accompanied the second phase of Anglo-Catholicism, but he did have a deep appreciation of the religious importance of space, surroundings, and sense. He was blunt about reminding his parishioners of the need for regular attendance at services, in spite of all pressures of work or season, and for reverent and attentive behavior in church. Christ himself, he reminded them, by his own practice acknowledged the importance of "place, posture, time" to religious devotion: how could they presume to think lightly of them? He was dissatisfied with the church at Hursley, "the eighteenth century arrangement of which really prevented the general inculcation of the more reverent observances which teach and imply doctrine,"[17] and when he published *Lyra Innocentium* in 1846 it was with the express purpose of using the proceeds to build a better church for the parish — not an uncommon gesture from devout and wealthy gentry of Keble's generation. The main purpose of the new design was to do away with the old high box-pews — not an original part of the medieval church — thereby forcing the congregation "to lay aside any bad habits which might have grown up out of sight," and to replace them with benches, designed so as to make it "nearly impossible" for their occupants "not to assume a really devotional attitude."[18] In the weeks before the congregation moved into the new building from the barn where services had been held during construction, Keble exhorted them to take full advantage of the opportunities for personal reformation and contemplation that the design and fittings of the new church would present to them, and he expressed in particular the hope "that our new Church may never be profaned by rude, irreverent, wilful behavior, as the old one too often was."

Such, then, in brief, are the situation and the audience to which the ser-

16. Battiscombe, *John Keble*, p. 178.
17. Yonge, *John Keble's Parishes*, pp. 108-9.
18. Yonge, *John Keble's Parishes*, pp. 122, 118.

mons in this volume are addressed. As pieces of literature, theology or rhetoric, they do not aspire to the same heights as Newman's sermons. This is no accident: Keble thought the pulpit an inappropriate venue for displays of eloquence, however moving and effective, and disciplined himself deliberately to avoid any such display in his own preaching. Newman records one occasion on which Keble was so distressed by the praise he received for a particularly fine sermon that he made a point of preaching a weak and poorly organized one the following week.[19] Despite this policy of stylistic humility, Keble's parochial sermons have a real and characteristic charm and even elegance of their own. It is not here, however, that their unique value as documents of the Oxford Movement lies. The purpose and value of the movement lay, as its leaders intended it to lie, not merely in the stimulus that it gave to such minds as Newman's, but in its effect on the life of the Church of England beyond the ivory towers of Oxford. Without question, the Church needs great minds able to tackle demanding theological problems and great hearts ready to throw themselves into painful battles and controversies. But it also needs humble souls willing and able to work in obscurity for and among the Church's humblest members. Keble, in the opinion of those who knew him best, was all of these. His thought and life as theologian, as churchman and as pastor were thoroughly of a piece. So acute a critic as Newman confessed himself unable to produce a coherent judgment on Keble's writings, precisely because, as he said, "I have not the skill to discriminate what is of intellectual origin in his writings from what is of ethical."

> All I venture to say of him in this respect is this: — that his keen religious instincts, his unworldly spirit, his delicacy of mind, his tenderness of others, his playfulness, his loyalty to the holy Fathers, and his Toryism in politics, are all ethical qualities, and by their prominence give a character of their own, or (as I have called it) personality, to what he has written; but these would not have succeeded in developing that personality into sight and shape in the medium of literature, had he not been possessed of special intellectual gifts, which they both elicited and used.[20]

19. Newman, letter to Miss Trent, October 29, 1875, in Newman, *Letters and Diaries*, ed. Charles Stephen Dessain (Oxford: Clarendon, 1975), vol. 27, p. 371.
20. Newman, letter to Miss Trent, pp. 372-73.

In the sermons that Keble preached to the "peasant flock" of Hursley, then, we see one of the great and formative minds of the Oxford Movement at its pastoral work, interpreting and communicating the movement's central ideas and principles to the kind of average people with average minds and average lives who always have and always will constitute the greatest part of the Church, visible and invisible, in England and elsewhere. The sermons represent, in Pusey's words, "the teaching which, with the experience of years spent among his people . . . he thought most adapted to their needs,"[21] and he was evidently well able to judge what was of use to "his people" and to communicate it effectively. It is a mark of genius to be able to communicate to all audiences, and as one of Keble's parishioners said of him, "I don't know what a great preacher is, but he always made us understand him."[22]

Keble's primary goal in these sermons is to transmit to his parishioners the Christian vision that he had inherited in its essentials from his father and had worked out in greater accuracy and detail in cooperation with Newman, Pusey and Froude, through the medium of his academic sermons and essays and his contributions to the *Tracts for the Times*. The literature that came out of Oxford during the heady days of the movement was typically occasional, and frequently openly polemical. Keble and his brothers-in-arms in the service of the Church squarely faced their enemies: the many faces of infidelity and apostasy, offspring of the Enlightenment and of sinful human pride and rebellion, which threatened the Church in both her temporal and spiritual roles — liberalism, rationalism, utilitarianism, Deism, Erastianism. Keble's historic Assize Sermon is one of the most prominent examples of this type of broadside on the *Zeitgeist*. The parishioners of Hursley, on the other hand, were sheltered from the storms raging in the universities and in learned journals throughout England and the continent, and it was no intention of Keble's to introduce them to the dangerous temptations of controversy. The informed reader can certainly detect between the lines the host of perilous "isms" that stalked the common rooms of Oxford. But Keble refers in the parochial sermons to the vexed doctrinal and ecclesiological questions that had motivated the Tracts only when he has reason to fear that the danger has

---

21. John Keble, *Sermons for the Christian Year* (London: J. Parker), from the Advertisement by Pusey, vol. 4, p. iii.
22. Battiscombe, *John Keble*, p. 176.

come close to home and needs to be confronted directly. When he warns his flock of the wolves prowling in the big world outside Hursley, he typically does so in general and exclusively moral terms, such as "rebellion" or "wilfulness" or "independence," terms that he applies as closely to the moral and religious lives of ploughmen and shopkeepers as to those of prelates and college fellows.

If little in the Hursley sermons is directly polemical, the sermons do share with Keble's Oxford works the view of reality that they seek to impress upon their audience. This view is profoundly sacramental: the visible world is permeated through and through by the invisible world. Faith directs human attention to the true nature of reality and acts as the true guide and motivator of human moral endeavor. Keble inherited this vision in large part from his study of the Fathers, and he seeks to transmit it to his parishioners by the patristic technique of typology. Typology, in its narrowest sense, is the method of scriptural interpretation which assumes that Scripture in its entirety points toward the person of Christ and the Paschal mystery. Most specifically it assumes that the Old Testament history is full of characters, events and objects that look forward to Christ: types that are fulfilled in the Archetype of the incarnate God.

Typological interpretation of the Old Testament, initiated by Paul and developed with great sophistication by the Church Fathers, had been fundamental to the development of an integrated Christian theology. But in Keble's day the Fathers and their methods of reading Scripture had fallen into disregard: several generations of liberal criticism had largely persuaded Keble's contemporaries that the Fathers' tendency "first, to regard things as supernatural which are not really such; and secondly to press and strain what may perhaps be really supernatural in an undue and extravagant way" rendered them "inadequate judges of Christian truth, infected sometimes with Platonic, sometimes with Rabbinical error" who "need not be regarded at all."[23] Keble's most important contribution to *Tracts for the Times* had been an apology for the typological or "mystical" methods of patristic scriptural exegesis. In Tract 89, "On the Mysticism Attributed to the Early Fathers of the Church," Keble responded to the modern disdain for the roots of Christian tradition by mounting an impressively erudite and thoroughly documented defense of patristic scrip-

23. *Tracts for the Times by Members of the University of Oxford* (Oxford, 1833-1840), no. 89, pp. 3-4.

tural exegesis.[24] He argued that its typological and spiritual elements do not eclipse or interfere with the literal sense, nor with the moral purport of the text, but are carefully restrained and disciplined by the analogous example of Scripture itself, and that they do not derive from Platonic corruption but are deeply rooted in the earliest and purest truths of Christianity. The tract is forbiddingly learned, both in style and content utterly different from the Hursley sermons. But one sentence speaks to the heart of Keble's pastoral aims and homiletic methods. The Fathers, he claims,

> with an instinctive skill felt when any exposition or conjecture, which occurred to them, was (to use their own word) Ecclesiastical, and when otherwise. It was a happy sagacity, which could afford to dispense with all manner of critical and argumentative development. They were natives, and could speak the language idiomatically, without stopping to recollect rules of grammar.[25]

Keble aspires on behalf of his rural congregation to no less than the typological cast of mind that enabled the great and learned minds of the Fathers to "dispense with all manner of critical and argumentative development" and to make the mind of the Bible and the Church their own. The most humble Christian can acquire the habit of seeing the world as a text rich with divine grace and religious meaning. Indeed, Keble claims, it is the mark of a true type that it should be accessible not merely to the scholar or theologian but to the ordinary faithful Christian. In a sermon on the Tree of Life as a type of the Cross he tells his congregation,

---

24. Tract 89 was conceived as the first part of a longer discussion and ends with the words "to be continued." It was followed by Newman's notorious Tract on the 39 Articles, which brought the series to an abrupt end, and Keble's conclusions never saw the press. On the controversy surrounding Tract 90 see Newman, *Apologia*, pp. 147-55. Tract 89 is directed primarily against scholars of the liberal or Broad Church party, who were influenced by the historical/critical method penetrating Britain from the continent. Although the revival of patristic scholarship was the legacy of the High Church party, evangelicals, who formed the majority of Victorian Christians, drew heavily on typology in their theology and preaching. For a masterly account of this topic, and of the predominance and influence of biblical typology in Victorian religion and culture, see George P. Landow, *Victorian Types, Victorian Shadows: Biblical Typology in Victorian Literature, Art, and Thought* (Boston: Routledge & Kegan Paul, 1980).

25. Tract 89, p. 40.

it may be well, before I go further, that I should just tell you what I mean by "a type of the Cross." I mean some person or thing, so described in the Old Testament, that the faithful people of God, when they should read or hear of it long afterwards, might be put in mind of the Cross.

Keble was not unrealistic about the capacities of his congregation; he knew that an attempt to elicit from them the accurate definition of theological terms and concepts would likely end in comical confusions with the innards of a pig. And yet he dared to hope that, if they persevered as "faithful people of God," they might learn to speak the same idiomatic language as the Fathers. This language lives in the minds of its speakers, who can use it freely and creatively. But although natives speak "idiomatically, without stopping to recollect rules of grammar," they still are bound by the language as they receive it, and the language of typology, Keble makes clear, is not the invention of human ingenuity, but is divine in its origins.[26] The Old Testament types, he says, "were no doubt intended not only to prepare the men of old for our Lord when He should come, but also to help us in thinking worthily of Him, now He is come."

Many of his signs and tokens are double edged — theological and exegetical on the one hand, moral and practical on the other, referring directly to the daily lives and religious duties of his hearers.[27] Christian holiness or "worthiness" is Keble's burning concern, and thus when he speaks the language of typology in his own voice he is most comfortable and at liberty with the second, moral aspect.[28] Because of the fluidity and variety of his associations, and because of his constant insistence on the pressing importance of his types and shadows for the moral and imaginative lives

26. This is the conclusion of Jean Daniélou's study of patristic typology. Despite the "diversities and deviations" within the tradition, he writes, "we meet an agreement of all schools upon the fundamental types. This proves that we are face to face with something which is part and parcel of the deposit of Revelation." Jean Daniélou, *From Shadows to Reality: Studies in the Biblical Typology of the Fathers* (Westminster: The Newman Press, 1960), p. 288.

27. W. J. A. M. Beek, *John Keble's Literary and Religious Contribution to the Oxford Movement* (Nijmegen: Centrale Drukkerij, 1959), p. 123.

28. It was normal practice from the early centuries of the Church for the exegete to assume a greater liberty when working in the tropological mode than was permissible in the allegorical. See Henri de Lubac, *Medieval Exegesis*, vol. 1 (Grand Rapids: Eerdmans, 1998), pp. 15-16.

of his hearers, the effect of Keble's enthusiasm for typology is only rarely pedantic or oppressive, although we can suppose that much of his congregation often came away with only an impression of linkedness and interconnectedness. Such a general impression would have served Keble's purposes quite adequately, as a means of proofing the minds of his flock against the rationalism and fragmentation of modern liberalism, in whatever form it might penetrate the neighborhood of Hursley.

The influence of Joseph Butler, as well as that of the Fathers, is evident here. Butler, together with Aristotle, was the recognized authority on moral philosophy in the Oxford of Keble's day, and Keble honored him both as a philosopher and as the upholder of Anglican orthodoxy against the barren infidelity of Deism. He learned from Butler (and passed on to the young Newman, who developed it along rather different lines in the course of his own career) the maxim that "probability is the guide of life." The scope of the human intellect should not be overestimated, and absolute certitude in religious knowledge is not to be expected, the human mind being formed by Providence to learn about truth as best it can from the world around it. The safest — "safety" being an utterly crucial word for Keble's religious vision — path through life is that guided not by the speculative intellect but by hints and patterns gleaned from an attentive observation of creation and of the practical realities of human life. This principle was ideally suited to Keble's pastoral situation: it shields its adherent from the more unhelpful elements of Enlightenment epistemology and thus in a sense is truly forward-looking, strange though it may seem to describe the almost pathologically conservative Keble as being ahead of his time. The inductive, analogical method by which the Fathers read and interpreted the sacred text and the natural world was far easier to communicate to his flock than the rigorous rationalism that threatened, in Keble's view, the very foundations of Christian belief in the Church of England. Moreover, unlike the hated "isms," this way of seeing and understanding the world is valuable even to those who do not fully understand its principles or implications.

In view of Butler's influence, it is curious that this devoted admirer of Wordsworth and author of *The Christian Year* made minimal use in his sermons of imagery taken from the natural world — curious particularly as his parishioners were more thoroughly familiar with the sights, sounds, and sensations of the changing seasons than were many of the more genteel admirers of *The Christian Year,* whose lyrical imagery of the natural cycle points to the supernatural cycle of the liturgy. Pusey, noting this omission, remarked that "until he had entirely trained himself to it, [it] must have involved considerable self-denial to his poetic mind."[29] Keble's language was constrained also by the Tractarian principle of reserve in religious language, which in its turn was in part a reaction to the excessive freedom of evangelical rhetoric, particularly on the Incarnation and Atonement, which Keble and his friends felt showed a lack of proper reverence.[30] Occasionally in the Hursley sermons Keble hinted at this principle, at the practices from which it arose, and at the dangers of impiety they brought with them; the unreserved language of evangelical or dissenting preaching and tracts must have been familiar to his congregation. He cautioned that,

> I hear and read the name Jesus very often used in far too familiar a way. Even serious persons oftentimes make too free with that holy name, and so and in many other ways they show plainly that whilst they are willing to take our Lord for their best friend and only Savior they have by no means learned to reverence Him as their God and Judge.

In his earnest desire to avoid irreverent freedom on sacred subjects and to communicate clearly with his congregation, Keble tends to adopt two distinct types of language in his sermons. The unornamented, direct style that Pusey regards both as evidence of Keble's humility and self-denial and as a debasement of his talents, Keble uses for the commentary, illustration and exhortation that comprise a large part of the sermons. Despite the strange absence of natural imagery from the parochial sermons, Keble does not hesitate to draw illustrations from the mundane sides of domestic or commercial life as a way of pressing a point home to his parishio-

29. Keble, *Sermons*, vol. 4, p. vi.

30. Charlotte Yonge describes this aspect of Tractarian teaching and practice as follows: "Reserve, reverent reserve, was ever a characteristic of the teaching of that school of divines of which the 'Christian Year' was the first utterance. Those who had gone before them, in their burning zeal to proclaim the central truth of the Gospel, had obtruded it with little regard to the season of speaking, or the frame of mind of the hearer; and moreover there was a habit of testing the sincerity of personal religion by requiring that its growth should be constantly proclaimed and discussed with great fullness of detail." *Musings over the "Christian Year" and "Lyra Innocentium"* (Oxford: James Parker, 1872).

ners. When the date or the text compels him to address directly the great doctrines and the mysteries of the faith, however, he substitutes for his own plain words "the words of the Church": creedal, liturgical, and scriptural language, words and phrases either taken directly from the Bible or the prayer book or closely imitating their tone and cadences.

The effect of this approach is of a piece with Keble's central aim in his preaching, and indeed in all aspects of his life and ministry. In the advertisement to *The Christian Year* Keble explains the aim of the volume and the nature and function of Anglican liturgy thus:

> Next to a sound rule of faith, there is nothing of so much consequence as a sober standard of feeling in matters of practical religion: and it is the peculiar happiness of the Church of England to possess, in her authorized formularies, an ample and secure provision for both.
>
> The object of the present publication will be attained, if any person can find assistance from it in bringing his own thoughts and feelings into more entire unison with those recommended and exemplified in the Prayer Book.[31]

The object of the sermons could be put in much the same terms: to school the religious thoughts and emotions in accordance with the correct and sober standard of holiness and piety that the Church provides in her lectionary, her collects and her services. Keble appeals, in his sermons as in his poems, to the imagination. As feeling and reflection move naturally in response to the shifting seasons of nature, so should they be moved deliberately by the conscientious Christian in response to the cycle of the liturgical seasons. The liturgy is the divine script for a moral and spiritual drama, both the reenactment of salvation history and the actual enactment of personal sanctification. The pastor's sermons, like a director's instructions to his cast, lead his flock through the acts, asking them to identify emotionally, intellectually and imaginatively with the seasons, moods, and characters of the appointed readings and collects.

Advent, like evening, is the natural time for self-examination and resolution concerning the year past and the year to come. Christmas is the

---

31. John Keble, *"The Christian Year," "Lyra Innocentium" and Other Poems, Together with His Sermon on "National Apostasy"* (Oxford: Oxford University Press, 1914).

time for solemn reflection and wonder at the incomprehensible miracle of the Incarnation and its transforming effect on human life. New Year is a time when "all, who are not quite childish and thoughtless, naturally pause and look around them, to see where they are, and consider how they are going on." Any Christian "who has read his prayer book with any degree of attention" knows that Lent is set aside by the Church for the "especial exercise of repentance" and self-denial, in preparation for a full and proper realization of the greatest act of the drama. "What is the purpose of the holy Church universal," Keble asks,

> in appointing this particular time of year during which for so many days we are to follow Him step by step through all the stages of his bitter Passion first and then of his triumphant victory over death? Of course, what is meant is, that we, by the help of God's Holy Spirit, should make what happened to Him as present to us and as near to us as ever we can, that we should, as St. Paul says, so "have the mind of Christ," that when Good Friday comes we should spend that solemn day with some faint touch at least of His heavenly patience, charity and self-denial.

The avalanche of "feelings and imaginations proper to the three great days" are such that Keble makes a rare recourse to natural imagery to convey the impression they make on a "thoughtful person."

> Friday was a day of earthquake, of darkness, and desolation, the day, so to speak, of a great storm, . . . Saturday was a calm and clouded day, a day of pensive rest and regret mingled with quiet hope, but . . . this Sunday morning is all brightness and sunshine.

The enactment of these turbulent and shifting feelings and imaginations is exhausting, and with an unmistakable note of relief Keble remarks to his congregation on the Sunday after Easter that "the two holy weeks are now over, the week of sorrow and the week of gladness. The battle is fought, and the victory won, and we are come back again to the usual quiet times."

This cycle, repeated year after year, should lead the Christian on an upward spiral of virtue and holiness, her thoughts and feelings, schooled by repetition, coming ever closer to those "recommended and exemplified in the Prayer Book." The collects serve as a useful test of this growth, enabling Christians to ascertain something of their spiritual condition by their ability to pray them sincerely. The collects for the Sundays before Lent, for instance, "are very well fitted, and were most likely intended" as lessons in the "great Christian duties" of faith, hope and charity. That for Quinquagesima, or the Sunday before Ash Wednesday, is "such that who-ever uses it with a Christian mind must have true Gospel faith in the great doctrine of the forgiveness of sins." On the Sundays after Easter "a thoughtful man, though ever so simple, may by attending to the collects and lessons learn some question to ask himself, which may help him to judge whether he is going on as one risen with Christ or not."

The moral and spiritual drama of the liturgical year revolves around the story of Christ and around the great doctrines of Incarnation and Re-demption. Keble's treatment of the mystery of God made man furnishes the richest example of the relationship between the contrasting forms of language in his sermons. Indeed the juxtaposition of the plain language that he habitually uses for instruction and exhortation, with the elevated liturgical language that he uses when speaking about the great mysteries of the faith, is naturally suited to the incarnational theology of the ser-mons. He effects sometimes startling shifts in tone to emphasize the gulf between the divine nature and the human world, and the incomparable humility of God in taking on human flesh. Describing the scene at the Jor-dan when John the Baptist preached, he sketches among the crowd the fig-ure of "a humble quiet young man . . . working at the carpenter's trade . . . a poor but respectable artisan," a description that applied doubtless to a number of his own congregation, and a figure whom that congregation would have been as little inclined as the crowd at the Jordan to identify as the subject of John's prophecy. "This poor young carpenter," he goes on, "was the Christ: the very Christ, the Son of God, begotten from everlasting of the Father, the only sacrifice for the sins of the world, the King and God of the whole creation, the Judge both of quick and dead." Shifts like these — on occasion he even moves to the archaic form of verbs, "he hath," "he seeth," when making the transition — give new life to doctrinal and litur-gical phrases and formulae with which his congregation had been familiar from their cradles. Keble aims less to sharpen their systematic grasp of doctrine than to awaken their imaginations to the mysteries of the divine economy of salvation. Thus he follows the example of the Fathers in draw-ing on and evoking a variety of scriptural images, with freedom and flu-ency. Christ is "that warrior stronger than Satan who will not let him possess his goods, his ill gotten goods, our souls and bodies, in peace"; he is the High Priest, keeping perpetual sacrifice in heaven; his body is the veil of the temple that was torn in two; he "became the second Adam to undo the mischief done by the first Adam."

As eager as Keble is to help his flock to enter imaginatively and emotionally into each act of the Christian drama, he prompts them also to be aware at all times of the whole of the divine economy, resisting the Protestant tendency to concentrate exclusively on the doctrines of Crucifixion and Atonement. Even on Good Friday he remarks that "we must look not to the Crucifixion merely, but to the Incarnation as preparing the way for it, and to the Holy Sacraments as flowing from it." The blessings of Christ's Crucifixion are inseparable from the blessings of his risen life: "He died once for all mankind; but He lives again, lives for ever, to communicate the benefits of His death to the Church which is His Body, and to each Christian in particular. While you remember His agony and bloody sweat, you must not forget his glorious Resurrection and Ascension." Keble's confident use of suggestive imagery and his reliance on patristic typology keep him from becoming embroiled in the exposition of some particular theory of atonement. And yet, while he is more comfortable than many of his friends with the favored evangelical language of the atoning blood of Christ, he resists as firmly and explicitly as Newman ever does the evangelical understanding of justification by faith alone and assurance of salvation. "How many are there," he asks,

> who go on carelessly, or even wickedly, for many years, it may be through the whole of a long life, and when they see death and eternity at hand, make themselves easy with the reflection, that, however, they never trusted in their own works or doing, they always depended . . . upon being saved at the last by the infinite mercy of Him who died on the Cross for them!

The complacent Christian, secure of final salvation amid the wickedness of the world, is as blindly foolish as the soldier in the thick of battle who believes that he is in no danger. The "comfortable" doctrine of assurance imperils the very souls it seeks to reassure by blinding them to the other element of salvation more often stressed by the Catholic tradition, the holiness and obedience that Keble seeks constantly to cultivate among his congregation. He warns his parishioners constantly against the peril of this false security. This "great mistake" arises from an impoverished understanding of faith as consisting merely in belief or mental assent, an understanding that Keble is at pains to correct. He presents faith not as a condition or an act but, according to a much richer tradition, as a virtue or faculty, as "that which receives our Lord's resurrection as the eye receives light." Faith enables its possessor to grasp the divine presence in the sacraments of the Church: to see Christ in the bishop at confirmation and in the priest at the Eucharist. Like other virtues it is essentially a habit, attained by resolute discipline and practice; the acquired faculty of "looking towards things out of sight, as real things; turning your heart and mind towards them; giving up the things which are in sight for them." Faith is indeed "the great matter of our trial," the deciding factor in the eternal destiny of the individual soul. But it does its work by awakening the individual fully to the reality of the invisible world.

Thus faith is the foundation of the Christian vision which Keble's sermons illustrate and try to inculcate. It is the necessary condition of the sacramental or typological vision, in that the sanctified imagination can embrace the mystery of the divinity and the humanity of Christ. This transformed perception of reality is much more than a simple assent to doctrine, but even so it is not simply thus that faith is salvific. The Christian is saved by faith not merely insofar as her eyes are thereby opened to the pressing and immediate reality of "things out of sight," but only insofar as her behavior is thus transformed. The "true doctrine of the Cross," Keble insists, is that "faith saves us so far, as it makes us partakers of His Death; but we must not depend on what we call our faith, if our mind and behaviour in other respects be not such as to keep us joined to Jesus Christ, dying with Him daily to sin, rising unto righteousness." Faith is both a virtue and the necessary condition of other virtues — it renders the other world so present that motivations to virtue appear more real and pressing than the most powerful temptations either to vice or to indifference that the visible world can offer. Keble never tires of pointing out to his congregation that their lack of energy in devotion and in the pursuit of virtue belies their protestations of Christian faith, however firmly they may think that they believe.

Whether the inhabitants of Hursley choose to order their lives in accordance with the world they perceive with their senses or in accordance with that which they perceive through faith, it is to the invisible world that they will have to answer at the last. The task of preparing his flock to face the day of judgment is, in Keble's view, the final purpose of his pastoral vocation. "As the husbandman's work in the field all looks on to the harvest," he says in an Advent sermon,

> as the sailor's work on board ship at sea all looks on to the haven where he would be; as the physician's work all looks on to the full recovery of the sick person; so the clergyman's work looks on to the salvation of the souls committed to his charge. Our teaching, our preaching, our prayers, our Sacraments, our visits from house to house, whatever we do as clergymen, has no meaning, unless there be a day of Judgment. It is all in order to that one day.

Keble insists that the danger of damnation for the ordinary Christian is a very real one, and that the majority of humanity, perhaps even the majority of his congregation, will find themselves among the lost. But he never dwells on, indeed rarely mentions, the doctrine of hell. He does not try to terrify his hearers with the flames of eternal perdition, but rather to inspire them with a fitting sense of solemnity and awe at the thought of the moment of judgment itself, the inevitable encounter with all-seeing, absolute righteousness. When the gulf between the visible and invisible worlds is destroyed on the last day, all things will be disposed, naturally, to their proper ends. "A person who had gone on for many years singing entirely out of tune would be very ill-prepared to join in any perfect harmony," he points out; "so are we unprepared for heaven if we are living in any respect unholy lives." He urges his congregation to encourage in themselves the "godly and wholesome" fear of their own lives and actions; "what if my worldly untuneable heart should exclude me for ever from that blessed company?"

The moral life thus has a distinctly sacramental aspect. It is the place where visible and invisible worlds meet. By means of their moral conduct, human lives approach the moment when the veil of sense will be drawn aside, revealing the sacred order of creation. The aim of the moral life is to shape the individual will into perfect accord with the divine will, in preparation for this moment. "Angels and glorified saints are quite free, because their will is quite one with God's will: we on earth are training ourselves more and more in this true Christian liberty, as the good Spirit trains us more perfectly in conforming our wills to the will of our heavenly Father."

The world of sense is providentially ordered as a rigorous moral classroom for the perfection of human wills. Keble pays careful attention to the details of this training for eternity, which is the real business of human life. His insight into the moral life is perhaps the most significant and original thing about the Hursley sermons, even as, despite his brilliant intellectual achievements, his personality and holiness were the basis of his great influence. The foundations of holiness and the sanctification of the will are humility and repentance, the fruits of self-knowledge and careful attention to the voice of conscience. The discipline of humble self-examination is as fundamental a necessity to moral development as the keeping of accounts is to the commercial life. Apart from its universal psychological value, self-examination for the Christian is "a holy exercise, ordained by Almighty God, to be, as it were, a rehearsal of the day of Judgment." Indeed, more than simply rehearsing judgment, repentance preempts it. The man who places himself in imagination every day before the judgment seat and carefully enumerates his sins to himself and to God will not be judged on the last day. For this reason Keble exhorts his parishioners to attend carefully to the promptings of conscience, to encourage scruples and to resist the perilous whisperings of the world that they should not be so severe with themselves. Conscience is the voice of God, and it demands to be respected and cultivated accordingly. If persistently ignored it will become less and less audible until the unfortunate soul finds itself, by its own hand, bereft of the means of repentance and forced to face the moment of judgment with no rehearsal.

As human souls are providentially guided and instructed by the instrument of the conscience, so are they purified and perfected through suffering. Suffering, like self-examination, is a two-edged sword, with both temporal and eternal value, a meeting point between the world of sight and the world of faith. The Christian gospel is one of sorrow. All the forms that God has chosen for his worship "have something in them to remind us in some way of suffering, affliction, pain, self-denial, death." The "great act of solemn worship" among the Jews was the sacrifice of an innocent animal. The central event of salvation history is the "violent and bitter death" that the great Christian act of worship commemorates. Those who worship God are called to identify themselves, inwardly and outwardly, with the divine suffering. Keble reminds his congregation repeatedly that in patient resignation and submission to physical, mental or emotional pain they are uniting themselves to the redemptive suffering of the incarnate God. As the Christian who cultivates the habit of humble introspection engages in "a holy exercise, ordained by Almighty God, to be ... a rehearsal of the day of Judgement," so the suffering Christian participates in the cosmic events of the redemption. The trials of the parishioners of Hursley have sacramental and theological significance and bear both directly and indirectly on their salvation. Opportunities for suffering abound along the Christian's path through life, a path clearly marked by the demands of duty. Duty holds a central place in Keble's moral vision; to be dutiful is to follow the example of Christ himself, who prepared himself for his passion by faithfully carrying out the tasks of his earthly ministry, teaching, healing and ministering to demanding crowds. The duty of the individual, in however humble a state of life and calling, is the means providentially ordered for the salvation of her soul. Faith reveals the details of individual life to be ordained, not simply by chance and the social structure, but by God. The moral classroom that Providence makes of life contains "no end of the many little crosses which, if quietly borne in a Christian way, will by God's grace do the work of affliction, and help to tame our proud wills by little and little."

Patient and uncomplaining resignation to the petty irritations and the more painful burdens of daily life — "losing what we value, missing what we desire: disappointment in other persons, wilfulness, unkindness, ingratitude, folly, in cases where we little expected it" — is complemented by a deliberate discipline of self-denial. No matter is too trivial to be of value as an occasion to tame the will. Keble suggested to one correspondent eager for some form of ascetical practice that she deliberately contradict her personal taste in her choice of clothes.[32] Acts of self-denial of this sort are valuable particularly because of their scale; the more minute and quotidian they are the more easily they can be used to form the settled habits of character that, as Keble learned from the Aristotelian tradition, constitute virtue. He explains the power of habit to impress on his congregation the importance of the myriad tiny decisions of daily life. Virtue is acquired in much the same way as any skill, by repetition "until it become what is called natural to you."

> Imagine one learning to sing or to play on any instrument or to practice any kind of mechanical craft. He is commonly so awkward at

32. Keble, *Letters of Spiritual Counsel and Guidance* (1870; repr. London: Harper Collins, 1995), p. 102.

first that he feels as if he never could succeed, but if he have a real good will he perseveres for all that and takes double pains. He does something right once, observes how he does it and studies to do it again. So he goes on improving by degrees . . . and thus at last he overcomes his difficulties and learns the desired art or trade. So must we . . . learn goodness.

Decisions form habits, whether of virtue or of vice, and habits, developed over time, form the will after their own likeness. A perfect will, one purified of selfishness and rebellion and conformed to the will of God, is the final goal of human life and the only security on the day when the invisible world is revealed. Thus unpretending humble dutifulness in the most banal matters has the power to raise the Christian to the level of the great heroes of the faith. "Think of St. Stephen on his knees . . . or of St. Paul in prison," Keble recommends,

> think of the noble army of Martyrs, how "they were stoned, were sawn asunder, were tempted, were slain with the sword." Or rather, think of some young person quietly going on day after day in the faith and fear of God, in dutiful obedience to those set over him, in chastity of body and purity of heart, and see how resolutely and courageously, yet how calmly such a young person will reject the enticements of evil pleasure and the false shame of such as would laugh at him; think of such a case as that, and you will well understand what "overcoming the world" is.

When Keble exhorts his parishioners to the practice of the virtues proper to their duty — honesty in the poor; patience in the suffering; truthfulness and obedience in children; chastity in the young; sobriety and propriety of language in the lowest class of laborer; generosity in the rich; devotion, humility, faith and charity in all Christians — he reminds them that the effects reach far beyond the apparent increase in order and harmony, and that they are doing a great and eternal work in their own souls.

For all of Keble's insistence on the sacredness of the mundane as a preparation for eternity, he warns his flock with equal urgency against mistaking the respectability of a "quiet decent life . . . with a mere decent ordinary religion" for true holiness, or easy-going good nature and the fashionable virtues of "toleration" and "liberality" for the Christian virtues of patience, forbearance and charity. We should not be misled by the popular conceit "that we are sufficiently prepared for receiving Christ if we be honest and punctual and kind in our daily calling . . . that there is no special need of devotion, that we have no occasion to exercise ourselves in withdrawing from the world in order to have direct intercourse with God in prayer and deep thought and heavenly contemplation."

It is a characteristically English defect, Keble asserts, to elevate a purely secular morality of respectability beyond its proper sphere and, in effect, to "make an idol of what we call common sense." Christ himself, although united in nature with God, prepared himself for his trial by spending his days in duty and his nights in prayer. No Christian should be so "wilfully imperfect" as to believe that he can dispense with attendance to specifically religious duties: regular and devout prayer and the reading of Scripture and devotional books, faithful attendance at church, attention to the service. Above all he cannot hope to form his soul and will properly except through an established habit of private contemplation on the objects of faith. The Christian should, when alone, "naturally begin meditating on heavenly things, the presence of God, the mercies of Christ, the hopes and fears of eternity." If he begins instinctively to think rather of worldly plans and concerns, he has proper cause for anxiety as to the state of his soul. Keble, judging by the sermons, expected a good deal from his parishioners in the way of devotional habits. To anyone who does not faithfully turn to prayer and self-examination morning and evening every day he barely allows the title of Christian, although we may question whether the sermons paint a realistic picture of the religious habits of Hursley's hard-working inhabitants. We do know that as harvest season approached he felt the need to remind them in strong terms that the two months of intensive and anxious labor ahead of them were no excuse for staying away from Sunday services.

Keble, then, dwells repeatedly on the need for individual Christians to prepare themselves for the ineluctable encounter with the Judge by scrupulous fidelity both in the performance of the humblest duty and in prayer, devotion and self-examination. The salvation of the individual soul, however, is by no means the full extent of his focus in the sermons, nor is it the exclusive purpose of the pursuit of holiness. "Let us all understand," he tells Hursley, "that it is our bounden duty in our several callings to do our best and pray our best, that others may be turned to God through us." Keble is deeply and constantly aware that the lives and destinies of individuals cannot be isolated from the lives and destinies of their communities. The individual, if she is to be saved, must participate fully in the life of the Church, seen both as a cosmic sacramental reality, the body and bride of Christ, and as a local community.

In the world of Keble's rural England, the parish was the central unit of social organization. The parochial system was valued by the Tractarians as having its roots in the pre-Reformation English Church and in the stable hierarchy of feudal society. But Keble saw the parish as far more than a remnant of the ecclesiastical organization of medieval England. Parish boundaries describe a moral community with a coherence far deeper than the economic structures of rural life. Each member of a parish is responsible for his influence on his neighbors for good or ill, and this responsibility and this influence are eternal. The integrity of the parish community belongs to the sacred as well as to the social order; it is an integrity that even death and judgment will not dissolve, as they will not artificially isolate a soul from those who shared its life in the temporal order. Keble turns on its head the sentimental Victorian tendency to look on the resurrection of the dead as an occasion for blissful reunion with loved ones who have gone before: the experience will be terrifying and shaming rather than joyful for individuals who encounter souls that they have helped to ruin by bad example, even by such trivial misdemeanors as "smiling, and being or seeming amused at what we know to be unclean and wrong; by looking curiously, when we ought not; by letting things pass, which we ought to reprove."

The pastor is at the center of the parish community in both its temporal and its spiritual dimensions and will be held peculiarly accountable on the day of judgment for his flock. On that day, Keble tells the inhabitants of Hursley,

> each faithful Bishop or pastor will have to present each one of his own flock . . . face to face, to his Savior. Yes, each pastor may say to his people, "I am to present you; and I and not another: you the very same persons, to whom I am now speaking, whom I am seeing with my eyes and looking upon, will have to meet me that day before the Throne; we shall see one another, we shall know one another, we shall meet face to face, and we shall be conscious of the immediate bodily Presence of the Son of God on His Judgment seat. If through Him we are found worthy, I, even I myself, am to bring you, even you yourselves, to your several places on His gracious Right Hand."

The picture of the little rural community from Hampshire shuffling all together before the throne of judgment and being introduced to the Almighty, one by one, by their pastor Mr. Keble is a surprising one and strikes the modern reader as gently ludicrous. But for all its oddity it is an unusually rich and telling image and peculiarly characteristic of Keble, whose ecclesiology penetrated every aspect of his thought — moral, spiritual and political. It is on the subject of ecclesiology, and particularly the nature and status of the Church of England, that the contemporary controversies that provoked the Oxford Movement come closest to the surface of the parochial sermons, and Keble allows himself to touch most directly on the controversial subjects from which he generally tried to protect his parishioners.

At the center of the Tractarian agenda stood the Church of England's claim that the chain of Apostolic Succession had not been broken by the events of the English Reformation, and that the Anglican Church, the *via media* between the extremes of dissenting Protestantism and Romanism, was truly the "Catholic Church in England." Keble applies the doctrine of Apostolic Succession directly to the experience of his flock and instructs them directly and explicitly on its meaning and import. The historical principle of succession by the laying on of hands is one of the primary means of God's activity in the Universal Church; it is also a crucial instrument of divine presence in the little world of Hursley.

> We in this village, for instance, have our Bishop, the Bishop of Winchester, and we can trace up each link in the chain of his succession quite back to the time of the Apostles, just as certainly as we can trace the natural descent of our Queen Victoria from the old kings and queens of England.

Seen with the eyes of faith, when the Bishop comes to Hursley for confirmations, or for the consecration of the new church, it is as one of those "whom Christ has made ministers and stewards of his mysteries," and through him it is really Christ who confirms and consecrates. Through his or her confirmation, each member of the parish has a direct historical, as well as a sacramental, connection with the apostolic Church.

The most crucial grace and function of the Church, and that to which all else points, is sacramental: in the sacraments the ordained minister of the Church not only instructs people about Christ and exhorts them to seek and serve him but also makes him actually present among them. The sacraments are at the heart of Keble's preaching, of a piece both with his theological vision and with his views on the proper status and nature of the Church of England. The repristination of classical sacramental theology and practice that had become increasingly neglected during the long dry years of the eighteenth century was the Oxford Movement's most enduring contribution to the life of the modern Church.

The effects of Tractarian sacramentalism eventually spread far beyond the confines of the High Church party, but the revival was not accomplished without considerable struggle and controversy. To a Church that had become accustomed over the preceding century to a rather loose understanding and practice of the sacraments, the Tractarians' insistence on the doctrines of Baptismal Regeneration and the Real Presence and their practice of frequent communion were regarded distrustfully as smelling of papistry. Newman's conversion served to heighten suspicions about the integrity and patriotism of these most committed of Anglicans, and public and official hostility in turn increased the High Church conviction that the forces of evil were attacking the Church through the agency of an increasingly secular state. This state of mutual suspicion resulted in the rather odd phenomenon of nuanced and erudite questions of doctrine and interpretation being debated in courts and newspapers and in forums more typically associated with matters of state and policy, not with matters of mystical theology. The Gorham case, in which the Privy Council overruled a High Church bishop on a question of baptismal doctrine, is the best-known instance.[33]

The Eucharist was likewise the source of dissension and suspicion, particularly as the effects of the Oxford Movement on this sacrament were much more evident. All Anglicans had always received baptism as a matter of course, and the contribution of the movement was merely to assert a much higher interpretation of the sacrament than had long been popularly held. As regards the Eucharist, on the other hand, both doctrine and practice were at stake. The High Church party asserted the doctrine of the

33. In 1847 the Privy Council ruled in favor of an evangelical clergyman whom Phillpotts, the High Church bishop of Exeter, had refused to institute to a living because he did not hold the doctrine of Baptismal Regeneration. The High Church party was horrified by the implication that an arm of government had a right to overrule episcopal power on a matter of doctrine. For a full account of the Gorham case see Owen Chadwick, *The Victorian Church* (London: Adam and Charles Black), vol. 1, pp. 250-71.

Real Presence of Christ in the Eucharist — a *via media* between Roman transubstantiation and the symbolic or purely commemorative theories of Protestantism. At the same time they encouraged more frequent celebration than had become common practice. In the first part of the nineteenth century it was possible to go to church weekly and receive communion less than once a year. Under the influence of Tractarian teaching more frequent celebrations were instituted, and gradually during the 1840s and 1850s the practice of first monthly and then weekly celebration became widespread throughout the Church.[34] Hursley was no exception; when the congregation moved into the new church, Keble announced "in fear and trembling" the institution of weekly communion. Several years earlier the controversies engendered by the Eucharistic theology and practice of the High Church party had penetrated the quiet confines of Hursley. In 1841 Bishop Sumner of Winchester, whom Keble frequently recommended to his parishioners as the token of Christ's presence among them, rejected for the priesthood Keble's curate because of his views on the Real Presence. Keble, probably not without some reason, interpreted the Bishop's act as an indirect attack on himself, and he tried unsuccessfully to draw the fire intended for the unfortunate curate. A decade later he served, with considerable trepidation, as advisor to two more prominent churchmen who found themselves under attack for their Eucharistic theology.

For all this, the bitterness of controversy never marks the sacramental teaching in Keble's Hursley sermons. When he speaks about the status of the Church of England a faint edge of defensiveness is sometimes evident, although doubtless only a few members of his congregation would have noticed it or understood its significance; but when his subject is the sacraments of the Church, no such tension is evident. Keble's understanding of the sacraments is so profoundly intertwined with the whole of his thinking that it is impossible to separate sacramental from pastoral concerns in the context of the sermons. In particular the doctrine of Baptismal Regeneration, over which battles were fought in the world outside, is mentioned in almost every sermon. Keble speaks of the vocation, destiny and duty of the souls of Hursley almost invariably with some explicit reference to the transformation they underwent in the waters of baptism. It is hardly an exaggeration to assert, as does Yngve Brilioth, that the Tractarian *via media*

34. Chadwick, *The Victorian Church*, vol. 1, p. 514.

between Protestant "justification by faith" and Roman Catholic "justification by obedience" is "justification by Baptism."[35] The bizarre reality of
water transforming a human soul from death to life is as fundamental to
the economy of salvation as the bizarre truth that "our redemption, and
that of the whole world, depended on a child in swaddling clothes." The
symbolism of baptism looks backward to the death and resurrection of
Christ, and forward to the daily life of self-denial, the continual death to
self and regeneration to divine life that constitute the Christian path. The
regeneration effected by baptism is not merely notional; Keble goes so far
as to suggest that the conscience, the voice of God in the soul, is granted
only at baptism, and that without it the individual remains in a "natural
heathenish condition," with no hope of attaining to self-knowledge and
salvific repentance.

If baptism is really transformative of fallen human nature, if it is really
the means whereby we will be readmitted to the garden from which Adam
was cast out, then "the sacrament of Holy Communion is the tree of life in
the midst of that garden." Keble's views on the Eucharist are at the heart of
his vision. In his treatise "On Eucharistic Adoration," described as "the
most technically theological of all his writings," he draws on both patristic
and Anglican sources to defend his view of the sacrament.[36] The depth of
erudition and conviction and the thorough immersion in the subject that
inform the treatise are as evident in the parochial sermons. In both treatise
and sermons he asserts a literal interpretation of the words of institution
and upholds unequivocally the doctrine of the Real Presence of Christ in
the Eucharist. Keble never gives his congregation any hint that such doctrines are disputed anywhere. Instead, he takes every occasion that text or
topic or season offers to press home both the reality of Christ's immediate
presence where the sacrament is being celebrated and the immense importance of that presence for all Christians. The sacrament is the central
mystery of both human and divine life, the place where the invisible world
penetrates the visible. The sacrifice that Christ offered on the cross he offers continually: openly in heaven before the angels; and on earth, veiled
in the elements. At the altar, to which everything in the church directs the
worshiper's attention, it is Christ, not the priest, who truly ministers the

35. Yngve Brilioth, *The Anglican Revival: Studies in the Oxford Movement* (London: Longmans, Green and Co., 1933), p. 283.
36. Beek, *John Keble's Literary and Religious Contribution to the Oxford Movement*, p. 152.

sacrament. To the altar, then, Christians must come to receive the nourishment that will enable them to continue the journey begun at baptism.

As passionately as Keble instructed his congregation on the sacredness and importance of the sacrament, he did not find it easy to persuade them to receive it. There is considerable evidence in the sermons that Keble faced a challenging pastoral predicament at Hursley with regard to the sacrament. Part of Newman and Keble's pre–Oxford Movement agitations within Oriel was their opposition to the practice of allowing, and even expecting, the most dissolute undergraduates to receive communion regardless of their conduct, a practice that Newman described as a "gross . . . profanation of a sacred rite."[37] Keble felt to some extent the necessity of handling the same issue at Hursley. To receive the sacrament lightly or unworthily, without proper preparation and penitence and without suitably devout thoughts, is a serious sin that does the guilty soul "the greatest hurt." Paul warned the Corinthians that the unfit communicant "eats and drinks judgment on himself." Keble is more explicit: their sin "is the same, as if they had gone by whilst Joseph was laying Him in the grave and had insulted His blessed body."

By far the greater challenge, however, to judge by the frequency with which Keble raises it, was not that of warning off unfit communicants, but that of encouraging his parishioners to communicate at all. All members of the church were baptized: he could simply remind them of the transformation they had undergone, and exhort them to remember daily the momentous significance of their baptismal promises. But with regard to the second sacrament he all but pleads with his congregation to claim the greatest privilege of their baptism. Numerous sermons give the impression that the people of Hursley were so well aware of the seriousness of the sacrament and the perils of unfit reception as altogether to prevent them from receiving it. Doubtless the simple and universal unwillingness to accept change — a phenomenon at least as evident in parish life as in any other human institution — was also responsible for keeping Keble's parishioners from communicating in the numbers and with the frequency he desired: the change from infrequent to weekly celebration must have been too great and too rapid for them to adapt to willingly or with ease. Whether from timidity and scrupulosity or merely from habit and indifference, it is evident that many of Keble's congregation did not receive the

37. Ian Ker, *John Henry Newman* (Oxford: Oxford University Press, 1988), p. 38.

sacrament, and that Keble found this very troubling and missed no opportunity to encourage them in the strongest terms to change their ways.

The doctrine of the Real Presence in the Eucharist was not merely a theological issue for Keble but one of immense and pressing pastoral importance. Christ is present in the Eucharist "with such grace as is promised to nothing else that is done here below." To reap the benefits of Christ's atoning sacrifice, the Christian must not only seek and accept forgiveness but also partake of Christ's risen life by the means divinely appointed for that purpose. To the *via media* formula of "justification by Baptism" Brilioth might well have added "justification by worthy reception of the Eucharist": Keble is as forceful on this point as on any. The sacrament is the means ordained by God to bring human souls into communion with Christ, and as such it is an indispensable part of the gospel and truly necessary to salvation. "To depend, as some do, on spiritual communion merely, the communion, as it is called, of faith and prayer alone," is to risk one's salvation, for there is no promise attached to such communion. Love, fear and obedience should all bring the Christian to the communion rail; those who willfully ignore such a pressing element of their duty have little reason to hope that they will be counted on the side of Christ. Keble encourages the newly confirmed to take advantage of this crucial moment in their religious lives to prepare themselves immediately to receive. He does not hesitate to issue sterner warnings to those who hold back from long habit and indolence: "Good intentions I dare say you have. I dare say you think you shall begin to prepare yourselves and come by and by. But remember that a wise and good man used to say that 'the road to hell is paved with good intentions.'"

The duty of regular communion lies "very near the heart and root of the doctrine of the Atonement." In fact, in his teaching on the Eucharist all of Keble's theological and pastoral thought comes together. Here the sacramental and typological principles are gathered into a point. Here the divine world that faith perceives penetrates the world of sense and demands a positive response of obedience. To refuse the demand and neglect the duty of communion is more than a simple failure of obedience; it constitutes a rejection of the life of faith, of the Christian vision that Keble labored to instill in the hearts, minds and imaginations of his parishioners. To neglect communion is, in fact, to capitulate to the liberal, rationalist, secularizing forces that threaten the status and future of the Church of England and imperil the souls of her children. The voice of secular reason, which disdains the mystical vision of the Fathers and regards the sacramentalism of the High Church party as superstition unworthy of the nineteenth century, is the voice of the serpent in the garden, the voice that led mankind to its ruin. "Think not to say to yourselves," Keble warns those inclined to belittle the importance of communion,

> these are but slight and easy things; how can so much depend on them? *How*, and *why*, are not good words, to be spoken by a creature to his creator. Remember by what sort of disobedience sin and death came into the world. Was it not by an outward action, the most easy and indifferent in itself, that can be imagined? was it not by just tasting of a fruit? In a word, was it not by a kind of sacramental act, a sacrament of death and evil? Why then should we hesitate to believe all that the word of the Lord tells us of our sacrament of life and good? If we will not believe what Christ tells us of the one, "In the day that thou eatest thereof, thou shalt surely live," what reason have we to think we should have believed what the same word told Adam concerning the other, "In the day thou eatest thereof, thou shalt surely die"?

In Christ's sacrifice at Calvary and in the Eucharistic feast, God has freed humanity from the deadly effects of Adam's sin. It is the goal of all of Keble's work and preaching to persuade the souls under his charge to avail themselves of that freedom, to fix their attention on the divine presence in the world, to attend to the guiding voice of Providence in every detail of their lives, and thus by duty, by devotion, by repentance and by the grace of the sacraments to prepare for the moment of judgment, when the veil is drawn aside and the invisible world made plain to all.

Keble's reputation, considerable among his contemporaries, has dwindled since his death. Not only has he, understandably, been overshadowed by Newman, but his own profound and pervasive conservatism can be alienating to the modern reader, who may be tempted to write Keble off as no more than quaint, and to dismiss his sermons as period pieces of purely antiquarian or scholarly interest. For this reason it is worth pointing out to the reader of these sermons that embedded in them are many themes and insights of burning interest and relevance to our own age. Keble fought passionately against the rationalism of the Enlightenment and the social progressivism of his own century. While we have thoroughly assimilated most of what Keble rejected, the academy and the Church — in a society characterized by a pluralism whose manifestations would have bewildered and terrified Keble — are still struggling with many aspects of the Enlightenment legacy. Many of the themes and methods of the sermons, which I have dealt with above primarily in historical perspective, speak directly to these struggles, and I would like to close by touching briefly on those concerns of Keble's which are most immediately relevant to the contemporary reader.

In the first place is the inseparability of the intellectual and the moral. In recent years the academy has come to regard with increasing suspicion the proposition — an article of faith for Enlightenment thought — that ideas are best understood if abstracted from any context and regarded with impartial detachment as free-standing entities. Keble understood that ideas and beliefs cannot be wrenched from their roots in the lives and practices of individuals and communities without losing much of their significance. Religious belief or the lack of it is not merely an assent of the reason to abstract ideas; rather, it is deeply influenced by experiences, fears, desires, temptations, acts and choices, and it has, in its turn, far-reaching moral and practical implications.

Closely linked to this is the inseparability of the meaning of texts from the tradition in which they were written and through which they are read. Keble's commitment to the typological and analogical methods of reading Scripture manifest his understanding that texts and traditions have an inner logic of their own that must be respected; to attempt to extract meaning from a text by subjecting it to a method derived from outside itself is to distort and misuse that text. Keble's defense of patristic typology against the attacks of a corrosive scientific rationalism prefigures some of the crucial themes of modern literary studies.

Finally, Keble was deeply aware of the inseparability of the individual's life from that of his or her community. We are becoming more sensitive to the fact that people are not primarily isolated individuals whose membership of groups is a matter of secondary importance, but that individuals not only belong to but receive their identity, to a considerable degree, from the communities and cultures to which they belong and cannot be properly understood or fully respected except in relation to those communities and cultures. Keble knew that Christian belief and life are not primarily private matters that occur in accidental conjunction with the individual lives of other Christians; rather, they are constituted by participation in the liturgical and ritual life of the Body from which they cannot be separated. To be a Christian is to live with others through the drama of the Church's year, to join with others, present and absent, living and dead, fellow parishioners and the communion of saints, in telling and retelling the Christian story, and to be transformed, heart and mind, by the telling of that story.

A NOTE ON THE SERMONS

The texts from which the sermons in this volume are selected were assembled and collected by Keble's nephew and published in the 1870s by J. Parker in eleven volumes, two volumes containing prefaces by Pusey. Sermon 22 is taken from *Village Sermons on the Baptismal Service,* a series of commentaries on the service that Keble delivered in 1849 and 1850, which was published in 1868, again by J. Parker, and again with a brief preface by Pusey.

In preparing the sermons for this volume I have borne in mind that Keble deliberately steered away from rhetorical or literary display and sought only to communicate to his flock the truth of the gospel as compellingly as possible. I have taken this as license to make some small alterations — primarily, although not exclusively, to Keble's heavy and eccentric punctuation — in order to remove what seemed to me to be unnecessary barriers to a contemporary reader's understanding of the text. Keble appears to have sometimes made scriptural quotations from memory (his memory, of course, of the Authorized Version) as they are not all fully accurate. I have reproduced Keble's versions as they appear in the original edition, and, for the convenience of the reader, have provided sources for all citations, whereas the original edition provides sources for perhaps 15 percent of Keble's scriptural references.

In making my selection I have kept in mind a number of goals. In order to give a sample of Keble's treatment of the central doctrines of Christianity I have included a sermon from each of the major dates of the Christian calendar. For the same reason, and because the cycle of the liturgical year was so important to Keble's pastoral and homiletic method, I have arranged the sermons liturgically, rather than according to the year in which they were preached. The only exceptions to this rule are the last three sermons, preached to prepare his congregation for, respectively, a baptism, the consecration of the new church at Hursley and an episcopal visitation.

Around this framework I have tried to build a selection of sermons that accomplished my other goals. I wanted to give the reader a taste of the variety of styles and moods of Keble's preaching: thus there are sermons that are primarily theological in content and method, and others in which exegesis or pastoral concerns prevail. The little sermon for Ascension Sunday, to give one example, was included as an instance of the rare occasions on which Keble allowed himself to be carried away by a spirit more devotional and poetic than practical or doctrinal. I have given rather little space to sermons that deal primarily with the theological, ecclesiological and sacramental issues that were the particular concern of the Oxford Movement — topics of considerable interest to the scholar or historian, but perhaps of little to other readers. Of much broader interest, and more fully represented here, are sermons that exemplify Keble's profound concern for and understanding of the moral and spiritual life and that give the reader a flavor of Keble's own personality. The two tasks are effectively inseparable, and indeed the most random selection of sermons could hardly fail to accomplish them both. Keble's personality is the key to the great influence he wielded over a mind such as Newman's and over the whole tenor and history of the Oxford Movement. The key to that personality is a deep and simple love for holiness, for the life ordered in all its details to the work of repentance, obedience and receptivity to the divine will. As no duty of daily life is too trivial to merit the careful attention of the Christian dedicated to the pursuit of holiness, so no sermon is too plain, no language too simple, no audience too humble for the profound expression of the beauty of the dedicated life.

MARIA POGGI JOHNSON

Conscience, an Earnest of the Last Judgment

Volume 1, Sermon 12

ADVENT

"If our heart condemn us, God is greater than our heart and knoweth all things."

1 JOHN 3:20

These words refer to the great duty, the universal, indispensable duty, of self-examination, and therefore they are well suited for our consideration, at this time of Advent in particular. For as the evening is the natural time for examining oneself concerning the past day and forming good resolutions for the next, so is Advent concerning the past and the next year. The great day of judgment, the second coming of our Lord, begins now to be set before us, with all its terrible circumstances foretold by Himself in order that we, truly judging and trying ourselves, may the more worthily keep our Christmas, the memory of His first coming, and not throw away His unspeakable favor.

And this so much the more as the world grows older and we draw nearer our own latter end. According to the words which you heard in the Epistle today, "Now it is high time to awake out of sleep, for now is our salvation nearer than when we believed. The night is far spent, the day is at hand: let us therefore cast off the works of darkness, and let us put on the armor of light. Let us walk honestly as in the day" (Rom. 13:11-13).

In this place the Church urges us to consider Advent as our morning twilight, as our preparation for the coming year. But as no one can rise up and go about his day's work properly without having well considered his own former failures and weak points, so we shall do rightly to regard Advent as our evening twilight also, using it as a time to pause and look back upon the past year, and asking ourselves such questions as these: "What have I done? How have I employed myself? What growth have I made in good habits? Where, in short, am I now, compared with where I was this time last year? Am I nearer God or further from Him? Were I to be taken at this moment, would my condition be better or worse?"

These are the sort of questions we should ask — not with any expectation of being able certainly to find out the right answer, but with the certainty of finding enough to alarm us at least and put us on our guard, and with the wholesome resolution to keep such awful thoughts continually before us and to live more wakefully, if so it may be, in the new year now beginning than we have in the past year.

Everybody, even the most worldly person, sees at once the advantage of thus looking into things and examining oneself from time to time. Everyone knows the absolute necessity of casting up accounts in trade or business, of reviewing at set periods the conditions of one's farm or shop or household, of stopping mischiefs in the beginning, before they get too bad to be mended. Everyone feels how good it must be for him to "stand in awe": to put his heart and conscience from time to time more immediately before his God, who he knows is always watching it, "to commune with his own heart and in his chamber and be still" (Ps. 4:4). Such exercises keep a man's conscience tender. They give him a better chance of remembering and repenting of sins past, of preparing and bracing himself against future temptation. If you want, for example, to break yourself of anger and passion, common sense teaches you that one most likely way is to consider every night how far you have transgressed in that way, and every morning what is likely to provoke you, so that you may prepare your heart for the danger to come and humble your soul for the transgressions that are gone by, both in the fear of God.

All these are what may be called the *natural* advantages of regular self-examination, and it has been recommended, and no doubt practiced, for the sake of such advantages as these by wise and good men who as yet knew nothing of Christ. But now we, who believe the Creed and know that Christ will come to judge us, have learned to consider this exercise in a far more aweful and mysterious way. To a Christian man — duly considering what Christ's Gospel teaches of the things out of sight and of the way in which it has pleased the Almighty to connect them with the things in sight — to such a one solemn self-examination, at certain times, is far more than a prudent precaution, invented or adopted by himself to keep his passions in order. To him it is a holy exercise ordained by God Almighty to be, as it were, a rehearsal of the day of judgment.

As our nightly sleep is an image of death, so the nightly self-examination of a thoughtful person is in some sort an image of the last great day. As the Holy Communion is the earnest and pledge of heaven, so the trial and judgment of our own selves, which we are ordered to practice before the Holy Communion, is a shadow of that aweful hour when we shall all stand before the judgment seat of Christ. As St. John the Baptist, with his severe calls to repentance, came before our Lord, so Christmas comes after Advent, the remembrance of judgment, the warning call, "Behold the Bridegroom cometh; go ye out to meet Him" (Matt. 25:6).

In a word, whenever God visits in graciousness, it will go well with those who have prepared themselves to receive Him by deeply fixing their hearts on the thought of Him as now and always present within us to be our Judge, and by examining themselves accordingly, as in that fearful presence.

I say "now and always present within us," for is it not true that what we call conscience, that inward sense of right and wrong which every man feels more or less within him, now accusing, now excusing, now whispering peace, and now remorse and self-reproach — is it not true that this is the voice of God? Is it not as the faint low murmurs which are sometimes heard in the air before a thunderstorm? And are we not sure that what they tell us of the sentence to be passed on our misdoings will be repeated in such tones as shall shake heaven and earth when the great day shall come?

A parent, for example, neglects or ill-uses his child. If he ever feel shame and confusion at thinking of it now (and surely all who sin against their own children must be more or less uneasy, however present temptation may drown their remorse) he may depend on it that the shame and confusion which he feels is hardly to be accounted a faint shadow of what must come upon him unless he repent, when that child and he shall stand together before the all-seeing eye and behold it fixed upon them. Or, to take a more common case, a child has been undutiful to a parent and trembles at the thought of what his parent may next say to him. How will it be with that son or daughter when he rises from the dead and feels that he is presently to meet that parent again, unless he quickly and earnestly repent?

And so in all other cases: the remorse, the misgivings, the scruples, the gnawing anguish which men feel while they are planning any sin or after they have committed it, are so many hints and tokens from Him of what it must all come to at last, without a great and serious change. "The spirit of man," says Solomon, "is the candle of the Lord, searching all the inmost parts" (Prov. 20:27). That is, if we will listen to the silent warnings of our conscience, which seem to be our own but in fact come from Him, we shall by degrees improve in the knowledge of ourselves: our secret sins, our deep and hidden dangers, the mystery of our own iniquity will become known to us, and happily so, if we profit by the knowledge and resort in good time to that better Spirit who alone can undo the mischief wherein we have entangled ourselves.

And this is the meaning of that other wise man who says "Let the counsel of thine own heart stand, for there is no man more faithful unto thee than it" (Ecclus. 37:13), as if he had said "When your conscience fairly tells you you are wrong, I beseech you, let the impression remain. Do not attempt to soothe or trifle it away — they are but false friends that would help you to do so. To listen to them instead of your conscience is listening to man instead of God. If your heart and conscience condemn you, God is greater than your heart and knoweth all things. They know next to nothing; they have no power to acquit or condemn." In such a case, therefore, be greatly afraid to take comfort from anyone against the plain reproof of your conscience.

This rule holds even in respect of that judgment which every man, Christian or heathen, passes by instinct on himself. How much more in the case of Christians, when we recollect what further inward light they have abiding within *them* and what a Judge is come down from Heaven to preside in the court of *their* conscience! That aweful Judge, that heart-searching light, is the most Holy Spirit of God, given to every one of us in baptism. So we are plainly taught by St. John in the chapter before the text, "ye have an unction, an anointing, from the Holy One: and ye know all things. The anointing which ye have received of Him abideth in you, and ye need not that any man should teach you; but as the same anointing teacheth you of all things, and is truth, and is no lie, and even as it hath taught you, ye shall abide in Him" (1 John 2:20, 27). The anointing was the gift of the Holy Ghost, coming on all Christians in baptism as it came on our Lord when He was baptized by St. John. If it teaches us of Christian doctrine, confirming us in the holy creed which we have been taught, surely it teaches of Christian practice too, confirming us in the holy commandments, which we have sworn to obey.

Here, then, is another reason, an unspeakable reason, why Christian persons should attend very much to the warnings of their own conscience. They may be — they very often most surely are — the warnings of the most Holy Comforter, of Him whom Christ has sent to dwell in our hearts to guide us into all truth. You think it strange that the children of Israel, plainly directed as they were by the cloud in sight over the tabernacle door which way to move, what to do and whom to serve, should ever have broken God's ordinances and moved backward instead of forward. Why, it is the very thing you do yourself as often as the voice within bids you forbear and you go wilfully on, as often as it bids you abstain, and you indulge. The perverse Jews had not more reason to know that God was guiding them in the cloud than we Christians have to acknowledge Him present and speaking in our hearts by His Spirit.

Depend upon it, it is no slight or mean gift, that unction from the Holy One. Having it, the Apostle says, "we know all things." The expression is remarkable, and answers wonderfully to those words of St. Paul, "I can do all things through Christ which strengtheneth me" (Phil. 4:13). To know all things and to do all things are great privileges indeed, and such as we never would have dared affirm of any but the Most High God Himself, but He, you perceive, affirms them of all Christians, thus making good His own declaration, so wonderful to think of, by another apostle: that we are partakers of the Divine nature.

Let us not then be afraid to trust our own heart whenever it tells us plainly that we are not in a good way. Let us rather be very much afraid not to trust it, not to obey it, for it is a voice from a place where God has promised to be. To use again the words of the text, "If our heart" — our natural conscience — "condemn us, God" — the Holy Ghost dwelling in our heart — "is greater than our heart, and knoweth all things" — knoweth much that our own heart hath either forgotten or never knew, the many sad circumstances and shades of deeper guilt in our sin. The Holy Spirit knows all this, and if our sin seem bad to ourselves, depend upon it, it is in His sight infinitely worse.

Thus, whether we regard ourselves as judged by our own conscience or by the sacred indwelling Spirit, either way we come to this very serious conclusion — that whatever our own heart reproves us for God is reproving, and will reprove us very much more. When we reject such warnings we reject the Holy Ghost; when we endeavor to turn away from them or only to dismiss them with slight notice, then we grieve the Holy Ghost and provoke Him to diminish His grace.

Here, I say, is matter for serious thought indeed, if we could bring the doctrine home to our hearts as thoroughly as we believe it with our minds and acknowledge it with our lips. I will try to set down its effect in a few cases, but first I will guard against a wrong use which may be made of it.

We know that there is such a thing as a mistaken conscience, imagining things wrong and inexcusable which are not so at all, and it is possible that such a one hearing, "If our heart condemn us, God is greater than our heart and knoweth all things," may be led to pain and grieve himself all the more. Whereas these words, if he would consider them, may suggest a way of thought which may calm him and set him right. If your heart condemn you — if you be inclined to vex yourself about something which you did at the time for the best but which has turned out ill — remember that God is greater than your heart and knoweth all things, and perhaps this matter may be of less consequence in His eyes than it appears now to you. Your great concern about it may be in part a snare of the devil, to turn you away from present and pressing duties. You had better commit it to God with penitence and prayer; leave it in His hand, and set about your day's work cheerfully.

This is so if the case were really doubtful, and you acted for the best. But it is another matter when the case was plain and your conscience spoke out and you disregarded it; then, I fear, you come under the more alarming sense of the text, and God's greater knowledge of your ways and thoughts will only serve to confirm your own heart's condemnation. Your only way of safety and wisdom will be most humbly to submit to this, to embrace and hold fast the thought as part of the cross which, however it burden and gall you, is your only salvation. Settle it in your hearts to believe, and carry the thought about with you everywhere, in your work and in your rest, that the serious misgiving of your own heart is the call of the Holy Ghost within you, and therefore whatever seems decidedly bad to you must, of course, appear much more so to Him. Endeavor to have this assurance quite familiar and ready in your mind, and use it to help you in putting away the many whispers of the evil spirit whereby, if he could, he would encourage you to stifle all that your own heart, all that God's good Spirit, may say of the charge that lies against you.

For example he is ready, not seldom, with the suggestion that, to be sure, your own conduct in such and such things does appear contrary to rule when it is thought over, but then, could we know all (so the evil one argues) we should probably find many more just as bad, of whom we and all men have now a very good opinion. Well, and suppose it were so, the question is not whether others are as bad or worse, but whether if I do such things I can possible be good enough to please God. And this is no question but a certain impossibility in the eyes of those who really believe and recollect that the voice of their conscience pleading with them is the voice of the Holy Ghost. Others may be impure in secret, and the same voice may plead with them also, or it may not plead so distinctly as with you. Of that you know nothing. But this one thing you do know, that the sacred voice has pleaded and is pleading in your heart against impurity, and now, if you sin, you sin deliberately, under the very eye of the Judge. You must take the consequences, and will have no reason to complain should you find them infinitely worse than you now understand: as much worse as might be expected from the difference between God's knowledge and yours concerning the real amount and guilt of your sins.

But it may be that the tempter takes another tone with you and tries to persuade you that, after all, there is not so much in what we call conscience. It is a matter, he may say, of opinion, of feeling, of fancy. There is as much difference in consciences as in tastes, and He who made all will make allowance for all. Anyhow, he will say, there must be great liberties allowed where people's judgments differ so very widely.

Now here again the thought of God present within and of conscience, His attendant, repeating His decisions in our hearts, seems well calculated to put such impiety to silence. Men's consciences do *not* differ so widely as the devil and his messengers would persuade us. Who is there over all the earth, who does not own the duty of children to honor their parents? Who that does not feel that for good, good should be returned? Trust the voice of God within and believe, in spite of those bad suggestions, that others hear it, or have heard it, as well as you. The proud Assyrian said, "There is no religion, no God, that can stand against me. Is not one place as another? Is not Calno as Carchemish? Is not Hamath as Arphad? Is not Samaria as Damascus?" (Isa. 10:9). But good Hezekiah believed his own heart which told him that there was a Lord God in Israel who dwelt between the

Cherubim and to whom he might come in all his perplexities, and the end showed which was right — the Assyrian was cut off and Hezekiah was saved.

Again (and this, perhaps, is the most numerous class of all) there are those who are inclined to dismiss all serious thoughts and scruples, for a time at least, altogether from their minds, as if they would come again in good time whenever it shall please God, so that meanwhile they might take things easy.

Now — not to speak here of the desperate madness of taking for granted that it will please God to give them as much time as they demand and to be found of them whenever they please to seek, although He has distinctly said "Some shall seek Him early, and shall not find Him" (John 7:34) — consider, I beseech you, what you would think of one who should hear God's voice actually calling to him from heaven and should answer, as St. Paul was answered by Felix, "Go thy way for this time; when I have a convenient season, I will send for thee" (Acts 24:25)? Would it not be unutterable profaneness? And yet, if the voice of conscience be indeed the voice of God's Holy Spirit speaking within us, this is what we really do say when we put away self-condemning thoughts. And when the world and worldly friends say "Do not be so over-serious; do not turn melancholy and gloomy before the time — there will be plenty of leisure by and by for meditating on such matters," is not this, in effect, advising one's friend to give that very answer to the Almighty Himself which sounds so profane when we read of it as given to an apostle?

I beg of you to turn this over in your minds, for surely neglect of inward scruples and warnings is one of the commonest of all sins, and very few there are — are there any? — who know how heinous a sin it is. Few, very few, are accustomed to believe and recollect and realize the presence of God's Spirit in a Christian's heart, as really to distinguish His warning or condemning voice in the low deep murmurings of their own conscience, when they are set on thinking of their own ways, past or to come.

For example: a young person is tempted to tell a lie to obtain some present satisfaction or get himself out of some present trouble. He does it with uneasiness for the first time, and the thought will come in and disturb him afterwards "that all liars" — these are the words of the Most High God — "shall have their portion in the lake that burneth with fire and brimstone" (Rev. 21:8). It would be well for a person in such a state of mind if some one were nigh to remind him that these scruples, these troublesome thoughts, are not his own. There is a great and good Spirit present in him and He puts them into his mind. Such a recollection might, perhaps, prevail on some to cherish these holy scruples and really to obey them, confessing and bewailing their falsehood in the hope that the pain and shame of doing so might be accepted by their Judge as a sort of holy revenge which they take upon themselves for their great sin — and not only confessing and bewailing it, but really turning from it forever. When your conscience tells you that you have told a lie, be that lie more or less shocking in its circumstances, still the very thought is the whisper of the Teacher within you, His warning never to do so again but to speak the truth boldly as you ought to speak, though it be to your own worldly hindrance: you who are a member of Christ and, through Him, of all Christians.

There will be whispers of a contrary kind, encouraging you to think lightly of the sin — nay perhaps even to pride yourself on the skill with which you have made the falsehood serve your own purpose for a time. But you will know from what sort of spirit those whisperings come, and will put them out of your mind accordingly. Else, if you unhappily listen to them and either please yourself with your deceit and what you have gained by it, or at least forget to repent of it, then the next time a tempting opportunity of the like kind arises (and it will not be long before the devil contrives one) the Holy Spirit, vexed by your former profaneness, will whisper to your heart less loudly. The prayers of your friends will avail less in your favor and your own prayers will savor more of hypocrisy and a double mind. If you fall again the third time your chance will be still less, and so on, till a regular habit of falsehood is formed and the Holy Spirit, grieved more and more, quite ceases to warn and make you uneasy in your sin.

Wherefore, whether it be telling lies or any other sin to which you are tempted, beware of overcoming or slighting the *first* scruple; beware how you turn away your ear from the voice, however still and small, which comes over your heart in secret, saying "that is not the way, walk not in it." For as surely as God has made you that voice, if it come of your natural conscience, is a true reporter of His judgment, and as surely as God's Holy Spirit has entered into you to regenerate you and make you a member of Christ, so surely is the same voice breathed from that Holy Spirit, to keep you from vexing Him and forcing Him to forsake you.

And be not afraid thus to call on God's Holy Spirit — I do not say in words, but in the secret thoughts of your heart — on every occasion. Slight though it seem to you, it is not slight if it prove the beginning of a sin. Since He vouchsafes to be present with you in all things, in what seems little as well as in what all men would call startling and awakening occasions, do have so much reverence as to try to remember Him in all things. Be what many will call particular and scrupulous. Encourage all thoughts of caution and holy fear, though even to yourself they may seem at first sight to come unseasonably and to be more than is required. For aught you know they may be the whisperings of God's most Holy Spirit, coming just when you need them. You may find hereafter that in receiving them you have been entertaining angels unawares — and not only angels, but the Son of God Himself. For such godly motions are His tokens, and if we love him so well as to attend to them and keep His words, he hath said "My Father will love him, and we will come unto him, and make our abode with him" (John 14:23).

• 2 •

Our Lord among Us,
though We Know Him Not

··

Volume 1, Sermon 37

ADVENT

"There standeth one among you, whom ye know not."

JOHN 1:26

In one sense, as you well know, Christ and His kingdom are not yet come. The trial of the world and of the Church is not yet over; the world is not yet judged nor the saints delivered; we are not yet in heaven or in hell but God keeps us yet awhile upon earth to see whether we will repent and amend or not, and our brethren departed He keeps either in Paradise or in their sad prisons of darkness, apart from their bodies until the time of the end come. And in this sense we pray continually that His kingdom may come; holy men like St. Paul have desired to depart and to be with Christ, and we read that while we are at home in the body we are absent from the Lord.

But in another sense the kingdom is come already and Christ is even now among us. We are come to Jesus, the mediator of the new Covenant, and He can never for a moment leave us nor forsake us. Thus the preaching of the Church even now is that Jesus Christ is both present and to come. He is with us as a God who hideth Himself, but before long He will so come that all will see Him. The veil will be taken away, and we shall wonder that we have all our lives dwelt so near to that brightest glory and have never yet discerned it.

Like to this double preaching of the Church was the preaching of St.

John the Baptist, the type and shadow of the Church's ministry. He too spoke of our Lord as not yet come; "One mightier than I cometh" (Luke 3:16). "He cometh" — I do not say He is yet come — and "the Kingdom of Heaven is at hand" — it is not set up in the world, it is only very near. But in another sense he pointed to our Lord as being already come, as the bright morning star shows whereabout the sun is before he has quite risen upon the earth. That is, our Lord was come in presence but not in open sight, not so as to put forth His power. And of this coming the holy Baptist bore witness in the verses appointed for the Gospel of the fourth Sunday in Advent — "there standeth one among you, whom ye know not," even as, just after, he spoke of His future coming in power and setting up His kingdom on the day of Pentecost — "He shall baptize you with the Holy Ghost and with fire" (Matt. 3:11).

We may well imagine what a stir it must have made among the multitudes who heard St. John speak, when he uttered such words unto them, "There standeth one among you, whom ye know not." We may fancy how they looked round upon one another, doubting of whom he spoke: how some of them watched St. John's eye and the turn of his countenance to see whether he looked towards anyone in particular. They perhaps were expecting that St. John would declare himself to be the Christ. We know that some of them had been in expectation, "musing in their hearts concerning John, whether he were the Christ or not" (Luke 3:16). And when he told them it was not he they might naturally suppose that it was someone even more remarkable in his outside appearance than St. John was, more poorly clad, more worn with watchings and fastings, or, on the other hand, one more noble and glorious, carrying all before Him by the brightness and power of His appearing.

Something of this sort no doubt was their expectation, and it must have sounded very strange to them when he said "he standeth already among you; ye know Him not," but I know Him. He is come from heaven, He is here on earth, He is in the country, nay more He is even now in this company. There He is, standing bodily among you, little thought or dreamed of by you. No doubt when they heard this many thoughts arose in their hearts but few, if any, came at all near the truth. Few, if any, could discern which of all that crowd was God Almighty present on earth. Some might look among the chief priests, the scribes and the Pharisees, those who seemed to be most learned, most depended on for their knowledge of Holy Scripture. Others might look among the rich and great ones, Herod's nobles if there were any there, or the chief of the soldiers who listened to St. John.

But all the while there was in the multitude a poor, humble, quiet young man, supposed to be a carpenter's son of Nazareth, a place of no great credit, who had lived now thirty years working at the carpenter's trade, going about the village like any other poor but respectable artisan. When people met Him they saw nothing particular in Him: no form nor comeliness, no beauty nor glory that they should desire Him. He was very likely one of the last persons in the crowd around St. John towards whom the generality would have turned their eyes, thinking "What if this should be He? What if this Jesus of Nazareth should prove to be the very Christ?"

And yet He was so, and no other. The poor young carpenter so very mean in outward appearance was the Christ: the very Christ, the Son of God, begotten from everlasting of the Father, the only sacrifice for the sins of the world, the king and God of the whole creation, the Judge both of quick and dead. He of whom all this is true was in that company, but they knew Him not. He was in the crowd; He was close to some of them; very likely they thronged and pressed Him, but they knew Him not. Some of them might know something about Him — for example, if there were any there from Nazareth they would know Him to be the person whom they called the "carpenter's son." Some few of them might have the same kind of knowledge of Him as St. John seems to have had before he baptized Him. The Baptist must have known our Lord from the beginning as a very very holy person. He must have heard what the shepherds had said of Him, yet he says "I knew Him not: but when I saw the Spirit descending and remaining on Him, I saw, and bare record, that this is the Son of God" (John 1:32, 34). He know not Christ's full glory until the Holy Ghost had descended upon Him. Those among the crowd who knew most of Jesus could not well know more than St. John knew before he baptized Him, and St. John himself says "At that time I knew Him not" (John 1:33). Well, therefore, might he say to the multitudes, "There standeth one among you, whom ye know not." Those among you who know most of Him account Him only a very holy man, raised up for some very great and gracious purpose, but in truth He is the Most High God, God Incarnate, God the Son come down from heaven and made man to die for us. There He stands in the midst of you, but ye know Him not.

Thus it was when the Baptist spoke, and it was the same all along, in all the stages of our Savior's life on earth. Whether He was among friends or enemies or indifferent persons He was not fully known, and when He had died and risen again and His Holy Spirit had made Him known as the true God to all believers, He could no longer be seen. He was gone away into heaven. Always and in every case He was "a God who hideth Himself" (Isa. 45:15).

If it were so then, my brethren, be sure it is so now. It is still exactly and literally true, in respect of every assembly of Christian people, few or many, whether they be come together for good or for evil, for business or diversion — "There standeth one among you, whom ye know not." Jesus Christ is always among us, to watch both over good and over evil, both over business and over diversion. We do not see Him — we only see one another — but he is not the less certainly among us. If we disobey Him we disobey Him to His face, if we affront Him we affront Him to His face, if we forget Him yet He is close at hand listening to every word we say and noting all down in His aweful book. Let us turn this over in our minds; let us go on thinking of it until we have got it well fixed in our hearts, so that whatever company we go into we may always remember that Christ is one of that company.

For example here we are now, in church, and we see a certain number of our friends and neighbors around us. We see them and we do not see Christ, yet we know that Christ is here for it is His own promise and we have been told of it over and over "Where two or three are gathered together in my name, there am I in the midst of them" (Matt. 18:20). Christ is here in the midst of us, but we know Him not: not even those among us who most earnestly desire and labor to behave well, not even the most devout of His worshipers can thoroughly know Him, He is so unspeakably high, holy and pure. How much less can the ordinary sort, who in general are but outwardly well-behaved, be said to know Him? And least of all is He known to the profane and wilfully inattentive. Yet is He among us all. In one corner of a church perhaps are some young people inclined to behave rudely, and fancying that they have found a place where nobody can see them — there they imagine they may amuse themselves at their leisure. Take care, my young friends. Christ is even now close to you, in that corner of the church as well as anywhere else. There is no whisper so secret, no sign or token of folly so slight and unnoticeable but He comes between those among whom it passes, hears the whisper, sees the glance or the movement. Take care, your Lord hears and sees all.

Elsewhere perhaps, in the same church, is some quiet person, young or old, with but few of his own house or near friends to encourage him in coming there. There is no one, it may be, at hand at all near or dear to him, to whom he can look for encouragement or sympathy in his devotion. Let this man again remember that *He* is standing among us, who is more than all fathers and children, wives and husbands, friends and neighbors, who has taught His true servants to say, "When my father and my mother forsake me, the Lord taketh me up" (Ps. 27:10), and therefore such a one may humbly cheer himself with the thought that Christ at least is present to say Amen to his prayers, and if Christ be there, surely he need not feel desolate — if Christ say Amen, surely the prayer falls not to the ground.

Above all things, when the memorial sacrifice of Christ, His sacrament of Holy Communion, comes on — when you leave your place and come into the chancel to kneel down and partake of that saving Body and Blood — let all endeavor to feel in their very hearts that *here* above all other places on earth our Lord Jesus, God and man, is present in a peculiar manner. To those who come worthily He is present with such grace as is promised to nothing else that is done here below, for they do verily and indeed eat His Flesh and drink His Blood: they dwell in Him and He in them, they are one with Him and He with them. Even so, the Holy Scripture teaches, they who come unworthily find Him also present in such sense as that they are guilty of His Body and Blood. Their sin is the same as if they had gone by whilst Joseph was laying Him in the grave and had insulted his blessed body. Therefore to all careless communicants the Church seems to cry aloud, "There standeth one among you whom ye know not." Take care how you deal with Him. For he comes longing to dwell in your heart — He cannot bear to be neglected, much less to be affronted and reproachfully used. And to all penitent but sad and dejected communicants she still utters the same words, "There standeth one among you." Yea, there abideth in the midst of you, even in the very deep of your heart there abideth One whom ye know not. The God of all comfort is there, though as yet you taste not His comfort; but wait on Him in loving obedience, and all will be right.

Now we will suppose that the holy sacrament is over and the Christian people are gone home to their houses. You are gathered together, families, fellow-servants, friends or neighbors, for innocent and loving conversation and refreshment. It is well. This also is God's blessing. But take good heed, I beseech you, that in these your home gatherings as well as in your solemn assemblies there is always present one more than your eyes can see; Christ is there though you see Him not. He expects you to turn towards Him and give Him thanks at the beginning of the meals which He allows you. He expects you, during the meal, to recollect that He is there, and as you would not act rudely and unmannerly if you were at a great man's table, at a feast where a king was present, so Christ expects of you to be sober and temperate out of true reverence to Him, and to guard your tongue from scandal and backbiting especially, because He is there setting down every word. Keep these rules, my brethren; behave at your common meals and meetings for diversion as persons who do not forget that they carry Christ about with them, having received Him in His holy sacrament, and a great blessing will attend you even on these ordinary occasions. You will not be the less cheerful, but your cheerfulness will be far more innocent and happy.

Next, imagine the Sunday over, the time of rest and refreshment at an end, and that you are gathered together for some purpose of worldly business — at market, for instance, or in a shop, or working together in any manner. Here again the saying will be true, "There standeth one among you whom ye know not." He who once spake from Heaven in thunder, "Thou shalt not steal," He who cannot bear any manner of cheating, fraud, injustice or wrong, He is with the tradesman behind the counter, with the dealer in the fair or market, with the thresher in the barn, with the servant in the storehouse or garden. He knows all the liberties we ever take, either in helping ourselves secretly or in bargaining unfairly to our own advantage. He knows all the falsehoods men tell in such matters, all the grudging and envious thoughts, the bitter and angry words to which they are tempted. He knows when the hired laborer neglects his due portion of work as well as He knows when the employer underpays him or grudges him his just wages in proper time. In all such temptations (and most of us at times are exposed to one or another of them) the great safeguard is to be aware of His eye fixed upon us. If we knew that some saint, some very holy person, was watching us, should we not think a good deal of it? Would it not make a great difference in our conduct? How much more when He standeth among us invisibly who is the Lord of all Saints? How pure should we strive to be in sight of the God of purity.

Indeed, my brethren, the thought of His so standing among us would be too aweful if really considered; it would be too much for us, it could not be borne, were it not that He has graciously told us how good and forgiving He is also. We should surely die upon thus seeing God were it not that it is the same God who made Himself man for our sake, the same Christ who died for us. But then we must be making much both of His birth and of His death, not neglecting them or making them void. Christmas, like other holy seasons, is given us for our trial in this respect. May we so keep it, this time at least, that it may not tell to our condemnation.

3

The Mystery of Christ's Birth, and of Our New Birth

....

Volume 2, Sermon 3

CHRISTMAS DAY

"My thoughts are not your thoughts, neither are My ways your ways, saith the Lord: For as the heavens are higher than the earth, so are My ways higher than your ways, and My thoughts than your thoughts."

ISAIAH 55:8-9

When a person wakes on a Christmas morning and turns his mind at once, as a thoughtful person naturally will, to the great and unutterable miracle of the day, it is somewhat of the same kind of thought as when we gaze earnestly on the deep heaven above us. The longer we gaze, the more certainly we feel how far it reaches, how utterly and entirely beyond us, how we might go on for ever and be more and more lost and swallowed up in the contemplation of it.

It should seem that the blue sky or firmament was on purpose so made, the light caused so to pass through it and our eyes so formed that as we look on it or but think of it spread above us, we may feel that we are in the midst of a power and wisdom which we can by no means understand, one which is at the same time close to us and yet infinitely far above us. The Scripture encourages this thought in many places. Thus God is called, first in Job and many times afterwards in the prophets, He "Who sitteth upon the circle of the earth, and the inhabitants of the earth are as grasshoppers; Who stretcheth out the heavens as a curtain, and spreadeth them out as a tent to dwell in" (Isa. 40:22; Job 9:8). "The inhabitants of the earth are as grasshoppers"; surely that word speaks to every man's heart, expressing how little and mean and insignificant we feel when we look up to the unbounded sky and think of ourselves, of how little room we seem to take in God's vast and wonderful world.

This is an overpowering thought. But the Scripture tells us something else, which makes it a thought full of all consolation. The height of heaven represents to our very eyes not only God's incomprehensible greatness and wisdom, but His infinite love also. For "look how high the heaven is in comparison of the earth, so great is His mercy also toward them that fear Him: look how wide also the east is from the west, so far hath He set our sins from us" (Ps. 103:11-12). The space in which our eyesight loses itself when we look up on a clear day, or when we look all around from a high place on some boundless prospect, is an appointed measure of God's love — a token from Himself of His pardoning and life-giving favor, shown to us as members of His Son. The Psalms repeat this over and over: "Thy mercy, O Lord, is in the heavens, and thy faithfulness reacheth unto the clouds" (Ps. 36:5). It is as if it were God's purpose that in that portion of the Scriptures which the rules of His Church should make most familiar to all — that is in the Psalms — Christian children should learn from the beginning the right use of the things which they see around them, and should never want something to remind them of saving truth, since even so common a thing as the sky, which they cannot help seeing with their eyes, is made to them a kind of sacramental token of infinite power, wisdom, and love.

As in many other places of the prophet Isaiah, so here in the text the Almighty commends to us this thought: that we should learn from the very sight of the heaven above us not to lose in our sense of God's mercy the deep trembling awe and reverence with which we ought to regard all His doings, not to dream that we understand them nor to conclude that they fail because we do not yet see the fruit of them, but to labor diligently in the ways of our duty, and for the rest to be silent before Him, and wait on Him with adoring patience. "My thoughts are not your thoughts, neither are my ways your ways, saith the Lord: for as the heavens are higher than the earth, so are my ways higher than your ways, and my thoughts than your thoughts."

Now this same lesson, which the very height of the heavens was intended to teach all mankind, seems to be brought before us Christians in a wonderful, unspeakable way when we are called on to remember our Lord's Nativity. For what, in fact, was that birth which took place today at Bethlehem eighteen hundred and forty one years ago, and in remembrance of which the whole Church has ever since kept this day holy? It is something so high and sacred that it seems almost presumption to speak of it. We have need first to pray that we may be forgiven for speaking unworthily. However let us speak of it, as we may, in the words of the Church.

We believe that on this day the only-begotten Son of God, begotten of His Father before all worlds, having been conceived by the Holy Ghost and made man, was born at Bethlehem of the Blessed Virgin Mary, that on this day God was manifested to men and angels in the flesh, so declaring and making known the Eternal Father, in whose bosom He is and whom no man hath seen at any time. We believe that He who was from the beginning, begotten from everlasting of the Father, condescended early this morning to have a beginning and birth of His own; that He who is God of God vouchsafed to be man born of a woman; that He who is called Light of Light prepared for Himself, as it were, a visible tabernacle, an undefiled human soul and body, wherein to dwell visibly for ever and ever; that the infant who was born in the stable and laid in the manger, is Very God of Very God, True Son of the Most High God, and Himself truly God as His Father is; that, although in His human soul and body He is made and created, as the first Adam was, by His own Almighty power, yet is He, as the Son of God, begotten not made.

He was seen lying in the manger this morning, just born, weak and helpless as another infant might be, yet He was even then, and had been for ever and ever, in heaven with the Almighty Father. He, that helpless Babe, wrapped in swaddling clothes as any child born yesterday, was the Lord and Creator of heaven and earth, of those who worshiped Him and of those who persecuted Him, of His Mother who had just borne Him, and of the angels who were at hand to sing glory to Him. By Him all things were made that are in heaven and that are in earth, "whether they be thrones, or dominions, or principalities, or powers, all things were created by Him and for Him; and He is before all things, and by Him all things consist" (Col. 1:16-17). This Great and Eternal God, pitying His creatures in their darkness and misery and accomplishing His own eternal purpose from the beginning, descended and was incarnate so many months ago, when the Blessed Virgin was visited by the angel Gabriel and the Holy Ghost came upon her and the power of the Highest overshadowed her. "For us men and for our salvation He came down from Heaven, and was incarnate by the Holy Ghost of the Virgin Mary, and was made man." And now, at the end of nine months, He made Himself visible to the world which He had created.

He began to show Himself to angels as well as to men, as St. Paul tells us in several places when he says that "to the principalities and powers in heavenly places was known by the Church the manifold wisdom of God" (Eph. 3:10), and that "these things the angels desire to look into" (1 Pet. 1:12). And accordingly the angels came, as all Christian children know, to sing their Christmas hymn in the hearing of the shepherds.

The very thing by itself, God Incarnate, was the wonder of all wonders, a matter surely as much above the thoughts and conjectures of man as the heaven is higher than the earth: that the Creator should become a creature, that the Lord most holy and true should join Himself to a sinful race, and become one of them, to deliver them from the evil consequences of their sin.

But even suppose the thought of God's becoming man had entered into any man's heart, the circumstances of His coming into the world were far unlike what we should have imagined. We should have expected some such appearance as the Psalms and prophets sometimes speak of: in the clouds of heaven, in terrible majesty, that He should "bow the heavens, and come down," that He should "touch the mountains, and they shall smoke" (Ps. 144:5), or at least that He should enter into His Temple in glory as the Ark of His Covenant had done of old. It would never have come into any of our minds to think of any thing so quiet, so poor, mean and ordinary in outward appearance, as the nativity of the child Jesus at Bethlehem.

Consider, first, the quietness of this great event: how in the silence of the night, in the town of no great size nor wealth, in an out-house of an inn, the Great God came visibly among His creatures as it had been prophesied concerning Him; "the dew of His birth was of the womb of the morning" (Ps. 110:3). As His eternal birth was in the secret and silence of God's nature, unspeakably everlasting, beyond all thought of the highest angel, so His mysterious birth at Bethlehem was a wonder in silence and out of sight. None knew it, as far as we are told, but His Virgin Mother and the holy Joseph. Everything, it would seem, was ordered so as to make it most suitable for the God of Israel "that hideth Himself" (Isa. 45:15).

Again, how poor and lowly was everything around Him who was come down to bring us all the treasures of heaven! His Mother the betrothed wife of a poor tradesman who had not, as it seems, wherewith to find her a lodging. The place a stable in which, according to ancient report, an ox and an ass were at that very time feeding. His cradle a manger. His dress such swaddling clothes as the children of the poor were commonly wrapped up in. The first persons who came to see Him plain simple shepherds, of no account among men either for their knowledge of the Scriptures or for their place or station or qualifications in other respects. And if they said high things concerning Him, having heard them from the angel, yet all was kept quiet, His Mother pondering them in her heart but nothing coming of it all for many years. What talk there was of the wonder in that immediate neighborhood very soon seems to have died away, and partly perhaps on this very account the angel bade Joseph return to Nazareth, that our Lord might grow up in quiet and obscurity, at a distance from those who might have heard of the wonders of His birth. The whole history, from beginning to end, is such as no one ever could have imagined: suited to His ways and thoughts who is far above out of our sight, but far unlike the ways and thoughts of mankind.

Imagine only what we should any of us have thought, had we been present in the place at that time. We should each of us have had, no doubt, his own fancies and imaginations, not one agreeing with another. Many would have hardly thought at all about it. Some would just have pitied the mother and babe, suffering what to them would appear such pain and inconvenience, and there would have been an end — they would forget it in a few hours. Some few, perhaps, who knew more of the circumstances before and were more considerate than others, might say to themselves, "What manner of child shall this be?" But none without especial revelation such as the Blessed Mary had herself, could have lifted up his thoughts to the real truth: that this is the Eternal Son, the Word of the Father, made a little lower than the angels for the suffering of death, the desire of all nations, the second Adam, the Way, the Truth, and the Life, the Savior of the world.

Never, I suppose, since the world began, was there such a moment as that to show how unlike God's thoughts are to our thoughts, and God's ways to our ways except, it may be, that more aweful, perhaps more surprising moment in which the Holy Savior, the God of heaven and earth, bowed His head on the Cross and gave up the ghost, being in the place of a malefactor between two thieves. It is in vain trying to think worthily of it. But such thoughts as the following, we may humbly hope, are some of those which the Almighty meant should be in our minds when we remember it.

We may learn not to doubt that God's purposes, however unlikely they appear to us, will be one way or another accomplished. He had declared by His holy prophets that at that time He would redeem the world and that the redemption should begin from Bethlehem, and we see how He fulfilled it in a way which no person present would ever for a moment have suspected. So He has declared that His Church shall last for ever and shall finally prevail against all the kingdoms of the world, and that all shall work together for good to them that love God, and for the punishment of His enemies. This work is even now going on and we are standing by, witnesses of it though not knowing how — nay, we are every one of us working in it, either with or against Him. At present we cannot at all see how it will turn out; many things appear to us going in the contrary way to what they ought to bring about the great purpose, and of many more we cannot see how they should, in any respect, advance it. But let us only wait awhile, and we shall see how, by the most improbable means, He shall work out the counsel of His will.

And not only in the great concerns of the world and of the kingdom of God but also in what relates to each of us particularly we are to be quite sure that the Almighty has His own purpose concerning us and that He is working around us and within us even with the most ordinary things. We think it a very small matter whether we perform such and such a task in its time, whether we resist or give way for once to such and such a common temptation, and all the while who knows but that in God's knowledge and purpose this small matter may be the beginning of great things, to us or to some other, through all eternity?

Recollect how it is in that which the Scriptures and the Prayer Book teach us to consider as having something more particularly to do with our Lord's birth; recollect our own baptism. The collect for Christmas day teaches that our Lord's taking our nature upon Him, and His birth on this day of a pure Virgin, answers in some remarkable way to our "being regenerate, and made His children by adoption and grace," that is, to our baptism. For then, as the Baptism service teaches, "we are regenerate and born anew of water and of the Holy Ghost," and then, as the catechism teaches, "we are made children of God." As Christ at his Nativity showed Himself in our human nature, so we at our new birth, St. Peter tells us, are "made partakers of His Divine nature" (2 Pet. 1:4). As He then became a child of Adam, so we now are made children of God. So great is the change wrought in Holy Baptism. Yet who that stood by and judged by sight, not faith, would imagine there was any change at all? Who would lift up his heart to believe that a little water and a few words spoken by Christ's minister would make so much difference in a little child, were it not that the Scripture of God, interpreted by His Church, so distinctly teaches it?

In this point then, also, we clearly see that our new birth answers to our Lord's Nativity — that is in the matter of its being so very far unlike what any one would expect. Why should we doubt that so great an end as salvation may come of so small an outward beginning as the sprinkling of the holy baptismal water in the three holy names, we who know that our redemption, and that of the whole world, depended on a child in swaddling clothes, born in an inn stable and laid in a manger? Surely, among the plain lessons which our Lord's Nativity teaches us, one of the plainest is not to despise what the Prophet calls "the day of small things" (Zech. 4:10): that is, to be very exact about our duty even in the matters which may at first sight seem trifling, not knowing of how much consequence they may one day prove to that which is the greatest matter of all.

Think this well over, my brethren. Think whether you yourselves, since this time last year, have not had more or less reason to be quite sure that God's ways and thoughts are far higher and deeper than ours, if it be only in His bringing great matters out of what seem to us very small beginnings. I hope that too many of us may not have to recollect this with bitter shame and remorse before Him who reads their hearts, as having been guilty within that time of grievous sin owing to this very cause: that they made light of small beginnings and of what they called trifling liberties which they permitted themselves to take with God's commandments. O! if the unhappy lost souls could speak from the next world, or send a message as that rich man in our Lord's parable wished to do, how certain we may be that they would warn us against the first trifling with the beginnings of mischief, the first scornful or idle neglect of what would be called little acts of goodness!

Let us think of these sad self-reproachings before it is too late for ourselves, and let us endeavor steadily to contemplate the great wonder of this day, the Son of God born of a woman and laid, like another child, in the manger at Bethlehem, with his prayer among others that our eyes may be opened to understand, in some measure, God's gracious and gentle beginnings with ourselves. As He our Lord and Savior Himself, from the very moment of His birth as on this day never ceased loving us and preparing all good things for us, so never let us quite take off our thoughts from His unspeakable love, of which this day is the crown. It is such love as we never can fathom, never can come truly to understand, but we may and shall understand more and more, as we turn our minds towards it more earnestly. To watch and study Christ in His cradle is the very mystery of humility and, if of humility, then of love, peace and joy. It is the very preparation, the beginning of eternal happiness; for in knowledge of Him standeth our eternal life, and such knowledge must begin from His lowliness. Jesus Himself is that little Child, like whom we must especially become, if we would be ever really fit for the Kingdom of Heaven.

4

Self-denial, a Main Lesson of the Gospel

Volume 2, Sermon 20

THE CIRCUMCISION

"Circumcise therefore the foreskin of your heart, and be no more stiff-necked."

DEUTERONOMY 10:16

It is a thing much to be observed, that many of the outward and visible signs which God has ordained His people to use in worshiping Him have somewhat in them to remind us in some way of suffering, affliction, pain, self-denial, death. Thus sacrifice, which was the great act of solemn worship among the Patriarchs and Jews, was the slaughter of some innocent animal and the pouring out of its blood before God. Thus the Holy Communion is the remembrance of our Savior's death — His violent and bitter death. Thus Baptism, the entrance into the kingdom of heaven, when performed in that way which the Church in her Prayer Book prefers is also a memorial of His death and rising again: of His death, by the burial of the child, just for a moment, under the water, and of His resurrection, by the same child's being immediately lifted out of the water into the minister's arms. It is a memorial of our Lord's death and it is also a token and pledge. It means a real death which the baptized person does at the same time undergo — an inward death unto sin and a new birth unto righteousness. It is a token of the sort of life to be led hereafter in this world — a life according to that death, as St. Paul said, "I die daily" (1 Cor. 15:31), a life in which a man has continually to keep himself in order, to deny himself many things which he would like, and to choose and embrace many things which he naturally dislikes. This is the sort of life of which Holy Baptism is the beginning; and it is signified to us by the very act of baptizing.

But of all Church ceremonies there is none which so distinctively sets before us our call to suffer as that which has, from the beginning, always gone along with Baptism: the signing the newly baptized with the sign of the Cross. The Cross is the very height and depth of all suffering. The very name presently tells us of a soul exceeding sorrowful even unto death, of sweat like great drops of blood falling down to the ground, of a burden too heavy to be borne, of reproach, scorn, shame, spitting, of scourging and a crown of thorns, of hands and feet and side pierced, of crying with a loud voice and yielding up the Ghost. All this and more, more than man's heart can understand, comes into a Christian's mind when he hears of the Cross. What, then, can we understand by the Cross marked on us from our very childhood, but that we too are to go on in suffering and self-denial and that, though our Lord's yoke is easy and His burden light to such as are renewed by His Spirit, yet in itself it is very bitter, "full," as the prophet says, "of gall and travail" (Lam. 3:5)?

Now such as the baptismal Cross is in the Christian life, such was circumcision among God's ancient people. It was His mark, made for life in the very flesh of those who belonged to Him, setting them apart, in a manner, for suffering and self-denial. It was a foretaste of the Cross and, as such, our Savior Himself received it. By permitting Himself, as on this day, to be brought and placed in the priest's arms and His sacred flesh pierced and blood shed, by the pain which His tender infant body now suffered He did, as it were, offer unto His Father the first-fruits of that full harvest of suffering which was finally to be gathered in upon the Cross. He sanctified our lesser sorrows, mortifications and vexations, as He was afterwards to sanctify in His agony and passion our more grievous and heart-searching trials: our great disappointments, our shame, want, sickness and death. Certainly, when we look at His course in this His lower world, beginning with endurance of the sharp circumcising knife and ending with, *My God, My God, why hast Thou forsaken Me?* it does seem strange that we should, any of us, expect to pass through life in ease and quietness, or think it hard if we have not our own way in all things. "The disciple is not above his Master nor the servant above his Lord. It is enough for the disciple, if he be as his Master, and the servant as his Lord" (Matt. 10:24-25).

Thus, whether we look to our Lord's own example or to the sacramental ways which He has ordained, both of old and now, to bring His people near Him, either way we are taught to "count them happy which endure" (James 5:11), to consider affliction and trouble as God's seal set upon those who particularly belong to Him, and to fear nothing so much as receiving our consolation in this world.

But if this be so, then just in such measure as we are going on prosperously and at ease have we need to mortify ourselves and keep our passions in order, that by our own doing, if so please God, we may provide for ourselves something like that due chastening which our afflicted brethren really have to endure. This, our self-denial, we must practice in little matters. It should accompany us in our everyday walk, as every Jew bore about with him the mark of circumcision visibly impressed on his flesh and as every Christian was continually reminding himself in old times, by the sign of the Cross, whose he was and whom he served. We must not keep our patience and self-command to be exercised only on great and solemn occasions. We must be continually sacrificing our own wills, as opportunity serves, to the will of others, bearing, without notice, sights and sounds that annoy us, setting about this or that task when we had far rather be doing something very different, persevering in it often when we are thoroughly tired of it, keeping company for duty's sake when it would be a great joy to us to be by ourselves. There are, besides, all the trifling untoward accidents of life: bodily pain and weakness long continued and perplexing us often when it does not amount to illness, losing what we value, missing what we desire, disappointment in other persons, wilfulness, unkindness, ingratitude and folly in cases where we least expected it. There is no end, in short, of the many little crosses which, if quietly borne in a Christian way, will by God's grace do the work of affliction, and help to tame our proud wills by little and little.

I say, "tame our proud wills," because Holy Scripture sets forth this as one of the particular objects for which circumcision was appointed, that God's people might learn by it not only to get over what are commonly called "the lusts of the flesh," but angry and envious and proud feelings also, as the text seems especially to hint: *Circumcise therefore the foreskin of your heart, and be no more stiff-necked* — as if stubbornness and obstinacy and, in one word, wilfulness (for that is the meaning of a "stiff neck") were to be cured by the same kind of discipline as sensual passions, lust and greediness. We know what power may be gained over these by duly and prudently mortifying the body. Fasting, for example, tends to cure greediness. When people are accustomed now and then to go without anything to eat, it makes them more moderate and less particular in all their refreshments of that sort. If they can go without, much more can they content themselves with less than they would like or with what is unpalatable to them, much more can they give up something in this and in other trifling matters for those who are in want or in sickness. In short, it is not hard to understand how the body, which greatly affects the mind, may be tamed and brought into subjection by a quiet and discreet method of fasting, accompanied, of course, with alms and prayer.

And a little consideration will show that the same discipline must do great good to the passions of the soul too. We see that St. Paul reckons among the works of the flesh not only "adultery, fornication, uncleanness, lasciviousness," but also "hatred, variance, emulations, wrath, strife, seditions, envyings" (Gal. 5:19-21) and, in a word, all wilfulness. Anything, however small, by which the Almighty accustoms people not to have their own way, even in respect of bodily comfort, is meant by Him to keep down all these bad passions, and not our bodily appetites only. For what are all our passions, left to themselves, but so many wills of our own, set up against or beside the will of God? And if, in any one respect, we do from the heart acknowledge the goodness and reasonableness of sacrificing our will to His, how can we quite forget that to do so is equally good and reasonable in every other respect? If we abstain from indulging our bodily appetites for the sake of pleasing God and obtaining His grace, is there not so far a better chance of our remembering Him when we are tempted to indulge discontented, unkind, proud thoughts or wilful tempers of any sort?

I do not, of course, mean that this benefit follows upon the mere outward exercise of fasting, but only if a person sets about it religiously, in the fear of God, in desire to draw near to Christ and in humble obedience to His will, made known in His Gospel and by His Church. Otherwise mere fasting, as well as mere prayer or mere reading or mere going to church, may be turned into a snare of the devil. But it is not therefore to be omitted any more than those other holy exercises, but to be practiced, as I said, in the fear of God, the want of which alone can ever make any person easy in depending on one or other holy duty so as to leave out the rest.

Therefore, as we keep under the body in order that it may the better serve the soul, so ought we very carefully to keep under the soul itself, watching and restraining within our hearts and in our behavior and even in our chance words, gestures and looks, every movement of the proud and wilful spirit. This indeed is the very thing which the holy prophet means, in bidding us *circumcise the foreskin of our heart*.

Nor let us rashly imagine that even when we are directly employed in serving God and doing our duty, we are safe against such wilfulness. Remember, we have a subtle enemy who can transform himself into an angel of light, who persuaded God's own people of old to think, without any manner of question, that when they were killing God's own apostles they were doing God service. Certainly, in proportion as we serve God and humbly obey Him we have a promise of protection against the snares of the evil one, yet as long as we are in this world we dare not expect to be *quite* safe. We are not safe in reading the Scriptures, we are not safe in prayer, we are not safe in almsdeeds, we are not safe in fasting, we are not safe in sacraments. In each and in all of these, there is room for the proud will of man to set itself up against the pure and acceptable and perfect will of God.

Thoughts, for example, such as these, will sometimes come into our minds in our public and private devotions: "Might not this prayer have been put in better words? Might not this service have been more wisely ordered? Might not this or that rule of the Church have been more discreetly omitted?" Such thoughts are permitted for our trial, whether, at the bottom of all our goodness, there be not some lurking seed of wilfulness. They are intended indeed for all mischief by the enemy, but God means them to be subdued by us and so to make our crown — so be it! — surer and brighter. What are we to do with them, when they come?

If they mingle with our devotions, if they interrupt our prayers, we must of course put them down at once, as we would any other worldly disturbance. If they make us openly disobedient to any rule of the Church, then surely they cannot be quite right: that surely is a case in which the stiff neck, the wilfulness of the natural man, requires to be subjected even by violence, and brought into captivity. We ought to obey God rather than man: God's plain command of humility and obedience and not giving offense rather than the scruples and doubts of our own (perhaps) deceitful hearts, and God's voice in His Church, with which He has promised to be, rather than the private opinion or example of this or that good person.

It is the neglect of this caution which has made so many heresies and schisms in the Church, so many mistaken and wrong ways of setting about God's work. They come of the carnal heart, the wilful mind, and therefore the apostle reckons seditions and heresies amongst "the works of the flesh," and they must be put down and guarded against in the same way as other "works of the flesh," by accustoming ourselves to deny and distrust ourselves in the very first beginnings of everything, no more expecting to have our own way all clear and comfortable in the service of God than in matters of this world, and making up our minds to obey, though we may not see all the reasons of the command.

This is good part of what Moses meant by calling on us to *circumcise the foreskin of our heart*. Whoever will really call himself to account as to how he has practiced this in the year that is past, and will resolve heartily, in the fear of God, to watch and deny his will and mind as well as his body in the year that now begins, he will at least have begun that year well. If he keep his vow, there are sure promises for him that he will be nearer God at the end of the year (if he live to see it) than he now is, through Him who, beginning this day from circumcision and passing by the way of the Cross, is set down at the right hand of God.

• 5 •

The First and Second Creation of Man

. . . .

Volume 3, Sermon 11

SEPTUAGESIMA

"The Lord God formed man of the dust of the ground, and breathed into his nostrils the breath of life, and man became a living soul."

GENESIS 2:7

Today the Holy Church takes us back to the beginning, the very birthday of man's nature and of the world, causing us to hear from the mouth of God Himself how we came into this our being, who brought us here and what are His great purposes towards us. Now this is what we never could have known of ourselves. We find ourselves each in his own place, so many men, women and children, every one with a soul and body of his own, and God has given the power and the disposition to think upon it all at least sometimes, and not to take everything which happens, as the dumb creatures seem to do, without consideration or reflection. Who and where am I? How came I here? And what is to become of me?

These are questions which in one shape or another every child of man that is not senseless cannot help asking himself. God has answered them for him. Know thyself, O child of Adam — know thine own high birth, and at the same time know thy meanness. Thou didst not make thyself; that thou knowest very well. Neither did thy parents create thee; they were but God's instruments for bringing thee into the world. But in order to know thine own beginning thou must go back to a time when instead of

68

these millions of men, women and children there was not yet a single man upon the earth. Thou must go back to the last of the six days of creation, to the first Friday that ever was. All the rest was now set in order: the sea from the dry land, the earth furnished with trees and herbs, the heavens with sun, moon and stars, the waters with fish, the air with birds, the dry land with beasts and cattle and creeping things. Then, last of all, God sets Himself to make man. Hear Him, hear the most Holy Trinity in a manner taking counsel together as though some greater thing than before were about to be done, some more especial preparation necessary. "Let us make man in our image, after our likeness" (Gen. 1:26).

It is like what our Lord did at the marriage feast; He kept the good wine until last. All His other works were indeed very good. When He beheld them, He delighted in them, but of this alone it is said, "In the image of God created He them" (Gen. 1:27). "In the image of God created He them," because, as you heard just now, when the great gap was to be filled up and a creature provided who should use aright all these wonderful treasures of the first six days, who should be capable of knowing God and loving Him and should be in God's stead, bearing rule and having "dominion over the fish of the sea, and over the fowl of the air, and over the cattle, and over all the earth, and over every creeping thing that creepeth upon the earth" (Gen. 1:26), it pleased Him not to send an angel down for that purpose nor to create a pure spirit only, but to make one who should in part belong even to the gross earthly world. "God formed man of the dust of the ground": not many men but one man, for it was His will that we should all come from one root. And how did He form him? "Of the dust of the ground" — of the same material as He had formed the cattle before him, as it is written, "God said, Let the earth bring forth the living creatures after his kind, cattle and creeping thing, and beast of the earth after his kind: and it was so" (Gen. 1:24). Out of the ground the Lord God framed every beast of the field. It was the body of man, not of course his soul, which was thus formed out of the dust of the earth. And so you see that in respect of that part of our being, the wisest, the noblest, the best of us all is akin to the beasts that perish. Except it were for a special act of our Almighty Creator keeping us alive, the saying of Job might be any moment fulfilled in us, "I have said to corruption, thou art my father: to the worm, thou art my mother and my sister" (Job 17:14). *That* is your kindred and mine by *body*, and we know how deeply from the beginning the holiest among God's people have felt this. Abraham, after so many special promises, confessed how bold it was that he should take upon him to speak unto the Lord — he who was "but dust and ashes" (Gen. 18:27). Job, when God's hand was heavy upon him, sat down among the ashes, and yet the more the judgment had done its work upon his soul, and he had learned the more to abhor himself as being more acquainted with God, his word was "I repent in dust and ashes" (Job 42:6). Joshua and the elders of Israel "put dust on their heads" (Josh. 7:6) when they felt God's hand smiting some of them before their enemies. David's comfort was to think that God "knoweth whereof we are made; He remembereth that we are but dust" (Ps. 103:14). Solomon's preaching was, "All go unto one place; all are of the dust, and all turn to dust again" (Eccles. 3:20). And sad experience proves it daily. The most unbelieving is forced to confess it, for why else should he bury his dead out of his sight?

See then, brethren, what becomes of the pride of beauty and of the desires and pleasures which so entrance and carry away man's poor deceivable heart. Look on a few years — it may be a few days — and consider what they must all come to: creeping things, noisome creatures and worms. This would be all if our bodies were all, and how many, alas! if the truth were told, are even now living as if their bodies were all!

And yet they know, they cannot be ignorant, what a different lesson the Word of God teaches them — yes, and their own heart and conscience too, would they but listen to its still small voice. Surely she or he that most lives in pleasure must now and then have inward misgivings that there is something better worth living for, and then how plain is the Scripture which says that He that formed man's body of the dust of the ground "breathed into his nostrils the breath of life." Think of that, dear brethren, think of it till your hearts tremble within you and you are amazed at yourselves that you have not thought of it more. What is this soul of yours, which makes you to be alive and not dead, which neither you nor any one else ever saw, but which you feel and know to be within you just as certainly as you feel and know anything?

Here you are, my brethren, in this church, sitting before God as His people. You know whether you are attending or not, whether you like to be here or not, whether you wish you were somewhere else. You know all this and can think of it. But an inferior animal, a dumb creature if there were one in the church, would know nothing of the sort: he would not be able to think of what he feels. What is it in you which makes you able thus to think when the beast is not able? It is your soul, my brethren, the breath of life which God breathed into your nostrils as He did into Adam's, and so "man became a living soul." The beasts and all living have something in them by which they live, and this too is called their *soul*, as it is written "Who knoweth the spirit of man that goeth upward, and the spirit of the beast that goeth downward to the earth?" (Eccles. 3:21). But nowhere is it said that God breathed it into them as it is said of Adam and, O my brethren, let us make much of the saying, for by this divinely breathed soul we are akin to the glorious spirits in heaven, who are all His spiritual creatures and children. Nay, we are more immediately akin to the great God Himself, who "is a Spirit" (John 4:24) and "the Father of spirits" (Heb. 12:9). In this part of our being especially He made us after His own image. In His own image, after His likeness, in the image of God created He man, male and female created He mankind, and both in His own image. Alas! that ever male and female should agree to corrupt one another and change by uncleanness that image of God into an image of the "beasts that perish" (Ps. 49:12): nay worse, of foul and filthy devils, spirits of fornication, defilers of soul and body!

But let us look once more at man — at our first father Adam, such as he was originally created. No doubt his body was beautiful and perfect in its kind, and his soul! Who can imagine its beauty and perfection, fresh breathed as it was from the very breath of the Lord God? And the man, observe, *was* the soul, for it is not said man *received* a living soul, or was gifted with it or the like, but man, Adam, *"became* a living soul": the living soul, breathed into the body by the Holy Spirit from on high, *was* the man, the man's very self. How beautiful and glorious soever might be the body, corruptible or incorruptible, it was not, it could not be, Adam's proper self. No more, my brethren, can it be yours. Your soul is yourself, not your body, and when death comes and the soul and body are parted it is not *you* that will be dead and be buried and crumble away in the forlorn grave. Not you — O no — your friends and neighbors, your parents if you leave them behind, your brothers and sisters and companions will look sadly towards your grave and say, perhaps, "There lies such an one, poor thing," but you will not be in earnest lying there. Your soul — the living soul which at the beginning had been breathed by the breath of the Almighty into your mortal body, that precious soul — if you died in God's fear and favor, will be far from dreariness and decay with God who gave it, in perfect rest from its own works, from the works of the world and the body, from evil and mischief, in the true sabbath, in the blessed paradise of God, in sure

71

and certain hope of the resurrection to eternal life when your body, the appointed friend and servant of your redeemed spirit, will be raised and joined to it again and become the partner of your true self again, never more to be divided.

Therefore be not too much cast down when you look on to your own death or when you look back on the death of any one dear to you in our Lord. Remember what He Himself said of such an one, "Weep not; she is not dead, but sleepeth" (Luke 8:52). "The souls of the righteous are in the hand of God, and there shall no torment touch them" (Wisd. 3:1).

But then, brethren, we must never, never forget what this consolation depends upon: this comfort wherewith we are bidden to comfort ourselves in all our troubles of soul and body, even to the parting of the two. This comfort depends entirely not upon the first creation of man in the person of the first Adam, whereby he was made a living soul, but upon the second or new creation of man in the person of the second Adam, our Lord Jesus Christ, whereby He, God Incarnate, became to us a quickening spirit. "The first man Adam was made a living soul; the last Adam was made a quickening spirit" (1 Cor. 15:45). You have heard these words, most of you perhaps, in the burial service. I beg of you to take particular notice of those words whenever you hear or read them. For they have in them the very secret of your eternal life. The first Adam was made a living soul. You heard how *that* was, in the lesson today, "God breathed into his nostrils the breath of life and man became a living soul." It was the free gift of God, and an unspeakable gift it was — the very perfection of the life of this world before man fell.

But alas! Man *did* fall, as we know too well: fell shamefully, sorrowfully and, had he been left to himself, incurably. What then did our blessed and most merciful Savior? He became the second Adam to undo the mischief done by the first Adam. There was a second and a far more wonderful creation; the Incarnation of our Lord Jesus Christ. In that astonishing moment described in the first chapter of St. Luke, when the Holy Ghost descended upon the Blessed Virgin Mary and the power of the Highest overshadowed her and she conceived in her womb and so became the Mother of God — in that moment came to pass that of which the creation of Adam was, as it were, a type and shadow. The Lord God formed a man, the man Christ Jesus, of the substance of blessed Mary, which substance itself came, through Adam, of the dust of the ground. And God breathed into that sacred body the soul pure and holy beyond thought and the eter-

72

nal Word, the Son of God, very and eternal God, took to Himself in the same moment that human body and soul never to be parted from Him. Thus He became a quickening Spirit — a divine Spirit so joined to an unspotted human soul and body that through Him as man eternal life and all things pertaining thereunto should pass for ever to all His fallen brethren of mankind who did not themselves reject Him.

This is the good news, the Gospel of Jesus Christ. In Adam, one and all, we were dead, but here is another Adam in whom, one and all, He offers to make us alive. And why do I say He offers? Nay, He has already done it, in respect of all who have been made members of Him by His Spirit in Baptism, for of such it is written, "we are members of His body, of His flesh, and of His bones" (Eph. 5:30). And this is again a third creation: a new creation for each one of us separately, when we are one by one brought to Christ, when we put on Christ, when we are grafted into Christ, when we are made members of His mystical body the Church, when we are put in a way to be nourished by the heavenly food which He invites us to, His very own Body and Blood.

Behold then and see if there be any privileges like unto your privileges, to whom the Almighty Father has given His own Son for a life-giving Spirit to cure the death and ruin which you had brought upon yourselves by defiling the soul and body which He gave you at the first. What could have been done more for you that our good God has not done? A body "fearfully and wonderfully made" (Ps. 139:14), a living soul to quicken that body with the life of this world, His own Son, your second Adam, to quicken both soul and body with a better — that is a heavenly — life, a task to do in His vineyard, His Spirit to help you to do it, everlasting joy with Him your exceeding great reward. "What could have been done more in my vineyard, that I have not done in it?" (Isa. 5:4).

Alas! my brethren, what will be the end of it all? What will come at last of these worldly and ungodly lives, these days and nights without true prayer, these oaths and hypocrisies, Sundays profaned and weekdays wasted, this great disregard of parents, masters, elders and all in authority, this anger and quarreling and envy, this uncleanness, fornication and excess, this thieving and cheating, this lying, slander, covetousness, fretfulness, which we day by day make a show of before Christ and His holy angels, here in the midst of His new creation? You know what came of our father Adam's fall from the purity of the first creation. What if you should fall at last, fall willfully, fall incurably, from your place in Christ's own

Body? And you are in great danger. Believe me, you are. Believe not him who says, "Ye shall not surely die" (Gen. 3:4). But rather believe Him whose word is, "let him that thinketh he standeth take heed lest he fall" (1 Cor. 10:12). O look around, is there no bad example? Look inward, are there no lusts of the flesh? Look onward, are no temptations before you? Then, lest you despond, look upward, and tell me do you see nothing, do you discern no-one there to encourage you? O yes — look up steadily, look up in faith and you will certainly have a glimpse of Him. He who found a remedy for your father Adam desires, be sure, to save you. He waits to be gracious unto you. If you live so long He will be here this very Lent, as in former Lents, to turn your heart if you will let Him. It is His appointed time, His day of salvation. O, prepare for Him. Do not cast all away.

• 6 •

Peril of Half-heartedness

....

Volume 3, Sermon 21

THIRD SUNDAY IN LENT

"He that is not with me is against me, and he that gathereth not with me, scattereth."

LUKE 11:23

Our Lord in today's Gospel gives us an account of the kind of warfare which is continually going on between Him and the great enemy. It is not so much like regular fighting in the open field, with large armies on the one side and the other coming to one large conflict which decides the matter once for all. But it is a never ending course of severe and dangerous conflicts in which one side disputes with the other the possession of every nation, every parish, every family, every individual person.

Thus in one of the parables which you just now heard (Luke 11:14-22) the devil is compared to a strong man, a great warrior in full armor keeping his palace. We seem as we read to have before our eyes one of the great lords of the Philistines or one of those who in our own country, when times were unsettled, seized upon castles and made them a kind of stronghold of robbery. Even so the prince of darkness and author of all evil, having once gained a footing in the world by the fall of our first parents, has never ceased to occupy one after another the houses and hearts, the souls and bodies of men. Born in sin as we are, and children of wrath, each one of us is by nature a palace or castle of the evil one, a place where he abides to do all the mischief he can, both to us and to all who come within reach of us. And as long as the Almighty permits this his goods, the possessions of the evil one, are in peace. He has his own way with the unhappy sinners who are possessed by him. There is no struggle, no distress, no misgiving of conscience — people come to be past feeling, they give themselves over to lasciviousness, to commit all uncleanness with greediness, they go contentedly down the broad way.

This is the full power of Satan of which St. Paul speaks: the condition of those who are without God in the world, a condition the more fearful by how much those who are in it are less aware of it. Out of this our natural heathenish condition God delivers men when He converts them and brings them by Holy Baptism to be members of Christ, as it is written, "He hath delivered us from the power of darkness, and translated us into the kingdom of His dear Son" (Col. 1:13), and again to St. Paul he saith, "I send thee to open their eyes and turn them from darkness to light, and from the power of Satan unto God" (Acts 26:18). And accordingly it has been very common in the Church of Christ, and is still practiced in some countries, to use in the Baptism service a regular form of exorcism, the priest in the name of Jesus Christ commanding the unclean spirit to depart from the child or person to be baptized. We may understand in much the same sense our own short prayer which we offer up just before the blessing of the water, "grant that he may have power and strength to have victory and to triumph against the devil, the world, and the flesh."

Jesus Christ thus coming to us in Baptism, or if we have sinned afterwards by true repentance and absolution, is that warrior stronger than Satan who will not let him possess his goods, his ill gotten goods, our souls and bodies, in peace. He cometh upon the old serpent as that seed of the woman promised of old time to bruise his head, and not without a severe conflict, that is His death and passion, that bruising of His heel, His lower nature as man, by which from the very first He undertook to save us. The Son of God, coming thus upon the evil spirit to whom we were in bondage, overcame him, took from him all his armor wherein he trusted: his power, craft, command of the world, the honor in which he is held by poor deceived mortals. All this Christ taketh from Satan when he getteth the victory over him and divideth it as lawful spoil by the rules of war among His own servants, the enemies of Satan.

How is that? How may it be said that the spoils of Satan are divided among Christ's soldiers? Partly, perhaps, because from that time forward

whatever portion any of us may have in the good things of this world —
riches, power, pleasure, skill, wisdom, knowledge etc. — is all given up to
Jesus Christ and His service. Partly, again, because redeemed man is intended in some sort to fill up the place in God's world which the fallen angels have left vacant, as it is written, "we shall judge angels" (1 Cor. 6:3) and
"we shall be made like unto the angels" (Luke 20:36). And so the spoils
which Christ takes from Satan are the souls and bodies before lost, but
now redeemed, regenerated, saved, and so far "divided" in that each of
them is employed by God's grace and providence in such particular work
as the great King knows to be most for His glory and the good of souls,
and will each have assigned his own special reward, his own mansion in
the Father's house.

In short, our Savior here teaches that not only those unhappy ones
who were actually possessed by unclean spirits in the way the Gospel describes, but each one of us, every child of Adam, has by nature a spirit of
an unclean devil which can only be cast out by the Holy and good Spirit
entering into each one separately and uniting him to the second Adam as
by birth he was united to the first. Every such case, every Baptism, every
effectual repentance and absolution, is a victory won over the strong man
armed by one stronger than he. It is a warfare which goes on continually
and will go on from Pentecost to the end of the world.

But now observe the next thing concerning this warfare which the
great captain of our salvation most expressly warns us of. It is a warfare in
which it is utterly impossible for any one to stand by and be neutral. In all
wars and quarrels here we know there are many who take no part at all but
only just look on. But in this war between Christ and the devil that cannot
be the case with anyone. We must all take a part in it, whether we will or
not. "He that is not with me is against me, and he that gathereth not with
me, scattereth." Even so, in another place He says, "He that is not against
us is on our part" (Mark 9:40). Do you hear this, my brethren? It is a fearful
sound, surely, for us all — more fearful than if a trumpet sounded from
Heaven for a signal which we must obey, to range ourselves on the right
hand or the left, on the side of Christ's enemies or of His friends. For such
a trumpet would only be an angel's voice but these are the very words of
the Judge, spoken to the very inmost conscience of every one of us. Some
of us may find it hard to receive them, just as it is hard, very hard, to bring
it home to ourselves that we must all without exception, every single one
of us, either go away at last into everlasting punishment with the wicked,

or with the righteous into life eternal. O, if we could indeed realize this, if we could keep it steadily before our mind's eye, how would it help us in the right way! What power would it give against temptation! And in like measure, if we could really settle it in our hearts to feel that we are, even now, in one or other of two great armies, if we could by faith constantly discern our King on the one side and the enemy on the other and ourselves ranged under this banner or that, would it not make us very serious? Would it be possible for us to go on as if our conduct signified little?

One thing at any rate is clear, if we will take our Lord really at His word: that such as feel quite easy in their minds and have no anxiety concerning their duty and their souls can hardly be on Christ's side and in the way of salvation. For as on the one hand we read, "happy is the man that feareth always" (Prov. 28:14), so on the other hand when the strong man armed keepeth his palace our Lord tells us his goods are at peace. That is to say that when the devil has his own way with us most entirely then we are quite entirely free from spiritual anxiety and misgiving of mind. We say to ourselves "peace, peace, peace" most confidently when there is no peace. I have heard people boast that they let nothing daunt them and that they always kept up a good heart, and I have had reason to fear that their hope was little better than an ignorant deadness to spiritual things and that they were going on at the very time in plain, open, grievous sin. Therefore, I beseech you, let us greatly beware of indulging easy views of our condition — I mean our condition towards God. Let us shrink from the thought that all is safe. Let us say often in our hearts "what if, after all, I should be lost?" Whatever else is right or wrong, there is one thing which we are quite sure must be wrong: for a soldier in the midst of the battle to go on as if there was no enemy, no danger at all, and for a Christian in the wicked world to feel entirely at ease about his soul and his behavior as if all would go right of itself. Such a one is surely against Christ, if he did but know it.

So too is he (no uncommon sort of person I fear) who thinks he may stand off for a while and take no part in this warfare until he is older or differently circumstanced. Then he fully means to be religious, but he thinks he may be otherwise as yet. He does not mean to be irreligious — from such a thought he unfeignedly shrinks — but is still not disposed to serve God entirely and always. What shall we say to such a man? That he is like a soldier in sight of the enemy refusing to put on his armor and declaring the hour of the battle to be not yet come, as if, when the order was given to charge, some should stand still and say to themselves and to another, "it

78

will be time enough by and by to take up our arms." Nay, who told you that you should be there to take them up? Who told you that they should still be within your reach? Who told you that you shall not by that time be in the other world?

Bear with me, my brethren and sons in the Lord, if I say distinctly that this way of putting off your duties is far too common among you. I will just mention one instance, and many of you will guess beforehand what I am going to say. You all know in your hearts — you have been taught from your childhood and have no doubt — that to be a good and thorough soldier of Christ, to be really and truly with Him and against His enemy, you must be one with Christ and Christ with you and you know also that this is promised only to those who eat His Flesh and drink His Blood as He bade them, in remembrance of Him. How can you put this duty away from you and yet hope to be counted on our Savior's side?

Good intentions I dare say you have. I dare say you think you shall begin to prepare yourselves and come by and by. But remember that a wise and good man used to say that "the road to hell is paved with good intentions." The greater number of those who go down that miserable road mean to repent at some time, only the time never quite comes. Our Lord did not say "He that does not purpose at some time or other to be with me" but He said distinctly "he that is not with me, not with me now, not fighting now on my side, now at this very time, he, be he who he may, is against me. He needs a great change: he is still in the snare of the devil."

But, some might say, surely we are on Christ's side. The other day we resisted such a temptation, yesterday we performed such and such a good work, and though we have perhaps today fallen under the same temptation and failed to do the same kind of good work, yet will not one tell against another? Are we not on the whole with Him and not against Him? I would ask you, my brethren, one question. Suppose in battle you saw a soldier striking a blow or aiming a shot or a dart now against his own comrades, now against the enemy, on which side should you imagine him really to be in the purpose and intention of his heart? Should you not judge this of him: that his secret purpose was rather on the side of the enemy, and that what blows he struck at them were rather to save appearances, or for some other selfish reason than for any loyalty or duty which he had in his heart? In like manner you may be quite sure that as long as you allow yourself to go on in any known wilful sin you cannot be quite sincere in any part of your duty: you are not a faithful soldier and servant, you do not love your King and Master. He who sees into your heart cannot reckon you to be with Him.

Besides, what is the real consequence even outwardly and before men when Christians thus allow themselves to be half on the devil's side? Much the same as it would be in an army when the soldiers should now and then turn against their own leader in the very moment of action. There would be no confidence; no one would know on whom he could depend; the end would be confusion and flight, as our Lord goes on to say, "He that gathereth not with me, scattereth." We see and hear and feel daily the like sad effect of our many backslidings and inconsistencies. The unlearned and unbelievers say "behold how these Christians, these men professing godliness, do in their hearts and works deny it. Why then need we care for it?" And they are bold to break off from God more and more. O! depend on it, it will never do, it is what neither God nor man will endure, for Christ's soldiers wilfully to go on striking one blow for Satan and another for Christ. They will find in the end that they have been against their Lord altogether.

Neither again will it answer in this warfare if any man think to be passively on Christ's side: that is to lie still and merely do nothing against Him. We cannot do so, my brethren, if we would. Even if the hands could be idle, the mind, the will, the heart must be employed, the whole soul must be tending this way or that, upwards or downwards, towards hell or towards heaven. I suppose there are not a few who, looking on the sad falls and strange inconsistencies of such as have appeared earnest in religion, are inclined to shrink from being earnest themselves, as though there were some deceit in it, and so they are contented to go on, not only cold and indifferent in their devotions but careless too, and loose in their rules of life, to their own and others' great danger and harm. I wish they and all of us considered more what the great shepherd here assures us; he that is not actively engaged gathering the flock with me is really scattering it. It is vain to think of being on Christ's side and not being earnest and active in His cause. Remember the wicked and slothful servant. What cast him into the outer darkness? Not his ill-using his talent, but his not using it at all.

Look round you, my brethren, and see: see what comes of lukewarmness and ordinary ways of being or seeming indifferent to the cause of God and His Church. The bad example speaks. One after another says "my friend, my neighbor is not particular, so why should I be? My friend, my father, my master does not communicate, so why should I? My mother, my mistress, my elder sister bears with unwomanly discreditable conduct, so why may not I keep company with whom I will?" Look into your own hearts and consider how much you are losing of God's grace and blessing. You might be fervent in prayer, you might be full of all good thoughts, holy seasons and communions might be a joy and a crown to you — what a pity to lose all this for want of courage and exactness in your doings! Look again towards the enemy and see how you encourage him. Depend upon it, he rejoices in every moment you lose, every opportunity you neglect. Look, above all, to that which you know, or may know, to be written in God's book as concerning your daily falls and backslidings: the positive sins of temper and will, at least, into which you are continually betrayed for want of a courageous purpose of being entirely and zealously on God's side. O! if we will but turn our minds towards it we shall see that heaven and earth all around us are full of tokens of how blessed a thing it is to serve Christ with our whole heart, and how fatal to serve Him with half a heart.

• 7 •

The Unchangeable Priesthood of Christ

· ·

Volume 4, Sermon 39

PASSION SUNDAY

"He is able also to save them to the uttermost that come unto God by Him, seeing He ever liveth to make intercession for them."

HEBREWS 7:25

We are preparing to keep the yearly solemnity of our Lord's death and passion. The Cross is once more to be lifted up in our sight, and Jesus Christ
to be evidently set forth crucified. In spirit we are to be present where He
is bound, dragged along, smitten on the face, blindfolded, buffeted, spit
upon, blasphemed. They condemn Him to death, they hale Him before Pilate, in scorn and spite they cry out "away with Him, crucify Him," they
give Him over into the hands of the heathen, and we shall see Him brought
very low, as a worm and no man, by the usage of those wicked soldiers —
scourged, crowned with thorns, wrapped in a ragged purple garment, a
very scorn of men and the outcast of the people. "He hath no form nor
comeliness, and when we shall see Him, there is no beauty that we should
desire Him" (Isa. 53:2).

When we see Him thus humbled, brought so very low for our sakes, it
may be that some of us may not rightly remember His glory. Those who
were by at the time could not know of that glory. Even the better sorts
among them, the women that bewailed and lamented Him, could not but
be grieved and shocked to see so holy a person so cruelly and shamefully

used, but they did not, they could not, know for certain how great and holy and glorious He is: the Most High God Himself, the Eternal Son of the Father, come down to suffer for us in the very truth of our nature, in all things like unto us only without sin. They could not know that He whom they saw dying on the Cross was very God and even we who do know it, who have been taught it from our earliest days, do not, I fear, always rightly remember it.

I once myself heard a well-meaning person say, when mention was made of our Lord's sufferings (it was long before I knew this place), "and to think of their behaving so to so good a Christian as He was." You see, my brethren, what that good person meant. She meant nothing but what was respectful, but you see also plainly that she was not used to think of Jesus as of the Most High God, equal with the Father, the God who at that very moment was looking down into her heart. And I suppose there are many like her in this. I hear and read the name Jesus very often used in far too familiar a way. Even serious persons oftentimes make too free with that holy name, and so and in many other ways they show plainly that whilst they are willing to take our Lord for their best friend and only Savior they have by no means learned to reverence Him as their God and Judge.

Beware of this, dear brethren — use yourselves to bow the very knees of your heart at every remembrance of Him who, though he so demeaned Himself for you, was, is and will be forever the Eternal Word of God, with God, Himself very God, of one substance with the Father. When you hear, verse by verse, of His sad sufferings in the lessons of next week, say to yourselves very often, "It was God Almighty who endured all this, God Almighty who sat down and ate the Passover with His disciples, God Almighty who broke the bread and blessed it and said 'this is my body,' God Almighty who washed His disciples' feet, who sweated blood in His agony, who permitted Judas to kiss Him, who was chained, dragged along, reviled and buffeted. The face in which they spat was the face of God. The body which they tore with their scourges was the body of God. It was the head of God which they crowned with thorns, the hands and feet of God through which they drove their cruel nails. It was God Himself, appearing among them, whom they put to death amid their railings and blasphemies." O, never forget it, never cease to think of it, else you will never think as you ought of your own sins or of His mercy. You will never have the right faith until you have accustomed yourselves to think of Christ not only as your Savior, but as God your Savior.

Our salvation itself, my brethren, depends upon this. If He were not our God He could not be our Savior: such a Savior as we need. To be such a Savior He is both God and man, and so His great names signify — Emmanuel, God with us, God making Himself one of us and abiding with us, and Jesus, the Lord, the Most High God, our Savior God, reigning for ever in heaven far above all suffering, made for a little while lower than the angels for the suffering of death, the worst of deaths, the death of the Cross, God of the substance of the Father, begotten before the worlds and man of the substance of His Mother, born in the world. And thus He was the Savior we needed. For being man He could suffer, as the apostle says "It behoved Him in all things to be made like unto His brethren" (Heb. 2:17). And as the children are partakers of flesh and blood, he also Himself likewise took part of the same. As man He could suffer, and as God His sufferings had that power and virtue in them that they were able to redeem a lost world. As man He took true blood of the Virgin Mary, and as God His blood was capable of washing away sins.

Because Jesus Christ is very God He was able to reconcile us by His death, and for the same reason, we being reconciled He is able to save us by His life. So the apostle tells us in the text — "He is able to save to the uttermost them that come unto God by Him."

We are not to think of our Lord's sacrifice as of a thing past and done in such sense that we sinners may have the blessing and benefit of it without anything done on our part and without any more merciful interference on His. True, he died once for all. The day of Calvary can never come again. Christ hanging on the Cross was "a full, perfect and sufficient sacrifice, oblation and satisfaction for the sins of the whole world." But even as He created the world once and the act of creation needs not to be again, yet still there is need of His constant preserving power to uphold the things which He hath made and to give life and being to each of his creatures in particular as they come into the world one after another. It is somewhat in the same way in the matter of redemption. He died once for all mankind, but He lives again, lives for ever, to communicate the benefits of His death to the Church which is His body, and to each Christian in particular. While you remember His agony and bloody sweat, His Cross and passion, you must not forget His glorious resurrection and ascension.

"I am He that liveth and was dead, and behold, I am alive for evermore" (Rev. 1:18). That is the Christ whom we have to wait upon, to follow to the Cross, to lay in the grave, now in the sad and aweful week which is drawing so very near us. The Holy Church bids us think of His crucified body and His saving wounds, not only as His friends and mourners saw them on Good Friday, but also as the blessed saints and angels see them even now in heaven. The Holy Church, I say, bids us think of Him so, in that she directs us to read at this time what the Epistle to the Hebrews teaches of Christ having come as an High Priest of good things to come, and having by His own blood entered once into the holy place.

The Son of Man, our High Priest and Savior, obtained eternal redemption for us by what He endured upon the Cross, but for you and me and each of us to reap finally the fruit of that redemption we must be partakers of that which He is now doing for us in heaven. Let us reverently consider what Scripture tells us of this. For only think, dear brethren, what a shame, what a danger it must be when our good Lord in Holy Scripture opens a door in heaven and allows us sinners to look in and listen and see and hear a little of what He is there doing for our good, and we choose rather to go to sleep or amuse ourselves with looking round upon each other or with anything else that comes into our poor frail fancies. Therefore I say again, attend to me, or rather attend to the Holy Ghost, and consider what the Bible tells us of our Lord's doings in heaven where He is now, in the way of saving our souls. How does he apply to you and me and the whole Church the blessed infallible medicine which He provided for us by His death and passion? How does He bring home His salvation to each one of our souls?

First, you know, He is our King in heaven and He sitteth there at the right hand of God. There, ever since His ascension, all power in heaven and on earth has been exercised by the man Christ Jesus, and all for the salvation of His elect, His own sheep that hear His voice. Heaven and earth, angels and men, all powers and creatures whatsoever, are wonderfully ordered and overruled by Him so as to work together for good to them that love God. And most especially He, as our King, sends down His royal gift, the Holy Spirit of the Father and the Son, to dwell in our hearts to unite us to Him, to sanctify and prepare us for joy and glory.

But that is not all. There is another high and wonderful office which "He that liveth and was dead and is alive for evermore" (Rev. 1:18) vouchsafes to exercise for us in heaven at His Father's right hand. He is not only our King but our priest. This is what St. Paul speaks of: "He ever liveth to make intercession for us" (Heb. 7:25). To make intercession is to intercede. You know what "intercede" means: it is when a person wants a favor of another and gets a friend or favorite of the other to ask the favor for him. So our Lord, not exactly as one praying, (at least Holy Scripture does not say so) but as a priest offering a sacrifice and pleading for another, appears before God for us. If He appears as a priest he must have some sacrifices to present, as St. Paul himself argues, "every High Priest is ordained to offer gifts and sacrifices: wherefore it is of necessity that this man have somewhat to offer" (Heb. 8:3).

What is the sacrifice which our Lord offers in heaven? The very same which He once for all offered on earth: the body which was broken and the blood which was shed on the Cross. It is that same body and blood which He took of the Virgin Mary, which He offered once for all with pain, suffering and death on Good Friday, but which on Easter Day He united again and on Ascension Day carried both body and soul into heaven, there to appear night and day in the presence of the Father for us. It is that same Blood, His own Blood, whereby he continually pleads for His Church and each one of His servants on earth, and is our advocate with the Father by that same love which caused Him to make Himself here a bloody sacrifice, a propitiation, a reconciling gift for our sins. Thus He pleads and intercedes in heaven, standing before the Father as a Lamb that had been slain. He does not forget us for one moment. As often as we say an earnest prayer in His name, as often as any poor distressed sinner begs mercy and grace of the Father "through Jesus Christ our Lord" as our Prayer Book teaches, so often, depend on it, our merciful High Priest in some unspeakable way makes His heavenly memorial of what he endured on Mount Calvary. And the Lord smells a sweet savor, and accepts our prayers as incense in His tabernacle for the sake of Him who unites them to His own sacrifice.

And as if this was not love enough, behold what He has done besides for us, according to the delight which He has in being with the sons of men and doing them good. Though He has taken up His blessed body and blood in its outward and visible form unto heaven, there to remain until His second coming, He has nevertheless in a sacramental manner left us that same blessed Body and Blood on earth, to be set before His Father in the way you know of, by the appointed use of bread and wine, and so to be pleaded on our own altars for a memorial of His precious death. And observe that this memorial on earth, as well as the memorial in heaven, is made by Christ Himself. Outwardly to the eye, indeed, it looks as if we earthly priests offered the sacrifice and made the memorial. But the truth is that we earthly priests are as nothing in that great work. It is not we that consecrate but our Lord Himself, though we say over the words. And since He has said, "I am with you always, even unto the end of the world" (Matt. 28:20), we cannot doubt that He is present especially when we sanctify and offer the precious Body and Blood of our Savior. He is there. He pleads for us on earth by that bread and wine which is His Body and Blood as surely as He pleads in Heaven by His natural body with its visible wounds, in the very form which He has shown to a few of His saints. The priest, be he who he may, is but an instrument in the Lord's hand, as the rod in the hand of Moses. Christ, the living and eternal Word of God, is the true priest, the true consecrator, just as in the other Sacrament it is He who really baptizes. The clergyman whom you see sprinkles the water, but it is Christ and Christ alone who baptizeth with the Holy Ghost.

So you see, my brethren, the offering in the Holy Communion is the same remembrance of our Lord's sacrifice on the Cross which He offers to the Father continually in Heaven, and it is the same Christ who pleads and offers it, here in an image and under a veil, there openly in His own human form in the sight of the angels. And for whom does our gracious Lord thus continually plead and offer Himself? For those, no doubt, whom He prayed for on earth, for those whom He mentioned in that wonderful prayer immediately after that first Holy Communion of which you may read in the seventeenth chapter of St. John. He prayed for his chosen apostles and in them for the whole Church, and not for them only but for all who should believe on Him through their word, for all Christians, for us, my brethren, for us, sinful and unworthy as we are, unless we unthankfully reject His intercession. For us He then prayed on earth and for us He now intercedes in Heaven.

What is the blessing, the special end of his prayer and intercession? Is it earthly joy and comfort, health in our bodies, peace in our homes, success in our undertakings and the like? No, my brethren, none of these did our High Priest ask for us in that prayer at His first communion, but what He did ask was "that we might all be one, as the Father in Him and He in the Father" (John 17:21). Christ in us and the Father in Christ, that we may be with Him where He is and may behold His glory which the Father hath given him. He pleads on our behalf where He now is, in heaven. In respect of all other things he orders them and pleads for them in such manner and measure as he knows will work together for good to them that love Him and keep His commandments.

Thus you see what a High Priest we have, "holy, harmless, undefiled, separate from sinners and made higher than the heavens, and able to save us to the uttermost" (Heb. 7:26). For what more could we ask or think of, were we the purest and highest angels in heaven, than being one with Him and He with us? Much more, being as we are sinful souls and bodies, worthy of nothing but hell. He is able and He is willing to save us, one and all, to the uttermost. But one thing is needful. We must come into God. We must not refuse or hang back when His loving voice calls. When His loving hand draws us on we must come unto God and we must come by Him. What is coming by Him? Not only praying in His name, but really doing and suffering for His sake — not only saying at the end of collects "through Jesus Christ our Lord," but joining in His sacrifice by worthy communion. Mind, I say, worthy communion. That word "worthy" gathers up all into a point. If that be right, all is right; without it there is no promise of life.

• 8 •

Christ's Own Preparation for His Passion
....

Volume 5, Sermon 2

PALM SUNDAY

*"In the day-time He was teaching in the Temple: and at night he went
out, and abode in the mount that is called the Mount of Olives."*

LUKE 21:37

This is the account set down by the Holy Ghost of the manner in which
our blessed Lord spent what may be called His Passion Week — the days
during which He stayed in Jerusalem after He had come up to His last
Passover, waiting for His hour to come, preparing, in a manner, for His
death and resurrection. He came into the city, as we read in St. John, six
days before the Passover, that is on the Sunday in that last week. On this
very day, as it were, He rode into the holy city as the prophets had foretold,
on a colt, the foal of an ass. That day he spent teaching in the temple, looking into the condition of all things there and working miracles, and when
it was now even-tide "He went out of the city to Bethany, and He lodged
there" (Matt. 21:17), most likely near the house of Lazarus, Martha, and
Mary. Now Bethany was on the Mount of Olives. When, therefore, St.
Luke tells us that our Savior went out on those evenings to the Mount of
Olives he tells us the same as St. Matthew where he writes that on the first
of those evenings our Lord went out to pass the night in Bethany.

As he did on the Sunday of that week, so he did on all the following
days until the Friday: the morning and daylight hours he spent in the tem-

ple teaching, instructing the multitudes and His disciples and warning His malicious enemies, who were all the while watching Him, and the nights he spent on the Mount of Olives, in what sort of employment we may guess both from what we read of Him before and from what followed near the end of the week.

We read of Him in the early part of the Gospel, when He first began to preach, that after a very hard day's work of healing men's bodies and instructing their souls, rising up "a great while before day," He departed and went "into a solitary place," and was there praying when His disciples came to look for Him (Mark 1:35). Again, after the miracle of the loaves "He departed again into a mountain Himself alone" (John 6:15), and was there until the fourth watch of the night (Matt. 14:25), that is until three in the morning. Another time, after much disputing with His enemies and long teaching in the temple the Pharisees went "every man to his own house" (John 7:53); they had houses to go to, with plenty of ease and all sorts of comforts awaiting them. But "Jesus went unto the Mount of Olives" (John 8:1). He chose not to have any home where He might lay His head. After His days had been days of charity He would have His nights be nights of devotion.

So it was during His ministry. And so it was, still more, when that ministry was drawing to an end. The very day before His Passion, having first eaten the Passover with His disciples and given them those blessed instructions which we read in St. John, He went out into a garden, the garden of Gethsemane on the slope of the Mount of Olives whither ofttimes He had been used to resort with His disciples, and there he was praying when the Jews and Judas came upon Him.

Our Lord's preparation, then, for His sufferings lay in these two things: active practical duties by day and earnest devotion and meditation by night. Now that means whereby He prepared Himself for the Cross itself and the grave and all His mysterious sufferings, the same means must be the best preparation for His people also when they are celebrating the memory and likeness of those sufferings. For what is the purpose of the holy Church universal in appointing this particular time of year during which for so many days we are to follow Him step by step through all the stages of His bitter Passion first and then of His triumphant victory over death? Of course what is meant is that we, by the help of God's Holy Spirit, should make what happened to Him as present to us and as near to us as ever we can, so that we should, as St. Paul says, "have the mind of Christ"

(1 Cor. 2:16), that when Good Friday comes we should spend that solemn day with some faint touch at least of His heavenly patience, charity and self-denial, and that the Cross should not be lifted up for us in vain but that we should go out of ourselves, forget and renounce ourselves and turn all our faith and hope and love towards our divine and only Savior as Mary Magdalene did and the other holy women when they stood by beholding His death. This, I say, is part at least of the Church's purpose in having such a day as Good Friday and such a week as Passion Week, to humble and chasten our minds, by way of preparation for that aweful day.

Now if we are to come as near as we can, frail feeble sinners as we are, to the mind of our dying Lord on the day of His death, it stands by reason that we should attend to, and in our measure imitate and practice, His proceedings while He was preparing for that day. If we would spend Good Friday with Him crucified, we shall do well to spend Passion Week with Him in the temple, and on the Mount of Olives.

For as we learned of our Lord Himself last Sunday, it is vain to expect any right understanding of any thing that God says or does, except one is so changed as to "be of God" (John 8:47). There must be a preparation of heart and mind, else the word spoken in our ears, the wonders wrought in our sight, will fail to come home to us. And if this be the case in respect of all Divine institutions, much more of so great a thing as the Sacrifice of His Son which is the salvation of the whole world. There will be no true receiving the doctrine of the Cross without a heavenly change in heart and mind, disposing us practically to take up the Cross. And, as was said, it should seem from our Lord's own way of spending His time when His death was drawing near that this will depend on two things: diligence in the duty of our calling and heavenly contemplation. Let us try to understand how each of these may help us to enter into the spirit of the merciful yet most fearful sacrifice, the memory of which will again be set forth before us if God spare our lives a week longer.

And, first, as to the effect of regular dutiful obedience in making us better able to feel our Lord's death as we ought, consider what it is that we mean by dutifulness. We mean that people do a thing because they know it is such as God will approve, without considering whether it is or is not pleasant or profitable to themselves. Thus we call a servant dutiful when he does a good part by his master in sight and out of sight alike, and the same with regard to a son and his father, a king and his subject, and to any other person who is accountable to one higher than himself. We call him dutiful when he forgets himself, when he goes out of himself entirely, and looks only to the one question of what his employer has a right to expect of him.

He, then, who in his ordinary life strives to be dutiful towards God is so far striving to forget himself. And when such a one shall come to contemplate the Blessed Jesus on the Cross his heart will secretly swell within him in a way unthought of before. He will say, or rather he will feel, to himself, "Here is, indeed, in unspeakable perfection, that which I have been faintly wishing and longing to practice — here is dutifulness taught in a way which the tongue of man can never express, nor his heart conceive worthily." How so? One may answer in divine words, the words of one of the proper Psalms appointed for Good Friday. There the prophet, in our Savior's person, says, "Lo, I come" — I come down from heaven to earth, I take on me the form of a servant, I stoop down under the Cross, and afterwards offer myself up on it. "In the volume of the Book it is written of me" — the Old Testament prophecies have pointed it out long before — that I should "fulfil Thy will, O my God: I am content to do it: yea, Thy law is within My heart" (Ps. 40:7-8).

Surely these words, taken as the words of Him who is God as well as man, are the highest expression of dutifulness that can be imagined, answering to those many sayings of our Lord wherein He at the same time declared Himself one with the Father, and yet spoke as if in a kind of subordination to Him such as, "The Son can do nothing of Himself, but what He seeth the Father do: for what things soever he doeth, these also doeth the Son likewise" (John 5:9), and again, "The Father hath not left me alone, for I do always those things that please Him" (John 8:29). What these words say, the sight of our Lord on the Cross showed forth in action. It was the perfection of all duty, utter forgetfulness of self, as looking only to that will which He prayed might be done in preference to His own. "He became *obedient* unto death, even the death of the Cross" (Phil. 2:8); whoever then studies to live in obedience is so far preparing himself to die with our Lord, if need be, on the Cross, and much more to keep devoutly the solemn memory of His death.

But whoever would do his duty thoroughly, no matter in what station or condition of life, must often endure things positively unpleasant to him and oftener deny himself what he would greatly enjoy. If you strive regularly to do a good day's work you will have often to go on when tired, sometimes in pain; to move, when you would be glad to sit still; to endure aching and soreness and pangs of body and mind when, if it were not for the whispers of duty and conscience within, you might be enjoying yourself, or at least remain quite at ease.

Now every little burden of this kind that a man has the courage to lay on himself will help him in some small measure to understand what Scripture says of the Cross of Christ. When we feel how hard it is, especially at first beginning, to endure for duty's sake but a very small degree of pain or anguish that we might free ourselves of, and how continually we are tempted, while so acting, to take out our own reward in praising ourselves for it, then we may begin faintly and dimly to imagine what that love must be which, for no joy of its own but only the joy of saving sinners, "endured the cross, despising the shame" (Heb. 12:2). He endured such pangs as the Psalms and Prophets describe — "I am poured out like water, and all my bones are out of joint: my heart also in the midst of my body is even like melting wax; my strength is dried up like a potsherd, and my tongue cleaveth to my gums. I was a derision to all my people, and their song all the day. He hath filled me with bitterness; He hath made me drunken with wormwood. Is it nothing to you, all ye that pass by? Behold, and see if there be any sorrow like unto my sorrow, wherewith the Lord hath afflicted me in the day of His fierce anger" (Ps. 22:14-15; Lam. 3:14-15; 1:12). I say, if a man does but lie awake one night with bodily pain and anguish he may well begin to have other and truer thoughts of such Scriptures as these than he had before.

And thus resolutely doing our duty, from the very pain which it sometimes brings with it, trains the soul to embrace the Cross. Who are more likely to turn towards their suffering Savior with all their heart and soul than those who are dutifully and affectionately waiting on the sick-bed of some friend or kinsman which requires more than ordinary self-denial? Persevere, then, in the work of your calling, pleasant or unpleasant, for His sake who called you, as our Lord was daily teaching in the temple; it will be half, one may say the first half, of your preparation for rightly drawing near the Cross of Christ.

But let us not forget that this preparation comprehends another thing equally necessary. There must be contemplation as well as action, devotional thoughts as well as dutiful obedience. Who can doubt that our Blessed Lord's nights spent in the Mount of Olives had at least as much to do with His hour which was at hand as His days of teaching and miracles in Jerusalem and in the temple? It will not do to imagine, as one may sometimes hear people affirming in a tone not quite so reverential as one should wish, that we are sufficiently prepared for receiving Christ if we be honest and punctual and kind in our daily calling. It is not a safe way of talking, which some have, that "they are not afraid to die, for they bear no man any ill-will, nor have done anybody harm, neither is the man living who has any reason to count them enemies." This is not, I say, a safe way of talking, though it is a very common one. For what does it, in fact, come to? It comes to this: that there is no special need of devotion, that we have no occasion to exercise ourselves in withdrawing from the world in order to have direct intercourse with God in prayer and deep thought and heavenly contemplation. This, if you consider it, is as much as to say that a man is just as likely to keep the way to Heaven and come thither at last though he never look that way.

But, unaccountable as this sounds when we put it into words, it is indeed, and in deed, and in real life, one of the most common of all errors and especially necessary to be guarded against in our country and in our time. For it somehow appears that we English people, of all people in the world, are most apt to make an idol of what we call common sense and to look at everything as those who are called men of business, to enquire after the visible apparent use of things, to be impatient of what we do not at once understand and to think that all must be right enough if people's lives and practices towards one another be right. Our spirit, left to itself, is too like that of the rich young man who having, as he thought, done all his duty to his neighbor from his youth up, asked of our Lord without fear "What lack I yet?" (Matt. 19:20). This, we have reason to think, is the disposition of our countrymen. They always want something solid, and dislike what seems fanciful and unreal. They are too much for sight against Faith, even in religious and spiritual things, and therefore devotion properly so called: worshiping God, lifting up their hearts to Him in public and in private, making leisure for prayer and holy and penitential exercises, keeping holy days and times, whether of humiliation or of festival joy. All these things we Englishmen are apt to think slightly of, because we do not perceive at once that outward fruit of them which we are accustomed to look for in every thing.

Is there any one here who does not know people who think little of public worship because experience tells them, as they suppose, that a man may be good and useful without it? And can it be reasonably doubted that many go on to despise private prayer also because they do not see why it should be necessary to a person doing his duty to his acquaintance and being useful in his generation? Now, while it is not so bad, yet it may be a part of this same undevout temper wilfully to despise and neglect any ordinance of the Church, any sort of direct devotion which she recommends to her children. Fasting, for example, is one sort of private devotion on which the Church has given very particular directions, as anyone may see in the calendar at the beginning of the Prayer Book. Yet how many persons are there who pass by these directions altogether, making no difference at all between fast-days and feast-days! No doubt most people do so in ignorance — their attention has not been ever really drawn to the subject. But as to whoever first began this inattention and whoever, being reminded, still goes on in it, have we not some reason to fear that it may be in them a symptom of the profane spirit of the world, to which all days and all times are alike? What would such a one have said to our Lord's devotions that last week of His life, by night, in the Mount of Olives? Would he not have thought it a pity that working so hard as He did, and having so much to endure, He should weary Himself out still more with watching and prayer all night? But we see that He, to whom alone the right way is perfectly known, took the way of self-denial and holy contemplation and added watching and devotional exercises, by night and when alone, to the pastoral and charitable works which engaged Him by day, and among others.

Add to this the reflection on who our Blessed Lord was: God Incarnate, so united, even as man, to the Most High and Eternal Godhead that he could not be for a moment left alone. Yet even He accounted it necessary, at set times and places and in a solemn manner, to keep up this intercourse of devotion with His heavenly Father. He who of all men, one should think, could least need it, has set the strictest example of intense prayer and retired meditation as the true way of preparing oneself for hard duties and conflicts in life, and for the last unknown hour.

I wish we thought of this more than we do. Here is our Master rising up to His prayers a great while before day, and we lie on in sloth and negligence. Here is our Master on the Mount of Olives after a hard day's work in the temple, and we, perhaps, fancying ourselves over-tired, come in and throw ourselves on our beds without one serious prayer or recollection. Here is our Master kneeling and falling prostrate, and we sit carelessly and perhaps look about us, while the Church is offering up the most solemn prayers.

You are deceived, my brethren, if you imagine that these are mere outward things, making no difference if the heart be right. Why are they set down as part of our Lord's behavior if they make no difference in God's sight? How can they be mere outward things if we do them humbly because we read that he did so? If place, posture, time, self-denial, helped Him in His devotions are we better than He (God forgive the word) that we should think ourselves above needing such help? If even He who was one with the Father used so much serious contemplation, took so much time, as it were, to recollect Himself when His death was coming on, can we imagine we are duly preparing for our death if we will not find or make leisure for calm thought and religious examination of ourselves before our prayers, and after we have done praying?

I say preparing for our death — for, indeed, that is the true light in which we are to regard all the services of this Holy Week. Good Friday, as the remembrance of our Lord's dying moments, is to a faithful Christian a sort of rehearsal and foretaste of his own departure. For such a person knows that his death cannot be a happy one except by partaking of the virtue of his Lord's death. It must be offered up as a sort of sacrifice in union with the only true sacrifice made once for all on the Cross. Our Lord, in His dying pains, did in a mysterious and heavenly manner bear the death-pangs of all His people, made them His own, and sanctified them, so that His death is in a manner their death, and theirs, His. This being so, how can we better prepare to keep the memorial of His death than by such holy and charitable ways as we would wish to be found in when we have to meet our own?

Be not, then, slothful, on this holy and blessed week. Make haste to be reconciled, you who are out of charity. Deny yourselves, you who live at your ease. Recollect yourselves, you who are careless in your prayers, and remember your Savior, while you have time — His warning in the verse before, "Watch ye therefore, and pray always, that ye may be accounted worthy to escape all these things that shall come to pass, and to stand before the Son of man" (Luke 21:36), and His practice, described in the text, "In the day-time He was teaching in the temple: and at night he went out, and abode in the mount that is called the Mount of Olives."

Old Testament Types of the Cross:
The Rod of Moses

. . . .

Volume 5, Sermon 55
This sermon is the third in a series preached at
evening services during Holy Week.

HOLY WEEK

*"And thou shalt take this rod in thine hand, wherewith thou shalt do
signs."*

EXODUS 4:17

The tree of life in paradise betokens the Cross, as being that whereon He
hangeth who is our only life, of whom Christians are invited to eat and live
for ever. Again, the wood which was carried by Isaac up the hill betokens
the Cross, as being that which He who should be our sacrifice bore on His
shoulders up Mount Calvary, being afterwards Himself to be borne by it
and offered upon it. And now we will think of another thing of which we
read a good deal farther on in the Bible. The *rod of Moses* is also a great type
of the Cross. For as Moses by his rod overcame the Lord's enemies and delivered his people from bondage, so did Jesus Christ by His Cross, and that
not only once for all in the beginning of His kingdom, but also day by day
continually for the good of each one of us. Let us, then, for this evening's
meditation, consider some part of what Scripture tells concerning this
wonder-working rod of Moses. Perhaps by God's mercy we may find some
instruction how to use our Savior's Cross, wherein we have a portion as
Christians, to our own good.

　　The first mention of Moses' rod is in the fourth chapter of Exodus,
where God is discoursing with him out of the burning bush in Mount Si-

nai. Moses, as a shepherd, had a rod or staff in his hand, and when he said "The Israelites will not believe me" (Exod. 4:1) the Lord appointed him that rod, wherewith he should work various wonders in their sight, and so convince them that God had sent him and encourage them to put themselves under his care. Yet the rod in itself was but a common piece of wood. No more was our Lord's saving Cross, which afterwards Almighty God used for the redemption of the whole world and entire discomfiture of His people's enemies. In itself it had no virtue, but as an engine of divine power it could do all things. And we may observe that all its virtue was given it by the Lord appearing in the bush. Now this appearing in the bush is that token of Christ's wonderful Incarnation, how that our most poor frail human nature became the abode of the Most High God and, instead of being consumed and brought to nothing by His intimate Presence, was ennobled and blessed and glorified to that infinite degree that, as the Creed of St. Athanasius says, it was even "taken into God."

I say then, as the rod had its virtue from the Lord appearing in the bush, so the Cross hath its saving power from the Incarnate Godhead of Him who hangeth thereon. He saves us by it, and by it He puts down our enemies, because He is God and man, suffering and dying for us upon it. Remember this, Christian brethren, in all your thoughts, at this aweful time. Remember that He who suffers, although He is true man (else He could not have suffered), is also very and eternal God, and fear and tremble before Him accordingly.

This rod is turned in the first place into a serpent, and Moses flies from before it, because the Cross is naturally the punishment of sin and the portion of sinners, and anyone would naturally shrink from it. Nay even our gracious Redeemer, who had devoted Himself from the first to bear it, felt His soul, as the time drew on, "exceedingly sorrowful even unto death" (Matt. 26:38) and prayed to His Father that, if it were possible, the hour might pass from Him. So when any one of us is bidden to take hold the Cross, to join with our Lord in any self-denial or suffering, we of course should be glad to draw back; we feel as if it were a serpent, as if there were enmity between us and it. But let us, at God's bidding, courageously put forth our hands and lay hold of it, and it will turn again to a rod; instead of destroying, it will support and guide us.

The next thing is, God directs the prophet, as in the text, to take the wonderful rod in his hand when he sets forth on his errands to the Israelites and to Pharaoh. "Take this rod in thine hand, wherewith thou shalt do signs." That is, both Christ Himself and His minsters should do all their wonders in the way of the Cross. Christ Himself did in a manner bear the Cross all His life long. He was "a man of sorrows and acquainted with grief" (Isa. 53:3) all the while that He went about doing good. He sighed and wept and groaned in the Spirit and was troubled, in the very act of healing the worst infirmities and raising the dead to life. And His ministers as they go about in His name must also bear the cross in His name, even as one of the holiest of them long ago declared to His people, "I determined to know nothing among you save Jesus Christ and Him crucified" (1 Cor. 2:2). And all pictures of our Lord in His glory represent Him, as you know, with the Cross in His hands, because the Cross is that by which He reigns, and by which His ministers prevail. Thus Moses, going to speak in God's name to the children of Israel and to Pharaoh, was a type of Jesus Christ first and afterwards of His Church, coming to all men with the message and power of the Cross.

But what are the great things to be done by this mean-looking and simple rod which the shepherd of the Lord's flock bears in his hand? It is the driving away their enemies and punishing them by the fearful miracles which we call the plagues of Egypt, and it is also the making of a way for His chosen people out of Egypt and helping them afterwards through the frightful wilderness. The rod of God was the outward and visible token by means whereof all these wonders were wrought. When the water was to be turned into blood, Moses and Aaron lifted up the rod and smote waters that were in the river. The water became blood by the same power which even now is present in Holy Baptism, to make the water, by the grace of the Holy Ghost, effectual to wash away sin by the blood of Jesus Christ.

When the swarms of frogs were to be brought up out of the river, then again Aaron's hand was to be stretched out with his rod, and so when the dust of the land was to become lice Aaron's rod is particularly mentioned, as if a holy priest or Bishop were to excommunicate some wicked country in the name of Christ crucified, and heavy scourges were to ensue. Again, in the last and worst of the plagues of Egypt, when the whole land was desolated with hail, when locusts were to be called over it, still the rod of Moses was used. Surely we are to understand by this that the effectual weapon for a Christian to use against all the enemies of his soul is no other than our Lord's Cross. We are to hold up the remembrance of His passion against the world, the flesh and the devil, against the sins that come nearest to hurt us, and we shall come off more than conquerors.

But more especially may a Christian discern, in type and shadow, the virtue of his Savior's Cross in that wonderful history which we hope to hear next Sunday: the passage of the children of Israel through the Red Sea. When that sea was to be divided for the people to pass through as on dry land, God said "Lift thou up thy rod, and stretch out thine hand over the sea and divide it" (Exod. 14:16). And in the morning again Moses stretched forth his hand over the sea and the sea returned to his strength, and the waters returned and covered the chariots and the horsemen and all the host of Pharaoh; there remained not so much as one of them. What is this but the Cross of Christ making a way for His chosen through the waters of the new birth, and overwhelming their spiritual enemies in the same? So that if the young child die before he commit actual sin he is, as the Church teaches, undoubtedly saved. The evil one with all his followers can no more come near that child to harm him than Pharaoh and his armies, being drowned in the Red Sea, could rise up to hurt the Israelites on their way. And as a token that this is all done by the power of our Savior's Cross the priest, we know, at the time of our Baptism made the sign of the Cross on our foreheads and bade us go on and fight manfully against sin, the world and the devil, as Moses, stretching out his rod, bade the children of Israel go on through the midst of the sea. Once again, on their way through the wilderness, we find the rod in Moses' hand working wondrously, and again it works in such a way as to show us plainly that it is the type of the Holy Cross. The Israelites are thirsty and there is no water to drink; Moses is commanded to take his rod wherewith he smote the river, and to smite the rock and bring water out of it for them. The rod helped them to a strange and miraculous drink, and does not the Cross help us continually to the spiritual drink of Christ's Blood in Holy Communion? His side, pierced on the Cross, is as that rock smitten by Moses which was the fountain of strengthening and refreshing to the children of Israel.

Thus, from beginning to end, we see that as the rod of Moses was the instrument of Israel's deliverance, so is Christ's Cross the instrument of our redemption. And so it must be from the beginning to the end of our lives. The thought and remembrance of the Cross is that which will help us above all others to get the better of the enemies of our souls. The Christians of old time made much of the outward sign itself. They used it, as the Jews did the words of their Law, on all occasions of any consequence: at going out and coming in, at sitting down and rising up. If we use the outward sign only that once at our Baptism, yet have we the same need as our forefathers had of the thing meant and intended by that outward sign. We have the same need as they had of calling to mind continually the passion of our Lord. We priests need it in our dealings with you, Christ's people, and you, Christ's people, need it continually in your dealings with your own consciences. Is not a priest, when he goes about the parish warning one man of grievous sin and encouraging and forwarding another in good ways, is he not a little like Moses, now contending against Pharaoh, now opening the way for the Israelites through the water? And if Moses could do neither of these things without the rod of God, his ordained instrument, of course neither can we do any thing for you, nor you for yourselves, without the Cross, without remembrance of the passion of Christ.

For only just consider, my brethren. When the world is strong upon you: when, for example, you know what your duty is but know also that you will be laughed at for doing it, would it not be a great thing for you to recall to mind the Cross and what happened round it? You are full of false shame; you are childishly afraid of the scorn and ridicule of certain companions of yours, very clever perhaps and amusing so that you can scarcely help laughing with them yourselves, and it seems to you an intolerable thing to be mocked and derided by them, and so you give up religious duties or join in profane jokes or otherwise encourage sin. But suppose at the moment you were so tempted Almighty God were suddenly to open your eyes and show you, as in a kind of miraculous vision, our Lord and Savior hanging upon the Cross and the scribes and Pharisees jeering round Him, I am sure it would make you afraid and ashamed to go on caring for the laughter of your foolish companions. You would say at once "I must take His part and not theirs." So it would be if we could actually see such a vision. And so by His grace it will be if, although we cannot see it, we yet force ourselves to think earnestly on it. Thinking earnestly on the Cross is carrying it about with you in your mind as Moses carried the rod of God in his hand. And as he by doing so prevailed against the Pharaoh and the Egyptians so you, by recollecting the Cross, may prevail, if you will, against the devil and against the temptations which now seem too mighty for you.

Therefore I beseech you, whatever you do, suffer not these blessed days of Holy Week and Easter to pass away without laying up a treasure of meditations on the wonders which now happened, such as may always be at hand when temptations and trials come on. Think much and deeply on our Lord's deadly pangs of the body; figure to yourself His sacred hands and feet pierced through and through by the cruel nails, and the whole weight of His limbs hanging on those wounds, and make a resolution, with prayer, to think of that pain the next time you are tempted to any sin of the flesh. *That* will be holding up the Cross for a weapon against foul and evil desire, as Moses held up his rod against the evil ways of Egypt, and be sure the Cross will not be held up in vain. If you have any great and hard work to do for God: the great and hard work, perhaps, of making a general examination and confession, for the first time, of the sins of your whole life: the great and hard work of thorough repentance and amendment, let not the devil frighten you by saying "It is no use trying; it is too hard." Nay, stretch the rod over the sea, and you will find the waters divide. Take up the Cross in earnest, not only in wish and fancy but in actual obedience; take it up and show it to the evil one and say "By this sign, so please God, I will overcome thee." Think deeply on what was done for you this week, and help yourself by such thoughts to real self-denial. Do this again and again; do it continually and see if you be not delivered. Keep Good Friday in mind all the year, and you will have a blessed Easter at last.

• 10 •

The World's Conduct to the Man of Sorrows

Volume 5, Sermon 10

GOOD FRIDAY

"He was despised and rejected of men: a man of sorrows, and acquainted with grief: and we hid as it were our faces from Him: He was despised and we esteemed Him not."

ISAIAH 53:3

There is not a verse of this chapter of Isaiah at which one might not very well begin, as St. Philip the evangelist once did to the eunuch, and preach the whole doctrine of Christ crucified. As it was in the counsels of Almighty God that His Blessed Son should endure for our behalf all the various afflictions which we have deserved, so this famous prophecy touches, one after another, the several sorrows which He endured. It speaks of His intense bodily pain: "He was wounded for our transgressions, and bruised for our iniquities" (Isa. 53:5). It speaks again of the grievous oppression, the wrong, injustice, undeserved ill usage which He had to sustain: "He was oppressed and afflicted, yet He opened not His mouth; He is brought as a lamb to the slaughter, and as a sheep before her shearers is dumb, so He opened not His mouth" (Isa. 53:7).

And here, in the beginning of the prophecy, mention is particularly made of that which was the root of all the rest and which many persons would feel as the bitterest of all: His being despised and scorned. "He shall grow up before" God "as a tender plant, and as a root out of a dry ground:

103

He hath no form nor comeliness; and when we shall see Him, there is no beauty that we should desire Him. He is despised and rejected of men; a man of sorrows and acquainted with grief; and we hid as it were our faces from Him: He was despised, and we esteemed Him not" (Isa. 53:2-3).

Now this is a prophecy, first and chiefly, of what our gracious Lord was to suffer in His own proper person. He was to be a man of sorrows, and *because* of His sorrows He was to be despised. Such is the pride and bitterness of our sinful nature ever since the fall of our first parents which began with the lust of the eyes — Eve indulging herself with the *sight* of the forbidden fruit — and which has gone on ever since: men refusing in general so much as to look at the afflicted, "hiding, as it were, their faces" from them, because such sights interrupt their enjoyments and satisfactions.

Something of this kind we may every day behold, in the behavior of those who are at all hardened by the world towards the afflicted and low-spirited when they come in their way. They may feel, indeed, some touch of natural pity, but far less than they ought to feel, far less than they used to feel when they were younger and before they were spoiled by long indulgence of selfishness. As it is, what are we to think of the ordinary behavior of persons in high health towards the sick, of flourishing persons towards the disappointed, of high-spirited and cheerful persons towards the feeble and dejected? People like to go on cheerfully and freely in their full relish for the pastimes or employments of the day, and it vexes them to be intruded upon by ill news and melancholy looks. Accordingly, do we not see a great deal of what one may truly call "hiding as it were their faces away," as if the very sight of the afflicted were a rude interruption of men's pleasure or business; as if God dealt hardly with them, to put them in mind of their own corruption and frailty by throwing such sights in their way?

Now, then, if you ever feel disposed in this manner to turn away from the afflicted, you will do well to check yourself with the question, "Am I not, in fact, behaving as those did who turned away from our Savior?" "He was a man of sorrows and acquainted with grief," and therefore "they hid as it were their faces from Him." Surely if we hide our face peevishly or contemptuously from any one of His afflicted and poor people, if we are impatient and displeased with everything except what encourages our mirth or what helps us in our day's work, we have every reason to think that we too should have hidden our faces from our Savior had we known Him in the flesh — we should have been impatient and displeased at being called on to look from our business or our diversion towards a person so lowly and little esteemed, so very full of infirmities and sufferings.

The history of our Lord's life and death is full of instances of this sort of temper, but none perhaps so remarkable as in the case of the two thieves who were crucified by His side. Even in the very agony of their own death — and that the most painful and shameful of deaths — both of them at first and one, it would seem, to the end, could find it in their hearts to revile our Lord for His sufferings. "If thou be Christ," they tauntingly said, "save Thyself and us" (Luke 23:39). They cast in His teeth the same reproach as the haughty Roman soldiers and self-satisfied Pharisees did: "He saved others; Himself He cannot save" (Matt. 27:42). Those dying and blaspheming malefactors were the very type of the world's proud and cruel nature, rejecting and disdaining all fellowship with the poor and afflicted and refusing to be saved by sufferings, even the sufferings of Jesus Christ.

But, secondly, the prophecy of the Man of Sorrows relates to the faith and religion as well as to the person of Jesus Christ. I mean that it represents to us not only the way in which both Jew and Gentile would treat Him while in sight of men, but also the way in which, both then and ever after, the world would receive the preaching of His Holy Cross. The preaching of the Cross is, in short, this: that the arm of the Lord, His saving power and mercy, is revealed from heaven in the person of Jesus Christ, His only Son and Word, of one substance with the Father, who was pleased to take upon Himself our nature in the womb of the Blessed Virgin, becoming very man as we are, and did in due time offer up Himself as a sacrifice and atonement for all our sins, so that no transgressor can be forgiven or obtain a blessing from God but through Him our only Mediator, and that the way to come to Him and be forgiven and blessed is, as He said, to take up His Cross and follow the example of His sacrifice.

This is the preaching of the Cross, and in both its parts it is most contrary to the mind of this world. The world, in the first instance, cannot bear to acknowledge that itself is unworthy of any blessing, any good thing at all, or that in order to redeem it such a deep and wonderful plan, such a condescension on God's part, was necessary. Especially those who are at all worldly wise are ever set against a plan which seems to them so very strange, so very unlike what they had expected. Thus it was in the days of our Savior; His Cross proved, to both Jew and Gentile, the bitterest of disappointments. The Jew was forced to give up at once his proud imagination of being one of a people who were to be lords over the whole world and to have their fill of pleasure and grandeur in the kingdom of an earthly Christ. The wise men of the Gentiles were forced to give up their haughty schemes of setting all things right by their own wisdom and goodness. Both Jew and Gentile, on becoming Christians, had to renounce what they naturally loved, to give up pleasing themselves and to embrace what they naturally abhorred: self-denial, mortification, patience, humility, very often pain, poverty, separation from dear friends, imprisonment and death itself. For these reasons when first the Gospel appeared the whole world was set against it — and why? Because it was the Gospel of the Cross. Because it was a Gospel "of sorrows, and acquainted with grief" therefore it was generally "despised and rejected of men."

Thus it was in the beginning of the Christian faith; men were actual unbelievers in our crucified Redeemer. They sought and found one excuse after another for continuing as they were, pagans and Jews, instead of humbly bowing down every thought into captivity to the obedience of Christ. Those days are over: the power and wisdom of God has proved too strong for the selfish pride of man. Even the worldly-wise, in despite of themselves, have now for many ages been compelled to admit, in profession at least, the doctrine of the Cross. Kings, as the prophet foretold, have "shut their mouths at" Christ (Isa. 52:15); the very highest of the great men of the earth can find no more to say against the Gospel. For very shame they dare not resist their own reason which tells them they must believe in Christ Jesus.

But although many are forced, as far as belief goes, to own that what the Scriptures tell us of Christ dying for us all is true, they cannot bring themselves practically to submit to the doctrine. They scorn the notion of taking up their own cross. In this sense very many who seem to themselves sound believers in Christ do in fact hide their faces from Him — they despise Him and esteem Him not. It is the last thing, indeed, with which they are ready to charge themselves. They are quite ready to profess, nay even to feel, that they cannot obtain everlasting salvation by any merits of their own. They look to Jesus Christ alone as deserving salvation for them, and if at times they find themselves wound up to certain strong feelings of assurance and of being nearer than others to Christ they consider themselves, for the present at least, quite safe, and have no fear at all but that they have really sure hold of the Cross.

But let no man be too secure. Laying hold of the Cross in order to eternal salvation is not a thing to be done once for all and then let alone for ever. It is a manner and way of life, not a mere feeling to come and go. It is, as St. Paul briefly expresses it, being "crucified with Christ" in mind and heart and temper and conduct. It is so living that angels observing you may say "it is not so much he that lives as Christ that liveth in him" (Gal. 2:20). In a word, it is giving up your own will and resigning yourself to Christ's will in all things.

People will say, of course, that they are not like this: they put in no claim to angelical perfection like St. Paul's. But before they flatter themselves that even in some tolerable measure they are *trying* to live in the spirit of Christ's Cross, let them compare their own ways of life with those which they know Christ approved of.

Christ said "Blessed are the poor in spirit" (Matt. 5:3), and when He was indeed rich (for He was the maker and owner of all things) "for our sakes He became poor" (2 Cor. 8:9). How many of those who profess to hold by His Cross follow His example in this respect, really preferring poverty to riches, contented and cheerful in a low estate and thoroughly convinced that God deals kindly with them in casting their lot among the poor — or, if He has given them riches, living evermore in fear of themselves, and drawing back on purpose from many indulgences, that they may be so far like the poor?

Again, Jesus Christ said, "Blessed are they that mourn, for they shall be comforted" (Matt. 5:4), and His Spirit long ago taught that "it is better to go to the house of mourning than to the house of feasting" (Eccles. 7:2). And when we consider the thing we see plainly that this is no strange doctrine at all: it is simply saying that grave thoughts of eternity must be better for an eternal accountable being than light thoughts of the present hour only. But what says the world in general to this? What say those (and they are many thousands of Christians) who are wholly taken up with the pursuit of pleasure and quite impatient of any interruption in it? They may, for a time, have tender and reverential thoughts of our crucified Savior when they think of Him, but their way of life being in reality a contradiction to the spirit and meaning of His Cross, it is much to be feared, and indeed it commonly happens, that these intervals of pious thought become rarer and rarer with them and the end is that they go on quite at their ease, as if they had never heard of the Cross at all.

If any one thing be more necessary than another, especially for persons beginning life, it is that they should learn by God's grace to guard against the first beginnings of this profane spirit, and should early accustom themselves to watch and pray lest, while they seem to be indulging only in the natural cheerfulness of youth, they be in fact conforming to the world and training themselves to despise Christ crucified.

One sign by which they may try themselves is the disposition they feel towards self-denial and towards those who are the great examples of the practice of that most Christian grace. For instance they read in Holy Scripture of Daniel fasting for the sins of his people, and being rewarded by an angelical visit and a promise from heaven of the redemption which should be by Christ Jesus. They read of St. John the Baptist and his rude and coarse and poor life in the wilderness. They read of St. Paul keeping under his body and bringing it into subjection. Above all they read of our blessed Savior fasting forty days and forty nights for the purpose, as it should seem, of heavenly contemplation, upon which followed a great triumph over His and our spiritual enemy and a visit from angels ministering unto Him.

Christians read of these things in the Scripture, and how do they feel disposed to them? Have they any desire, according to their ability and measure, to imitate the self-denying ways of the holy apostles and prophets, of the Baptist and of our blessed Lord Himself? Or do they not rather shrink back from the thought altogether, as something Jewish and now gone by? Do they not reckon in some way or another on being good without abstinence and self-denial? Would they not feel a little inclined to ridicule and discourage the attempts of others if they saw any smitten with the love of Christian discipline and trying to practice it according to the rules of the Church? This is a question the answer to which may help them to know a good deal of their own disposition to profit by the Cross of Christ. If they are unwilling or ashamed to deny themselves a full meal or a day's amusement in order to holy mortification, what reason have they, if tribulation or persecution arose, to expect such grace as may keep them from falling away? If they be so unfaithful in that which is least, in the first rudiments of self-denial, who shall give them that which is greatest, a martyr's crown in the kingdom of heaven?

Again, you may know a good deal of your own true mind towards the Cross of Christ by considering how you feel and behave towards the religious scruples of others. For example there is a great deal of difference between men in respect of the liberties they take in business. Some will make profits and take advantages in bargains from which others draw back, accounting them inconsistent with strict Christian honesty. If any man feel inclined to scorn and slight these latter as being ridiculously and strangely scrupulous, knowing little of the world and the like, this is but a poor token of their temper towards the Cross and those who take it up. So as to speaking the exact truth in conversation, keeping promises punctually and the like; it is bad enough to fail oneself in those duties, but to scoff or discourage others who attend to them better is surely a much worse sign.

One very common and very dangerous trial is when notions and practices forbidden by God's law and His Church are become customary under whatever pretense. For example, consider the notion that people may choose their own religion according to their own fancy of what will most edify themselves, and the consequent practice of running after strange teachers, without regard or reverence to the warnings of the Church. These things are now become so common that I suppose it must require Christian courage, something like taking up the Cross, in any one who resolutely sets himself against them on true Church principles. Surely, then, this is a time in which we ought to be much on our guard as to how much we join in the disrespect and scorn with which the world is sure to treat every opinion or person which it calls *bigoted*. If there be such a thing as Christian truth and a Christian Church, surely they are to be upheld, and we must cling to them in spite of any loss of credit, ease or purpose. To damp any such purpose and make light of any such sacrifice is no light error, but rather a mark that the person so judging is one of those to whom, if he had lived in our Savior's time, the very Cross of Christ would have been foolishness.

In this and in all parts of duty, deeds not words, settled behavior not passing emotions, a self-denying mind not an eager feeling of confidence, are what they must practice who desire to wait, with our Lord's true disciples, round the very foot of the Cross and not to go away like the mass of the people, just smiting their breasts and returning to the world and their sins. And the one great principle to guide and help us in carrying the Cross into our daily lives is that which our Lord Himself has given; "Whosoever shall be ashamed of me and of my words in this adulterous and sinful generation, of him also shall the Son of Man be ashamed when He cometh in His own glory and His Father's and of the holy angels" (Luke 9:26).

Remembering this let us watch ourselves in our several stations more and more carefully, thinking no matter or part of our conduct too trifling to be governed by the rule of the Cross. Let it be our happiness, our joy and honor to live and, if it please God, to die, like true disciples of the crucified Jesus. I do not mean, of course, that we can have such a mind at once, but let us at once set about trying to have it. Let us leave off hiding our faces from what the world dislikes to see: from the poor, the mean, the sickly, the disappointed, from whatever is "despised and rejected of men," but rather welcome such persons and wait upon them to the very best of our power, as beholding in them, after a sort, so many images and representations of our despised and rejected Savior. Finally, whenever need so requires, let us take up our cross boldly. Let us be, in the best sense, free and independent, steadily persisting that we will judge of our duty by the rules of the Gospel and not of the world. Let us fear nothing so much as rude or insincere treatment of the Cross. For on our portion in it depends our only hope of escaping eternal ruin.

The Holy Women at the Sepulcher

Volume 5, Sermon 19

EASTER EVE

"The women also, which came with Him from Galilee, followed after, and beheld the sepulcher, and how His Body was laid: and they returned, and prepared spices and ointments, and rested the Sabbath-day, according to the commandment."

LUKE 23:55-56

The history of our Lord's death and passion may be called, in a certain sense, the religious history of the whole world. It might, perhaps, be true to say that all the persons gathered round His Cross, whether as friends or as enemies, stand for so many sorts of people and their several ways of behaving to Him, not in those times only but in our times and in all times. There were Jews, to represent the open enemies of Christ and His Gospel; Pilate, to be a sample of those (not a few) who, being convinced in their hearts that the Christian way is the only right way, yet deliberately give it up for fear of doing themselves harm in this world; Judas, a type of those most miserable ones who, being specially entrusted by Jesus Christ, fall into such sins as to give the devil an opportunity of entering into them and tempting them to betray their trust; the Roman soldiers, to represent those unthinking persons who do as the world bids them, right or wrong, though it be never so much against their Savior.

On the other hand, by God's great mercy, there were also a few faithful and pious servants of our Lord. There was St. John the beloved disciple and the blessed Virgin Mother, emblems of the highest degree of faith and love. There was the penitent thief who died confessing Him. There was St. Peter, who was even then weeping, probably at a distance, as counting himself unworthy to draw near the Cross of Him whom he had so lately denied. There was the centurion owning, like a thoughtful heathen on the way to Christian belief, "Truly this man was the Son of God" (Mark 15:39). There were Joseph and Nicodemus, rich men both and both disciples of Christ, but in secret for fear of the Jews. There were, lastly, the pious women of whom the text makes mention, on whose example, and the blessing they received, I wish to say something today.

It is not for nothing, depend upon it, that the history and names of those women are so mixed up with the accounts of our Lord's burial and resurrection. What is said of them was, no doubt, meant as an encouragement to all quiet and simple persons who should follow them in doing good and waiting on their Savior. They are patterns of two things which God especially delights to honor: humble, unpretending, yet earnest devotion, and quiet exercise of the duties of their calling, according to their condition and station in the world.

They were patterns of devotion: for they followed Christ from Galilee, which must have been great self-denial. It was much for men such as the apostles to forsake home and parents, kinsfolk and friends for the sake of keeping close to our Lord — for women to do so was a still greater thing in proportion to the feebleness of their nature. Again, they ministered to Him of their substance: Mary Magdalene especially, and Joanna, who were wealthy persons. St. Luke had told us long before that such was their practice towards our Lord. They acknowledged in that way His inestimable mercy in healing them of infirmities or casting out evil spirits. Therefore their continuing near Him even in His death was no sudden impulse of natural pity or any other strong feeling. It was just persevering in a course of duty which they had entered on long before. Christ, it seems, had accepted their services, offered in grateful acknowledgment of His mercy, although He had refused to permit the person out of whom a legion of devils had gone to stay with Him when he earnestly besought leave to do so. These women, more highly favored, were allowed to wait still on our Savior, and so waiting they grew in faith, so as not to shrink from attending even on His very Cross. Neither fear of the Jews nor any kind of shrinking, so natural to weak frames when death is near, especially death in torment — neither, I say, of these feelings kept them back or drove them away from their Lord's departing moments. While indifferent people "smote their breasts" and returned, "his acquaintance, and the women that followed from Galilee, stood afar off, beholding these things" (Luke 23:19).

It was no more than might be expected that the same affectionate temper should cause them to be deeply and religiously anxious for His blessed body after His death. When Joseph and Nicodemus came and took Him down from the Cross (where it is noted as an instance of boldness in Joseph that he feared not to go in unto Pilate with such a request), the women followed after without any doubt or scruple. They seem to have had no thought of fearing the Jews. Neither would they consent to leave to Nicodemus and Joseph the whole trouble and expense of our Savior's funeral, though *they* both could well afford it and were ready to do much, for the one had already bought one hundred pounds of myrrh and aloes and the other had given up his own new tomb for the purpose. Nevertheless, the holy women would by no means endure to be bereaved of their part in the blessed and pious work. They noted carefully how and where the body was laid with a view to yet one more task of love: the last, as they imagined, which they could undertake for Christ. They made haste and prepared spices and ointments, in order to do Him such further honor as they could as soon as ever the Sabbath should be past.

But here comes in that other point in which, as I said, the Holy Spirit appears to hold them out as patterns to us. With all their earnest and courageous love, they still preserved the quietness and simplicity of the character which properly belongs to women. We do not read of their breaking out into any kind of wailing or lamentation. They waited, it seems, by the Cross in resignation, noticing everything with that presence of mind which God often gives to His faithful servants for their own and others' good even in times of deepest distress. Having seen the blessed body in the grave, they do not stay by it to mourn and lament but they lose no time in buying and preparing spices, recollecting (which is another instance of their thoughtfulness) that the Sabbath was near at hand and that then they could not have bought the spices.

How it was so near at hand you may easily perceive if you bear in mind that the Jews counted their days to begin from six in the evening of the day before. For instance, when it was now six on Friday afternoon they would reckon Saturday, or the Sabbath, as actually begun. Now, it was three in the afternoon before our Lord gave up the ghost, and we find that Joseph was much hurried to finish the laying of the body in the grave before the Sabbath should begin, and therefore it must have been *very* near six when the women set about preparing the spices, and having done so, says St. Luke, "they rested the Sabbath day, according to the commandment."

The use I would make of this is to observe that the holy women did not suffer their earnest zeal and affection for the honor of their Master to prevent their keeping, as far as was possible, the outward and ceremonial commandments of God also. They did not permit their deep feeling, even on such an occasion as this, to carry them away, as sometimes is the case, and cause them unnecessarily to leave undone any ordinary and regular duties. And this I take to be a great instance of that kind of self-denial which is peculiarly to be practiced by women: namely, constraining themselves in the midst of deep care and affliction to remember even lesser duties at proper times, much more such duties as the observance of God's day of rest. It is a thing to be much considered by those who allow themselves too easily to be excused for slighting our day of rest, the Lord's Day. And it is slighted, remember, not only by unnecessary work but as much or more by neglect of public worship — by refusing to acknowledge God in the assembling of ourselves together.

Observe this, you who so quietly miss the prayers and communions of the Church on every slight excuse of household business or other inconvenience; you who will not rise a little earlier or otherwise put yourselves out of the way in order to get things forward, that you may present yourselves the more regularly before your Savior, to beg His blessing and receive His grace. Observe the holy women who were likeliest to know what would please our Savior, having been waiting on Him so many months. They would not, if they could possibly help it, permit even their attendance on His sacred body, the highest of all labors of love, to cause them to break the rest of their Sabbath. They made haste; they put themselves out of the way to get the spices and ointments prepared before Friday was over, that they might leave the whole Saturday free for holy rest.

But the moment that rest was over, very early in the morning of the first day of the week, their affectionate reverence for our Lord had made them active again. They came unto the sepulcher at the rising of the sun. They came as soon as ever they could, "bringing the spices which they had prepared; and certain others with them" (Luke 24:1) who perhaps were moved by their good example and, in reward for their following it, were now to be made partakers of their blessing.

They brought the spices which they had prepared, although they were by no means certain that their doing so would be of any use, for on the way to the tomb we find them speaking, with the same thoughtful anxiety as before, about the great stone which Joseph in their sight had rolled to the door of the sepulcher. As they went, they said, "Who shall roll us away the stone from the door of the sepulcher? . . . for it was very great" (Mark 16:3-4). This, with many other circumstances, shows that they had not the least notion of the wonders which God had prepared to reward their faith withal when they came to the tomb.

Accordingly, the sight of the angel abashed them — "They were afraid, and bowed down their faces to the earth" (Luke 24:5). So utterly unprepared were they for the joyful message that some of them, when told "He is risen" were, it seems, as much troubled with fear and amazement at the sudden interference of the Almighty as they were comforted at the assurance of the resurrection of Christ. "They went out quickly and fled from the sepulcher; for they trembled and were amazed: neither said they any thing to any man; for they were afraid" (Mark 16:8). They did not, so to speak, come to themselves until they actually met our Lord, and heard from Him, "All hail," and were graciously permitted to hold Him by the feet and worship Him (Matt. 28:9).

I do not deny but there might in all this be a deep mysterious meaning, a lesson for us all, as to our Lord's usual way of making Himself known to His servants. As long as He is known only by the hearing of the ear, by the message of His angels or of men doing the angels' office, so long the doctrine concerning Him is full of confusion and amazement. Men may not indeed disbelieve it, but it startles and perplexes them, and takes no settled shape in their minds nor any fixed hold of their hearts. For those blessed ends it must be communicated to them by Christ Himself. He must enter in and dwell in their hearts by His Spirit, and give them in some way His blessed body to touch.

It may be that something like this is shadowed out in the Gospel history of the women's coming to the sepulcher, but at any rate we are sure from that history that they had no notion at all of what would happen. It came upon them by surprise. They thought of nothing but doing their daily duties, and of showing their love to Christ dead and buried in the best way that circumstances allowed. And behold, God made them first of the chosen witnesses to whom He showed Christ alive; their faith was the first-fruits of the faith of the whole Church, coming even before that of the Apostles themselves.

It is not hard, and to many it ought to be most consoling, to perceive what the Holy Ghost intended we should learn by this gracious example. Plainly the whole history is full of encouragement for those virtues and graces in particular which the women of Christ's flock are most continually called on to practice. God's providence has cast on the female sex a number of homely and minute duties which many are apt too hastily to plead as an apology for their more or less neglect of religion. Here you have a plain instance of how those duties themselves may be turned into part of religion. Industry, for example, in household work of any kind may be quickened by the thought of getting that work over some minutes sooner than usual, so as to be able to draw near God once the oftener in His church, or at least to approach Him seriously in private prayer. Charity in thoughtful waiting on men's souls and bodies, even in the least matters, which seems also to be a great part of the province of females, may be greatly animated by the recollection that Christ reckons such things as done to Him. Works of mercy, even the meanest, performed or intended to any of His living members, are as sweet odors which the holy women brought on the first Easter morning to anoint the lifeless members of His natural body. They may not perhaps be wanted for the particular purpose and the cost and price of them may in some cases seem thrown away for the time. But the willing mind which brings them will not lose its reward; it thought to do a little good, to satisfy a kind feeling on earth, and God will find a recompense for it in heaven as much above what it now imagines as Mary Magdalene's seeing our Lord that morning was above what she had promised to herself in the consolation of waiting on His dead body.

Let me, in conclusion, once more beg you to observe that this great blessing was quite independent of an exact understanding of the doctrines of religion, or of anything answering to what we call scholarship, the want of which is so often pleaded as a good reason for being more or less irreligious. The women at the sepulcher were probably in that state of mind which causes the persons who are in it to be accounted by many as poor ignorant women, however full of good meaning. Let not such then, whether men or women, be discouraged. Let them be up early and take rest late, over busy in good works, waiting on Christ's members and making time to wait on Himself in His church. Let us all, in such little matters as we can, deny ourselves for His sake, and we shall be sure in time to find that virtue which comes out of Him to all those who touch but the hem of His garment.

• 12 •

The Sight of God Incarnate

....

Volume 6, Sermon 12

EASTER DAY

"In my flesh shall I see God: whom I shall see for myself, and mine eyes shall behold, and not another."

JOB 19:26-27

When a thoughtful person has been able to have strongly in his mind the feelings and imaginations proper to the three great days of which this is the last, I should not wonder if he had on the whole some such impression as this: that Friday was a day of earthquake, of darkness, and desolation, the day, so to speak, of a great storm, that Saturday was a calm and clouded day, a day of pensive rest and regret mingled with quiet hope, but that this Sunday morning is all brightness and sunshine — sin forgiven, death overcome, the cares of earth forgotten and its miseries healed, heaven opened and the angels of God ascending and descending upon the children of men.

What now is it which makes all the difference? The answer cannot be all spoken in words, but it would come home to our hearts if we could go and ask the faithful friends and followers of our Lord, the apostles and the holy women who waited on His death and burial; if we could watch how changed they are to-day, in look and voice and manner and everything from what they were yesterday. Yesterday they sat alone and kept silence. Today they are running to and fro, eager to meet one another and each looking as one charged with good tidings. Yesterday their eyes were cast down to the earth, like men who had met in common with some great disappointment and were almost ashamed to look one another in the face, neither being able to help the other's perplexity. Today they exchange cheerful looks and words of congratulation, as though a great weight were taken off their spirits and all were now, as people say, going on right. In short, the difference between to-day and yesterday was, to the faithful friends of our Lord, almost like the difference between heaven and earth.

For what is it which causes heaven to be what it is? Why is there the fulness of joy and rivers of pleasures for evermore? Surely because they see God's face as a man seeth the countenance of his friend. "He will dwell with them, and they shall be His people, and God Himself shall be with them, and be their God." "The glory of God did lighten" the city, "and the Lamb is the light thereof." "The Throne of God and of the Lamb shall be in it, and His servants shall serve Him, and they shall see His face." "They need no candle, neither light of the sun, for the Lord God giveth them light" (Rev. 21:3, 23; 22:3-5). And our Lord's own account of the bliss of the other world is that He will receive His disciples to Himself; that where He is, there they may be also.

The happiness of heaven, then, is seeing God. And because our Lord and Savior is God incarnate, God the Son made man by taking to Himself a soul and body such as ours, therefore to see Christ was, to faithful men, a kind of heaven upon earth and losing sight of Him, as they did at His passion, was like being banished from heaven. Of course then His coming in their sight again was the greatest happiness they could have; it was like opening heaven's gate once more when it seemed to be shut against them; it was a joy with which nothing else can be compared save that unspeakable joy which their own resurrection will bring with it, when they will not only see our Lord but meet Him in the air and be taken up to dwell with Him for ever.

I do not say that those holy and happy persons, St. John, St. Mary Magdalene and the rest, were all of them at the time fully aware that He whom they had seen die, and whom they now saw risen again, was the very and eternal God. They very likely came by slow degrees, some at one time and some at another, to the full knowledge of that astonishing truth. But thus much they knew for certain: that they could not be happy without seeing Him, that there was no other to whom they could go, that in the light of His countenance was joy and peace, and that when He hid His face, they were troubled. Many persons have this feeling at many times towards one or other of their fellow-creatures, but then it is a dangerous feeling. So to depend on any of the things which God has made comes near to idolatry, and to setting that thing in the place of God Himself. But in regard of our Lord Jesus Christ there was no such fear. They could not be wrong in setting their hearts upon Him, for He is God Himself. And in Him, though as yet they might not themselves quite understand it, they felt that they had that blessing which the holy men of old, kings and priests, patriarchs and prophets, had from the beginning longed for.

The sight of God was the very blessing which Adam forfeited in Paradise, and which poor fallen human nature, so far as it was not utterly corrupt, has ever been feeling after and longing for. Adam, oppressed and alienated in his mind by sin, hid himself from the presence of the Lord God among the trees of the garden and was cast out from the nearer vision of God, but both he and his posterity retained still a blind consciousness of what they had lost and a blind hope of recovering it. Which of us has not felt this at times? Who has not yearned, now and then, after some better happiness than he has yet known? That better happiness is the presence and enjoyment of God. Holy Job spoke darkly of it when he spoke the well-known words which our Church comforts and warns us with at every funeral, "I know that my Redeemer liveth, and that He shall stand at the latter day upon the earth, and though after my skin worms destroy this body, yet in my flesh shall I see God: whom I shall see for myself, and mine eyes shall behold, and not another." Moses had the same longing when, in answer to God's assurance of favor — "Thou hast found grace in my sight, and I know thee by name" — he prayed and said, "I beseech thee, show me thy glory" (Exod. 33:18). David in the Psalms over and over declares the sight of God to be his only happiness. "Whom have I in heaven but thee? And there is none upon earth that I desire in comparison of thee. My flesh and my heart faileth: but God is the strength of my heart, and my portion for ever." "Thou shalt shew me the path of life: in thy presence is the fulness of joy, and at thy right hand there is pleasure for evermore." "I will behold thy presence in righteousness, and when I awake up after thy likeness, I shall be satisfied with it" (Ps. 73:25-26; 16:11; 17:15).

All these, all the holy men before the time of our Lord's first coming in the flesh, looked on by faith to the happiness of seeing God. But the apostles and those who were about Him when He came actually had that happiness. They enjoyed in their lifetime that privilege which Job had to wait for till he came to the other world. In their flesh they saw God. Their very own eyes, and not another's for them, beheld Him. Some of them even touched God, and handled Him with their hands. One, highly favored above all, bare Him in her womb, fed Him from her bosom, nursed Him on her lap, was His Mother and He her child.

This was the happiness of those who knew Christ after the flesh, but as yet it was a dim happiness — they did not thoroughly know it themselves. Only when by His death and burial it departed from them for a short time were they sensible that it was indeed their happiness, that He being gone there was none else to whom they could go. When they knew He was risen it was their life and joy, the light of their eyes and their souls' delight, their comfort, their hope and their all come back again after seeming to be lost.

This is why Easter was so bright a day to them. It was not merely a dear friend returning from the grave. It was not even their having a sure pledge of their justification before God and the forgiveness of their sins. It was their actual happiness, that which alone could make them blessed in time or in eternity, returning when it had seemed to be forfeited.

And now He graciously permitted them to know more of it than in the first days of His humiliation, before He suffered. He seems to have withdrawn the veil gradually and to have allowed them to find out, as St. Thomas did, that He with whom they had been so long a time was no other than their Lord and their God made man. In this way He showed Himself to them from time to time forty days together, and then withdrew Himself out of their sight, yet promising to send His Holy Spirit which should make Him really, though invisibly, nearer to them than He had been as yet.

And upon the faith of this promise we and all Christians even now live and, if we have not forfeited our baptismal blessings, are happy. We are happy, did we but know and thoroughly believe it, as members of Jesus Christ, but our happiness is so far dim and imperfect in that we do not as yet see Christ. His apostles and disciples who saw Him in the flesh were happy to be permitted so pure and glorious a sight, but their joy too was in one respect imperfect, and no less imperfect than ours is; though they saw and touched Christ outwardly, they were not as yet made members of Him. Thus as the apostles, so we, with all ordinary Christians, have somewhat as yet wanting to our joy. I will repeat it again, that it may be quite plain. The apostles saw Christ, but were not yet members of His body. We are members of His body, but do not yet see Him. These two things, which are now separated, are to be united in the other world and, being united, they will make us happy for ever.

But what are really our thoughts about this happiness? Is it happiness at all, according to the ways of thought and behavior which we are got into? Suppose, for example, there were any person here who is living in known uncleanness, either in heart or in deed, "fulfilling the desires of the flesh and of the mind" (Eph. 2:3), what sort of happiness am I telling him of when I say to him, "Jesus Christ is risen from the dead, He who hates all impurity, He who has laid it down for a law that one had better cut off a right hand or eye than suffer it to lead us into sin. He is risen from the dead, and you will see Him with your eyes, for you too will rise with your body at the last day"? What kind of joy, again, can it prove to the covetous, grudging heart when we tell him, "You may certainly look forward to the time when He who praised the widow for the gift of her two mites, He who said that it was more blessed to give than to receive, will come again and you shall certainly set eyes on Him"? Of course to such sort of persons, continuing such, the resurrection of Christ as a pledge of their seeing Him again can be no real joy but quite the contrary. They, in their secret hearts, would much rather the words of the profane wicked soldiers could be made out true — they had rather, if they could, believe that His disciples came by night and stole Him away while the guard slept. Such persons, all persons who are going on in deadly sin, must be greatly changed before the news of our Lord's rising again shall really be felt by them as good news coming home to their own hearts.

And even to good and thoughtful Christians who go on trying and trying, however imperfectly, to walk blameless in all the commandments and ordinances of the Lord — even to such the notion of seeing God in flesh like our own will oftentimes seem almost too aweful to bear. It will bring a natural dread upon their spirits. It will cause them to cry out, with him who had seen the angel in whom He was, "We shall surely die, because we have seen God" (Judg. 13:22). They will think again and again, "Who can stand before this Holy Lord God? Certainly not I, with my many sins, negligences and ignorances." Should such thoughts overpower you at any time and tempt you either to be reckless or desponding, do not give way to them. You may know for certain from whom they come: resist them accordingly, and they will quickly flee from you. Your Judge is most unwilling that your heart should sink and that you should feel as if you could not be accepted, as if repentance even and contrition came too late for *you*.

Therefore, behold, He has mixed up the account of His resurrection, so aweful to sinners, with the most affecting tokens of His mercy. From the moment of His rising to the hour of His ascension, He is never weary of giving them signs by which they might know Him, however glorified, to be the same mild and merciful Jesus, the same Son of Man whom they had known so well on earth. Was He, before He died, full of tender care for St. Peter? In His first message after His resurrection, His angel made loving mention of Peter by name, saying "tell His disciples, and *Peter*" that He is risen from the dead (Mark 16:7). Yea, and He Himself calls them brethren; "Go tell *my brethren* that they go into Galilee, and there shall they see me" (Matt. 28:10). Why? Because they had all lately forsaken Him. Had our Lord in His humiliation the feeling of an intimate friend towards St. John particularly? To St. John, above others, He showed Himself in His glorified state as you may read in the book of Revelation.

Then see in how gracious and condescending a way He ordered all His appearances to them, eating with them and blessing their food as He had been used to do, repeating over again the miracle of the extraordinary draught of fishes, at nearly the same place and with nearly the same company, as if on purpose to prove Himself unchanged in affection. These and many more gracious signs He performed so that neither His apostles nor we might ever doubt His being the same merciful son of Mary, the same true brother to us, now He is so highly exalted, as he was in His manger and on His Cross.

Think not that our Master's condescending grace in all these things was confined to those disciples only. O! surely it reaches to us, and to as many as believe on Him through the apostles' word. Though He be at the right hand of God, His human body and soul are there with Him, and all His brotherly love and pity for the lost children of men and His tender fellow-feeling towards those who stand afar off and smite upon their breasts.

All these blessings of our Lord's presence are sealed and made sure to us with the promise of the Holy Ghost which makes us members of Him, in His baptism first and afterwards in the Holy Communion. There, if not outwardly in our own flesh yet under the shadow and veil which He Himself ordained, we may see God as often as we draw near in faith and repentance. Then and there He grants unto us to be partakers of the same blessings as those first communicants were when after His resurrection, as on this day, more than eighteen hundred years ago, He made Himself known to them in breaking of bread. For it is not one Savior, one Eucharist to them and another to us, but to them and us and all from the beginning it is the same Savior, the same Baptism, the same Communion, the same merciful God. And upon Him, one and the same Jesus for ever, we shall all look when with one and the same voice He shall have raised us at the last day.

Try and labor, my brethren, for love and for fear's sake: for love of Him and for fear of hell. Try and labor to have this thought steadily present and without all question in your minds: that as surely as He rose again this morning from the dead with a true body which He showed to His disciples and took up with Him into heaven, so surely shall we all behold Him with these very eyes of ours. Hitherto we have seen Him, as it were, with other men's eyes: with the eyes of His holy apostles and martyrs who have told us how He appeared to them, either in heaven or on earth. But the hour is coming, and now is, when we shall see Him for ourselves; our eyes shall behold Him, and not another's. Upon one and the same Jesus, one and the same God, we shall all look, but He will appear to each one of us with a different countenance, according as we have behaved to Him here. As we see Him then, in wrath or in mercy, such He will be to us for ever and ever, and His countenance will be according to our works.

13

The Faith That Overcometh

....

Volume 6, Sermon 20

FIRST SUNDAY AFTER EASTER

"This is the victory that overcometh the world, even our faith."

1 JOHN 5:4

The two holy weeks are now over — the week of sorrow and the week of gladness. The battle is fought and the victory won and we are come back again to the usual quiet times. If we have had any good thoughts of giving up ourselves more entirely to the love and service of Him who died for us, now is there especial danger of our forgetting them and falling back again into our old careless ways. It is much as when some good and kind friend is taken out of our sight by death. The thoughts of him seem for a time very fresh and strong upon our minds and we feel as if we could never forget him, but too soon the world returns upon us and, unless we watch and discipline ourselves, we grow again in a little while as cold, hard-hearted and selfish as ever.

Above all things let us beware of this kind of falling away from the wholesome remembrance of the death and resurrection of our Lord. We are most plainly taught that He not only did and suffered these great things for us, but also that He hath wrought a great work in us. We have been made members of Christ so that His doings and sufferings, His death and resurrection, are in some very true sense ours. And now if we cast them away from us, as we do by living unholy careless lives, good were it for us if we had never been new-born, never sealed with Christ's saving Cross nor washed with His purifying Spirit.

God forbid that such should be our miserable lot. To prevent it, let us steadily consider what manner of persons we ought to be who know not only that Christ died and rose again for us but also that we have spiritually died unto sin and risen again unto righteousness in Holy Baptism. "Examine yourselves," says the Apostle, "whether ye be in the faith: prove your own selves" (2 Cor. 13:5): whether Jesus Christ be in you, whether you have those marks and characters which belong to such as are risen with Christ. Perhaps you will say, in your heart at least, "this is a very great work; I am but a poor unlearned person and I know not how to begin. When you bid me examine myself it does but bewilder me — I cannot command my thoughts." Whoever has this feeling, let him turn to his Prayer Book and let him diligently mark what he reads or hears out of that. Though he be never so dull and ignorant, yet if he try in earnest and beseech God to help him he will surely be able, on each Sunday, to gain some one good thought which may assist him in profitable self-examination.

On each of these Easter Sundays for example, a thoughtful man, though ever so simple, may by attending to the collects and lessons learn some question to ask himself which may help him to judge whether he is going on as one risen with Christ or not. And the natural question for to-day in particular would be "Have I that faith which overcomes the world?" All the particular services this Sunday point towards faith as the great matter of our trial. Faith is looking towards things out of sight as real things, turning your heart and mind towards them and giving up the things which are in sight for them. This faith is the great and immediate lesson taught us by the resurrection of Jesus Christ. For thereby we know that there is another world in which we are very soon to find ourselves, both soul and body, and that such as we are towards Jesus Christ when we die, friends or enemies, in communion or cut off from Him, such we must abide forever. These things are out of sight, and to have an eye to these things is faith. Faith is that in us which receives our Lord's resurrection as the eye receives light, and as the brightest light shows nothing to the eye which is obstinately closed against it, so is Christ risen, in a certain sense, nothing to the unbelieving heart. Have we then, my brethren, all of us this faith? Do we think of our Lord in heaven really and truly as we think of our friends and relations who are out of sight? Do we really contemplate His presence and put it home to our hearts that He is watching us as we acknowledge the presence of any person whose eye we see turned towards us? When we pray, do we really speak to Him? Or do we only say over certain words to ourselves or others? If we have been going on carelessly in our devotions I do not very well know what is to be said about our faith. Certainly we have no right to boast of it, nor to be severe on others for want of it; certainly we shall do well to pray as the disciples did, "Increase our faith" (Luke 17:5).

But we must not judge of our faith from our devotions merely, nor merely from what passes in our minds when we try to meditate directly on divine things. For so there might be a grievous mistake both ways. Some persons, feeling themselves at certain times greatly lifted up and deeply moved by church services or holy readings, might too easily make sure that they themselves had faith and were in a good way. Others, finding their hearts dull, cold and wandering, might too easily condemn themselves and be cast down without cause.

Therefore faith in Jesus risen, such faith as a Christian should have, is somewhat more than merely believing, and distinct from having eager feelings at times. It must be so real, so strong, so active and ready at hand that it shall really enable us to get the better of temptation. According to St. John's saying, it "overcometh the world." The world is the visible and outward course of things, amidst which we live and move. It is something different to each one of us but each one finds it the same in this respect, that by things in sight it tempts and draws him away from things out of sight. The laborer's world is his hard day's work, his family cares, his regular or occasional holydays — all tempting him in their several ways to forget God and Christ and his own never-dying soul, and to live on from hour to hour as he best may, without provision for eternity. The world, to him who is richer and more at ease in his possessions, is the company and the way of life which inclines him to say to himself, "Let us eat and drink, for tomorrow we die" (1 Cor. 15:32) or to "heap up silver as the dust and fine gold as the dirt of the streets" (Zech. 9:3), or to "love the praise of men more than the praise of God" (John 12:43). To overcome this world is really to turn away from the things which seem desirable in it and to give them up for the sake of better things out of sight, and when our faith has this effect on us — when it actually causes us to forego earthly things in order to secure the things eternal to please God and show duty to Jesus Christ — then it is a faith which overcomes the world.

The apostles, for example, had such faith. Of them and of the first

Christians generally St. John appears to be speaking when he says "This is the victory which hath overcome the world, even our faith." They had already got the better — their contests had been so hard, their dutifulness to Jesus Christ so entire, that even in this life they might be said to have secured their crown. Think of St. Stephen on his knees, praying for his murderers while the stones were being showered on him, or of St. Paul in prison, working with his own hands that he might not be chargeable to the Church and offend any weak brother, or of St. Peter quietly submitting to be reproved by St. Paul. Think of the noble army of martyrs, how "they were stoned, were sawn asunder, were tempted, were slain with the sword" (Heb. 11:37).

Or rather think of some young person quietly going on day after day in the faith and fear of God, in dutiful obedience to those set over him, in chastity of body and purity of heart, and see how resolutely and courageously yet how calmly such a young person will reject the enticements of evil pleasure and the false shame of such as would laugh at him; think of such a case as that and you will well understand what "overcoming the world" is. You will see also that, how high soever the apostles' seats are above ours, still our resistance to sin, if sincere and constant, is the same *kind* of things as theirs, nay the same with our Lord's own resistance when, with one word, "get thee behind Me" (Luke 4:8), He subdued and drove away from Him the prince of this world, its kingdoms and their glory. So great is His condescension that He counts us to be doing likewise if we do but silence for His sake some ordinary temptations. If a poor child, for instance, draw back his hand and refuse to touch what is not his, or if any man overcome the longing of vain-glory and really try to hide his good deeds because Christ has so bidden him, our Lord will add it in His book to the treasure of His saints — nay of His own holy deeds. It is done in His name, and it shall in no wise lose its reward.

You may think perhaps in your heart that no doubt the life of many may show abundance of such single good deeds. You may feel in your own conscience that occasionally, from time to time, you could do such yourself. But how, you may ask, can one make such faith *habitual?* How are we to get into a way of *always* acting with an eye to Christ, *always* drawing back the greedy hand, closing the wanton or envious eye, shunning instead of courting the praise of men? I answer that if you can do this once you can do it twice and three times, and so on till it become what is called natural to you. See how it is in arts and trades, when people set to work in earnest.

Imagine one learning to sing or to play on any instrument or to practice any kind of mechanical craft. He is commonly so awkward at first that he feels as if he never could succeed, but if he have a real good will he perseveres for all that and takes double pains. He does something right once, observes how he does it and studies to do it again. So he goes on improving by degrees; every day or week or month he is able to do something which he could not do before. He fails often but he will not let that discourage him: rather it makes him the more diligent and thus at last he overcomes his difficulties and learns the desired art or trade. So must we overcome the world and learn goodness.

Can you not tell by your own experience what a power there is in a resolved and positive will, whether it be for good or for evil? And again, what a turn is given to our wills by the remembrance of things out of sight? A little child is left alone and is tempted to touch something forbidden. It recollects its mother's words and draws back its hand. This is but a shadow of the power of faith when we call to mind some Gospel precept, some awful saying of our Lord or St. Paul, and control some unruly desire or action accordingly, or when we say a short prayer or renew the sign of the Cross in our foreheads and the temptation departs from us.

Moreover we see with our eyes what strength there is in a heart truly dutiful to God, for ridding us of those temptations which come upon us from evil companions. It was well said by a wise and holy man, "If you let men alone, they will let you alone." When people once see that you are determined not to yield to them and that you will not follow them to do evil, they will not think it worth while to go on tempting you much longer. They will abuse or scorn you for the time, as the case may be, and then they will leave you to yourself. Sometimes it may seem that bad men are even afraid to go on molesting God's servants in the discharge of their duty to Him, like those officers of the Chief Priests and Pharisees who, having been directed to seize our Lord, returned to their employers saying "never man spake like this man" (John 7:46). There is a secret power in steady faith to keep even the worst in order.

And if it be so in respect of bad example and the corrupt ways of mortals like ourselves, still more, may we believe, will our faith avail to drive away our invisible enemies, the most dangerous of all, the evil spirits. They can judge, probably, more truly than men can of the reality of our faith and know more of the awful and mighty helps which it engages on our side from God and His good angels. "Resist the devil," says St. James;

set yourself against him "and he will flee from you" (James 4:7). It may take some time to convince men like ourselves of our being in earnest in any good profession. They can only see the outside of us, but the devil, it is likely, according to his subtlety, may sooner perceive the settled purpose of our hearts and may depart from us as he did from the Lord when he found it was useless to tempt Him. Besides, who can tell what majesty and virtue there may be in true faith to rebuke that wicked one when he draws near, so that the very presence of a true believer may be even painful and tormenting to him, and each of Christ's members be to him in a measure such as Christ Himself was when He forced him to cry out "What have we to do with Thee? Art thou come to destroy us? I know thee who thou art, the Holy One of God" (Mark 1:24).

As faith is thus powerful against all sorts of enemies, so is it a help equally belonging to all sorts and stages of the Christian life. Little children learn it of their parents when they are first taught to kneel down and pray to God and to make a difference between church and other places. Elder children need it to keep them from lying, from profaneness, from disobedience — no other reason can be given why these sins are unhappily so common but that our young do not really and practically believe. They do not believe that God is listening to them and that for all this He will bring them to judgment.

Then as to those sins to which young persons, as life goes on, are especially tempted, we know what was Joseph's safeguard: "How can I do this great wickedness and sin against God?" (Gen. 39:9). Joseph remembered God's presence and came off conqueror in a great and grievous trial. Christian faith has something more to remember: Jesus Christ crucified and risen again and so united to us by His Spirit in Holy Baptism that He feels our wilful sin as crucifying Him anew. If we sin against our own bodies, we affront the members of Christ. When persons remember this and keep themselves in order accordingly, that is "the victory that overcometh the world," even faith in Christ crucified and risen again. And so to the very end of our time, covetousness, discontent and greediness, the sins of elder life, are all to be resisted and overcome in the same way. Believe in the Lord Jesus Christ and thou shalt be saved from them all. Let us endeavor and pray to do so. Let us have the grace to call on Him in all temptations. Let us be very much afraid of good words and good feelings without good deeds. Let us beseech God to write on our hearts the lesson of the Church in today's collect, that it is in vain to think of being justified except we be serving Him in pureness of living and truth. Thus may we, by His special blessing, maintain a reasonable hope that we are not wanting in the first great mark of those who are risen with Christ. Overcoming the world daily, we may hope that we have faith.

14

The Drawing of Jesus by His Ascension

Volume 7, Sermon 5

ASCENSION DAY

"Draw me, we will run after Thee: the King hath brought me into His chambers: we will be glad and rejoice in Thee."

SONG OF SOLOMON 1:4

We of Christ's Church are, on this day, as persons out of whose sight a dear friend has just gone, watching the door through which He vanished out of our sight. Jesus Christ has been so long, three and thirty years and more, going in and out among us and now in a moment He is gone. A cloud receives Him out of our sight. He is gone and we, His flock and people, may seem to be left alone on earth. We have gone out with Him to the Mount of Olives, to the garden where His sad sufferings had their beginning. He has led us out on this road as far as Bethany, the village where He had last had something like a home on earth, choosing the place of His departure in such a way as if He would bid farewell at once to all the troubles and all the comforts of this world and leave His blessing on both. I say that, if we have read the Gospels in faith, we have in spirit accompanied our Lord with His apostles for the last time to that well-known and chosen spot. We have heard His parting commands, He hath lifted up His hands and blessed us, and in adoring wonder we have seen how in the very act of blessing He was parted from us and with quiet and gentle motion was lifted up into heaven and slowly and gradually taken out of our sight, a cloud coming between Him and us, as it comes between the stars and us.

Jesus Christ, our Savior and Redeemer, is gone away from us into heaven, and we are left here on earth. What shall we do? Shall we wait kneeling here on the hill watching, as it were, the door through which He vanished? Shall we gaze on that spot of the heavens until He return, as He promised, again? This indeed to a loving heart might seem most desirable of all things, so to go on contemplating our departed Savior, even as those who from their hearts are mourning for a deceased parent or friend sometimes feel as if they would gladly go on thinking of him all their lives, and give up every thing else — as the aged Jacob, when he was told that Joseph was lost, said "I will go down to the grave to my son mourning" (Gen. 37:35).

Something of this sort might well suit the inclinations of some loving hearts. But His will was plainly declared that His disciples should not so gaze up after Him, nor so mourn His departure as to withdraw themselves in any degree from the tasks He had set them. By His angels He sent us this message: "Why stand ye gazing up into heaven?" (Acts. 1:11). And to His apostles, when He was preparing them for this day, He said, "Because I have said these things unto you — because I have said I go away sorrow hath filled your heart. And yet, if ye loved me, *me* chiefly and not yourselves, you would rejoice, because I said I go to the Father" (John 14:28). He told them beforehand that true love would make them rejoice when they saw Him go out of their sight and now, when the time is come, we read that they worshiped Him and returned to Jerusalem with great joy. It was to them as it has been to the Church ever since, a matter of the deepest joy and thanksgiving that Christ is gone up out of sight to His Father's right hand.

So the bride in the Song of Solomon, the mystical Bride in the text, invites us to rejoice that "The King hath brought me into His chambers: we will be glad and rejoice in Thee." Why are we all to be glad and rejoice? Because Jesus Christ, the great Bridegroom, has begun to lift up the Church, His Bride, into heaven. In the womb of the Blessed Virgin, of her substance, He took to Himself a pure body and so first espoused to Himself our human nature, marrying, if I may so speak, the manhood to the Godhead so that the two should never more be divided but for ever united in His most sacred person. And now by His Ascension He hath unspeakably glorified, and that for ever, His human soul and body, made, as it was at the first, like us in all things, sin only excepted. He humbled it in the garden, at the Cross and in the grave, and now He hath glorified it far beyond His humiliation. He hath taken His soul and body as a spouse into the bedchamber, and thereby hath given to each soul and body of Adam's seed an invitation and power to have a share in that glory. Well then may we, as well as the apostles, be glad and rejoice on Ascension Day!

We are not then merely to gaze after Him; we are not to stand bewailing ourselves of His absence; but this one thing we are to do. For the whole of our time until He come again or call us into His presence we are to set about fulfilling His dying commands. *That* is the point. He is gone but will come again some day — no one can tell how soon — and in the meantime we are to do all His bidding.

And what is His bidding? That we should run after Him; that we should obtain a place in the same heaven where He is gone before in order that we should even now ascend thither in heart and mind. But because the Church knows that we cannot by mere wishing obtain such a mind as this therefore she prays, and teaches us to pray. "Draw me," she humbly and seriously prays, "and we will run after Thee," as if she should say, "I know well that in me, in my flesh, dwelleth and abideth no good thing. Therefore it must be quite changed and renewed, and this is far too hard a task for me. I commend it therefore to Thee, O Lord. Take me in hand, I beseech Thee, and draw me constantly and mightily towards Thee and towards that heaven where Thou art gone. Attract and entice me towards Thee, unworthy as I am, by all sorts of loving and affectionate dealings. Draw me towards Thee by Thy good providence, ordering the events of my life, the friends and acquaintance that I meet with, my joys and sorrows, my health and sickness, my employments and diversions, secretly and wonderfully in such sort as shall most turn my soul from the world and turn it towards Thee. Draw me towards Thee again by the reading and hearing of Thy most holy and heavenly Scriptures, causing me to light in the proper time upon those verses that will do me good, to hang upon them, to taste all their sweetness or, if need be, all their bitterness, and not to let them go until they have become, as it were, part of my mind and are in a way to do me the whole good Thou intendedst by them. Draw me by the noble and winning examples of the holy men, women and children, whom Thou from time to time hast blessed with a double portion of Thy Spirit. Show me Thine own brightness upon them and incline my heart to delight in it, for left to myself I know too well I shall but neglect or even hate it. Draw me, once more and most of all draw me, I pray Thee, by Thy most holy and lifegiving Sacrament. There, above all, help me to taste and see how gracious Thou, O Lord, art. There let me touch Thee, as Thou didst promise to St. Mary Magdalene, now that Thou art ascended to the Father. Let me in the Sacrament of Thy love touch but the hem of Thy garment and by that draw me onward and upward, till, my old impure self being thoroughly put off and cast aside, I being wholly and only Thine, may dwell only and wholly with Thee."

This is the Christian soul's prayer when she muses earnestly on her Lord's Ascension. Thus day and night she seems to say to Him, "Draw me." But that is not all. She knows well that her holy prayers and heavenly desires, if not embodied in deeds, would soon cease to be holy and heavenly — they would vanish in the air like thin clouds which never drop down in wholesome dew. This the enlightened soul greatly fears, and therefore she cries out not only "draw me." Not only does she pray with all her might for the grace without which she can do nothing, but she is careful to add always, "We will run after Thee: we will act, and that heartily and zealously, according to the good desires which Thou breathest into us." "Draw me" is her devout petition. "We will run after Thee" is her humble and courageous vow, her good resolution made on her knees before God.

And we know that these two things must go along with every good prayer: a devout petition and a humble and courageous purpose. But now mark well the word in which the devout soul expresses her holy intention. She says, "We will *run* after Thee." She does not say walk, but run. Why? She is full of love. She is like a loving child who has caught sight of his father at a distance, and we see that when that happens the child does not creep slowly towards his father but runs to meet him as fast as ever he can. So should we, permitted as we are to behold our Lord with the eye of faith, afar off on His Throne in heaven. We must not walk but run towards Him or, if we cannot run because we are weak through sin, at least we must endeavor to walk our very best. The child who for love runs out to meet his parent does not mind his playthings if they happen to lie in the way or, if he minds them, he does not stop for them. No more should we mind the playthings, the toys of earth, when, according to the Church's invitation, we are hastening after our Lord.

But you will say, "It is so hard to disengage oneself from these earthly cares; they have so wound themselves about us, like clinging weeds, before we were aware." And in truth it *is* hard. But observe that Jesus Christ, because He knows it is hard, has told us how we may get strength to do it. Because we have to run after Him and He knows we have little strength, therefore He teaches us to say "draw me" as the little child that wishes to run and cannot, stretches out its arms and asks for help as well as it can. Since then He has taught us to pray, we may not doubt that He will help us to run after Him any more than the young child doubts the mother's or nurse's will to help him. He will set your heart at liberty, that you may run the way of His commandments. He will help you to untie for ever the bands and chains of evil habit which fasten you, as yet, more or less down to earth, so that you may be free to ascend to Him in heart and mind and with Him continually dwell. Morning by morning and evening by evening say to Him in earnest, "Draw me," and day by day you will find yourself better able to run after Him. Again, endeavor day by day to run after Him, to be more alert in His service, and you will be helped morning by morning to pray to Him more earnestly.

And even as those who are teaching young children to run very often go before them and run a little way themselves and then turn and entice them onwards, beckoning to them with all kinds of affectionate endearments, so our loving Lord, before He went up into heaven, had in our sight hastened along the very worst of the rough way which He calls upon us to tread and now, with unutterable yearning love, He turns towards us from His holy eternal Rest, and beckons us onward by a thousand signs which we shall see and understand more and more as our hearts are more open to any kind of goodness. Every hour something happens by which He speaks to the believing soul and says, "Behold me here preparing a place for you: are you preparing yourself for the place?"

O may we often, very often, think of Him in this manner — of Him and of this His own Ascension Day! May the remembrance of Him caring for us in heaven sweeten and allay the troubles of this life, quicken all our languid obedience, and above all keep us from the horrid ingratitude of affronting Him by wilful sin!

O holy and merciful Savior, Thou hast been lifted up from the earth, in order to draw all men unto Thee. Thou knowest how corrupt, how childish we are. Draw nigh unto us, O Lord, that we may draw nigh unto Thee!

• 15 •

Baptism with the Holy Ghost

Volume 7, Sermon 21

PENTECOST

> *"John truly baptized with water; but ye shall be baptized with the Holy Ghost not many days hence."*
>
> ACTS 1:5

Our Savior here makes a promise which sank deep into the heart of the holy apostles and was understood by them to be very full of mysterious and gracious meaning. He was just on the point of departing out of their sight and sitting down at His Father's right hand, and He turns their thoughts more and more to the great promise which had always been the end of His preaching: the promise of the Holy Ghost to come down from the Father and set up the kingdom of heaven. He renews this promise to them for the last time in such a way as to signify that it was connected, in some mysterious way, with the former baptism of St. John, though that was by water only and this with the assured presence and power of the Blessed Spirit also. "John truly baptized with water; but ye shall be baptized with the Holy Ghost." It was the great point of our Lord's farewell blessing. No wonder that the blessed Apostles treasured it up in their minds and applied it more than once as a prime law and rule of the kingdom of heaven.

Thus St. Peter, when he was blamed for admitting Cornelius and other Gentiles into the Church as well as the Jews, told them how he had seen with his eyes the Holy Spirit come down upon them, and how that heavenly sight recalled to his mind our Lord's own words. "As I began to speak," says the holy apostle, "the Holy Ghost fell on them, as on us at the beginning. Then remembered I the word of the Lord, how that He said, John indeed baptized with water, but ye shall be baptized with the Holy Ghost" (Acts 11:15-16). And so St. Paul long after, finding certain disciples at Ephesus who knew no baptism but that of John, spoke unto them as one who would have them think so seriously of the baptism of St. John which had gone before as to receive Christ, who came after, the better and more truly for it. When they said that they had been baptized with John's baptism, St. Paul's answer was, "John verily baptized with the baptism of repentance, saying unto the people, that they should believe on Him which should come after him, that is, on Christ Jesus" (Acts 19:4). And in his last regular discourse to the Jews which, being rejected, he turned to the Gentiles, he said, "God, according to His promise, hath raised unto Israel a Saviour, Jesus: when John had first preached, before His coming, the baptism of repentance to all the people of Israel" (Acts 13:23-24).

By all these places it is very evident that there is some deep and heavenly connection between the beginning and the end of the Gospel — the baptism of St. John, and that of the Holy Ghost. Between these two, I say, there is such a connection as all would do well to take notice of, our Lord Himself recommending it to the very serious thoughts of all His people. So too at the beginning of the Gospel we find no less distinct reference to this, the designed crown and end of it. The very form and object of St. John the Baptist's ministry was, as we all know, by baptizing with water to prepare the way for One who should baptize with the Holy Ghost. Twice indeed, to a few chosen disciples he said, "Behold the Lamb of God" (John 1:29), but to the whole multitude his saying was (before he knew for certain that Jesus of Nazareth was the person), "I indeed baptize you with water unto repentance, but He that cometh after me is mightier than I, whose shoes I am not worthy to bear: He shall baptize you with the Holy Ghost and with fire" (Matt. 3:11). And after he had come to know Jesus by what occurred at His baptism, still when he had to speak of Him to the multitude it does not appear that he pointed out to them the Lamb of God, but he spoke generally, and described our Lord as before. "There standeth One among you, whom ye know not, of whom I said, He cometh after me but is preferred before me: He shall baptize you with the Holy Ghost, and with fire" (John 1:26-27; Luke 3:16). The baptism with the Holy Ghost was the great thing, which they to whom Christ was preached were taught to look on to from the beginning. It was, if I may say so, the sign of the Son of Man. So that when it actually took place in that wonderful manner, as on this day, Christians and especially the apostles looked back to the sayings of St. John and said to themselves, "Now we know their meaning, now we see how God has been gradually preparing us for this His greatest work of all, the setting up of His kingdom by the coming of His Spirit to dwell in the souls and bodies of His people."

In particular they would then seem to know better than ever they had known before concerning the astonishing baptism of our Lord Himself. They would perceive that there was a sort of mysterious connection and correspondence between St. John's baptizing our Lord with water and the whole Church being baptized by Christ Himself with the Holy Ghost. The Church, we know, is the Body of Christ. His natural body is in many respects a kind of type of that spiritual body of which His person is the head and which has all its life from Him, made manifest in the flesh. The water therefore poured upon His visible body by St. John was a token and type of the baptismal water, by which sinners were in all time to be born again and made members of Him. And the Holy Ghost which descended in a bodily shape like a dove and lighted upon Him was a type and token of the same Holy Spirit descending, as in cloven tongues like as of fire, with a hovering, perhaps, and dove-like motion, and settling on His mother and His disciples, the first members of His mystical body. Who knows too but the sound as of a rushing mighty wind, which came suddenly from heaven and filled all the house where they were sitting, might answer in some wonderful way to the voice from heaven which said, "Thou art my beloved Son; in thee I am well-pleased" (Matt. 3:17)? seeing that those who then received the Spirit were truly made sons of God, adopted by Him as true members of Christ Jesus, and thenceforth, their eyes being enlightened, they discerned in all the house where they were sitting, in all the Church and the world around them, nothing but voices and tokens of His mysterious presence? As many as receive Him, to them He gives the privilege thus to become the sons of God, even to them who believe on His Name. He gives them power, not only to be accounted but really to become His children, by true sacramental union with Christ His Son.

Thus it may appear that our Lord's baptism by St. John was the pledge and in a manner the beginning of His Church's baptism by Himself. He then, as our Head, received the Holy Ghost for us. He was anointed with It as St. Peter says, "anointed with the Holy Ghost and with power" (Acts 10:38). And as the precious oil upon the High Priest's head ran down unto the beard and went down to the skirts of his clothing, so the Holy Spirit, poured upon the head of the Church, did on this day begin to flow over her members one and all, and shall do so until the end of the world, when she shall have attained her full stature and the number of those chosen to be grafted into her shall be complete.

Behold here, as in all things, the merciful condescension of our Redeemer: how when He wanted nothing He condescended to receive all, that we might receive it through Him. That He might baptize us, He consented to be baptized Himself; that He might confirm us, to be confirmed; that He might ordain some among us, to be ordained. For so the Holy Scriptures and the Church represent the deep meanings of His baptism by St. John. By His heavenly touch He sanctified the waters, not only of Jordan but of all the earth, to the mystical washing away of sin. By receiving the Holy Ghost presently afterwards He sealed to us not only the baptismal gift but also that further gift of the Spirit which the Church teaches us to call Confirmation. And since St. Paul affirms that the saying "Thou art My Son, this day have I begotten Thee" (Heb. 5:5) was the Father's commission to glorify Christ as our High Priest, we have reason to think that His baptism was also a pledge of that holy gift which He gave His apostles when He made them priests in His Church. And in a word, for whatever holy and divine purposes God intended to give the Spirit in due time to the Church and her members, for all of them together we believe that He gave the same Spirit to the divine and most merciful Head of the Church. Christ received the Holy Ghost without measure, that unto every one of us He might give grace according to the measure which He saw to be proper for each.

Since it was for us only and not at all for Himself that He received that good Spirit, we need not fear to say and believe the very highest things regarding the privileges with which He has endowed His Church and kingdom, for which He hath obtained that unspeakable gift. We may truly say that as He was anointed to be prophet, priest and king, so His Holy Spirit has anointed His whole Church, and what is more each particular Christian, to be in some sort prophet, priest and king in His stead. The Church, Christ's Body on earth, is a prophet in our Lord's absence, because the Spirit which dwells in her is a Spirit of prophecy, enabling her to foretell things to come, guiding her into all truth, opening her understanding that she may understand the Scriptures. As Christ's prophet, and our teacher under Him, the Church has provided us with Creeds, declaring to us the true meaning of the Holy Bible and which of all the truths which it teaches are particularly necessary to salvation.

And not only in Creeds but in liturgies and in catechisms and in many other ways the holy Church throughout all the world does the office of a prophet to God's people, warning them of their duty, calling their attention to God's written Word, giving them sure tokens when He is especially near them, showing them how He will be praised and worshiped and what prayers and sacraments they should offer Him. Nay, and all the Lord's people too are prophets now that He hath put His Spirit within them. They all know Him, from the least to the greatest, so far as that He has made them aware of their duty. They know what great things He has done in coming into the world and dying for them, and how infinite the consequence of their hearing or refusing to hear. They are prophets because they can look on into eternity. They are prophets because they have in them the Holy Spirit of the Father and the Son teaching them, in answer to their diligent prayer, what to do and what to avoid.

Again, Christians are priests likewise, and kings, "a royal priesthood, a peculiar people" (1 Pet. 2:9). So speaks St. Peter, and St. John gives glory "unto Him that loved us, and washed us from our sins in His own blood, and hath made us kings and priests unto God and His Father" (Rev. 1:5-6). And the whole Church is so far made partaker of Christ's priestly office that she is entrusted by Him to offer up spiritual sacrifices, to do that in remembrance of Him which He did the night before His death, in order to our being all made partakers of His most blessed Body and Blood. The apostles indeed and their ordained successors alone have commission to do it with their hands, but in virtue and effect it is the offering of all Christians for themselves and for one another. So indeed are all her solemn prayers and intercessions. If it is a great thing to have one righteous man praying earnestly and fervently for us, much more to have the whole Church, because the Church is the Body of Christ, anointed with His Spirit, the Spirit of grace and supplication, and encouraged to intercede for His members by very special promises. And inasmuch as she sacrifices and intercedes, she is so far a priest. The grace of His mediatorial office runs over, as it were, and is communicated, in a lower and ministerial sense, to His Church.

Now as to our Lord's third office, that of king on His throne. The sayings of Scripture are quite express that we shall reign with Him for ever, that such as overcome shall sit with Him on His throne, that we are even now raised with Christ to sit with Him on God's right hand in the heavenly places. And it is the same where either prophets or apostles make mention of the whole Church as one. She is called the bride of the lamb who is King of kings, and Lord of lords. She is the queen, "the king's daughter, all glorious within" (Ps. 45:13), standing on the right hand of Him who is most mighty. To her is given that kingdom and dominion which all people, nations and languages are to own and obey for ever and before which the kingdoms of the world are to become as dust carried away by the whirlwind. Thus is the Holy Catholic Church invested with her Lord's kingly office also, anointed to it with the Holy Ghost in mystery and type at His baptism and really on the day of Pentecost, when the kingdom of heaven began.

What could the Lord have done more for His vineyard that He hath not done in it? What if, after all, when He looks that we should bring forth grapes He finds us bringing forth no better than wild grapes? The same Scriptures which instruct us so largely in the Church's privileges and our own teach also no less plainly what fruit He expects both of the Church and of us her members. The Spirit which rested upon our Lord in baptism, and then upon His whole Church at the day of Pentecost and, thirdly, on each of us individually when we were baptized and made members of Christ — this Holy Spirit the Lord declares by His prophet to be the Spirit of wisdom and understanding, the Spirit of counsel and might, the Spirit of knowledge and of the fear of the Lord. Wisdom first, and understanding: that is, as it may seem, right thoughts concerning those things both in heaven and in earth which Christian people ought to pursue and seek after. These are the first tokens of God's Spirit: a true judgment of things eternal as compared with things temporal, and of things in this world, as they may or may not be made helps towards eternal blessings. We have reason, then, to hope that we have not forfeited or thrown away the blessed Spirit of God given us at our baptism, if we find and feel that eternal things take up the chief place in our will and mind and that we are accustomed to measure other things by the hurt or good they do to our immortal souls.

Again, Christ's Spirit is a Spirit of counsel and might. He shows people the right way to obtain what they seek after, and gives them the heart, the courage and the good will to set at once about that way, however disagreeable to flesh and blood. It is a good sign as to our having the Spirit when we are ready at once to do those things which our conscience tells us ought to be done, without asking questions and without making excuses or difficulties. When we are bold to say at once to foolish irreligious friends and companions, "I *will* not go with you in sin, and there is an end of it"; when we make ourselves good rules, or what is still better, observe the good rules of the Church and keep resolutely to them; when we mind the laughter of idle people less and less, and the secret whisperings of our conscience more and more; when, having considered beforehand and made up our minds what is right to be done and strengthened ourselves with prayer and Holy Communion, we steadily deny ourselves in order to perform our good intentions, not listening to our own indolent scruples nor to the frivolous objections of men — all these are good marks of our still being possessed with the Spirit of counsel and might who was given us at our baptism.

But most especially He is the Spirit of knowledge and of the fear of the Lord. Those who have not in any degree made void His gracious influences have a sort of inward light within them — an instinct such as that by which children know their parents — which tells them at once what ought to be done, without long calculation and reasoning. And most especially He causes the fear of the Lord to be present with us. He brings it home to our hearts that God is looking on and that whatever we do must not be done at random as an account is surely taken of all: an account the result of which will no less surely be made known to men and angels when Jesus Christ comes to judge us. When we have this thought entirely rooted in our minds, and the dreadful picture of the last day filling our hearts and imaginations so that we are really afraid to sin and ashamed to be cold and lukewarm in serving God, then may we hope that the sacred Spirit of whom we were born again unto righteousness has in no wise departed from us. Then may we trust the Lord Almighty that we have still the portion which He freely gave us in His Son. Then may we, in all humility and thankfulness, endeavor to go on unto perfection without such restless, devouring anxiety as if we had still the first foundations to lay.

This is what Christ would have us be, whom He hath Himself baptized with the Holy Ghost, and what we might all be at this moment had we duly kept, according to our power, the covenant we then made with God in Him. This is what we might be, and what He gave us power to be. What we are, is another question: a most painful one for very many of us to answer, yet one which must be laid to heart and sincerely answered, as in the presence and hearing of Him whom we cannot deceive, else we shall but go on from bad to worse, and any peace and calm of mind we may now seem to enjoy will prove no better than a deceitful soul-destroying dream from which we shall awake before long to everlasting incurable shame and anguish. Let us not shrink from asking ourselves, again and again, every day of our lives, the serious questions, "Am I living as one who has been baptized with the Holy Ghost, made one with Christ, endowed with grace to be in some true sense a king, a priest, a prophet under Him? Am I wise to love heaven better than earth, strong to keep my good resolutions, full of humility and fear, as constantly remembering the last dreadful day?" Let every man's own heart make him the true answer to these most aweful questions. Let him compare what he is with what he might be. And then although, blessed be God, there is no ground for despair in any, yet surely there will be found in most of us deep reason for humiliation and penitence through the whole time of our life. Too happy, if even so we may be forgiven and saved at last!

The Holiness of God, towards Us and in Us

Volume 7, Sermon 39

TRINITY SUNDAY

"They rest not day and night, saying Holy, Holy, Holy, Lord God Almighty which was and is and is to come."

REVELATION 4:8

"They rest not day and night." It is remarkable that these are the very same words which further on in the book of Revelation are used to describe the torments of the damned: "They have no rest day nor night, who worship the beast and his image, and whosoever receiveth the mark of his name" (Rev. 14:11). As much as to say that after the sabbath of the grave is over and the body is once more awakened and joined to the soul, there shall be no more sleep for ever. The good shall never rest from their happiness nor the wicked from their torment. The one is as certain as the other.

And yet in another sense the condition of the saints in heaven is entire and perfect peace and rest, as it is written, "Great is the peace that they have who love thy law" (Ps. 119:165) and our Lord's own promise is "Peace I leave with you, my peace I give unto you" (John 14:27). Rest is their reward, and yet here we read, "They have no rest day or night." From care, from wearisome labor, from anxiety, from all pain and disquiet of mind and body they are at rest for ever, but it is not the rest of sleep or of mere inactivity; it is resting from all lower works so that they may be at leisure to think of God, to adore and praise Him, to draw nearer and nearer to Him in heart and spirit for ever. "They rest not day and night, saying Holy, Holy, Holy, Lord God Almighty which was and is and is to come."

My brethren, this is indeed too high and hard a subject for sinful mortals, swallowed up with the cares of this lower world. We cannot enter into it more than very faintly, but even the little we may understand would be enough, were we but willing, to lift our souls far above the things that we see and make us long, as the Psalmist did, for the wings of a dove that we might flee away and enter into that rest.

For consider: when it is said that those blessed spirits are for ever crying out "Holy, Holy, Holy, Lord God Almighty" none of us, of course, is so childish as to think only of the mere saying or singing the words over and over again. Of course we understand that the heart goes along with the words and that each one of the heavenly spirits, in every moment of the solemn services which they are continually performing, is evermore thinking more and more deeply on the meaning of those aweful words. The employment of happy souls, now and for evermore, is to see God and know Him and love Him more and more perfectly. "They rest not day and night": because the work they are upon is so great and high that it can never be ended, and so full of joy and comfort and refreshment that they can never tire of it. The wisdom of God — that is, God Himself — says "They that eat me shall yet be hungry, and they that drink me shall yet be thirsty," as much as to say that in heaven it is far otherwise than it is in regard to those things which most delight our frail hearts. Here we very soon come to enough of a good thing, and from enough we presently go on to too much, but of that true joy in heaven God will so make us partakers, if we do not prove unworthy, that while we feel we always have enough, yet more and more will ever be most welcome to us. In one word, the joy of the saints is in God, and therefore it has no end, for God is without end. "They rest not day and night," nor ever desire to rest from praising Him.

And what is it for which most of all they praise and honor and adore Him, and desire to draw near to Him? It is His holiness; their endless song is "Holy, Holy, Holy, Lord God Almighty." Holiness in Scripture seems to mean that perfect goodness of God whereby He is most opposite to all sin and imperfection. "God is light," says St. John, "and in Him is no darkness at all" (1 John 1:5), as if he should say "God is goodness and in Him is no evil at all." "This," the same St. John adds, "is the message which we have heard of Him, and declare unto you" (1 John 1:5). This is the great message of the

Gospel: that God will have nothing to do with sin and that He has made Himself a way, by His Son and Spirit, for freeing us His people from all sin for ever.

The joy, then, which we hope by and by to taste in God's presence is altogether a pure joy, a joy in holiness, a joy in Him who is most holy. You cannot taste it, you can have no true notion of it, as long as you give yourself up to any kind of sin. A person who had gone on for many years singing entirely out of tune would be very ill-prepared to join in any perfect harmony, and just so are we unprepared for heaven if we are living in any respect unholy lives. The chant of the angels is not for such. They could not join in it, they could not understand it, even though by some miracle they were taken up where the angels are. Oh may the good Spirit of God write this lesson deep in our hearts and save us from the madness of thinking to be ever happy without being holy!

May he teach us also to have in perpetual remembrance what he has taught us of Himself and of the great things which He has done for us, that we may love Him and serve Him and follow him — His very self and not an image of our own contriving which we vainly fancy to be like Him. For so the heavenly anthem instructs us by repeating the word "Holy" three times, no more and no less: that we might know Him who is Holy, Him whom the saints and angels are for ever praising, to be three persons yet one "Lord God Almighty, which was, and is, and is to come."

Much in the same way does the Church instruct us every year by the return of this Feast of Trinity. After we have been keeping our solemn days of remembrance of the wonders of God's mercy one by one, this day is appointed to gather them, as it were, all together, and to acknowledge Him who wrought them to be three persons in one God. We know it is His will that we should do so, for so in the beginning of our Christian life it pleased Him to reveal Himself to us, causing us to be baptized in the name of the Father and of the Son and of the Holy Ghost. And so in the crown and end of that life, when we shall see Him as He is, we are to praise Him with the word Holy thrice repeated, in acknowledgment of the same three divine persons. From beginning to end, and all along, we are to look upon Him as three in one, and each of the three infinite in holiness. And therefore, from time to time as long as we live, we must praise Him in such hymns as the Creed of St. Athanasius and the Gloria Patri at the end of the Psalms. And when we endeavor, in our weak way, to joint devoutly in such hymns, we may with humble courageous hope think of the angels who are now and ever singing them in heaven, and of the promise given to the faithful: "I will hear thee, and thou shalt praise me" (Ps. 50:15). The beginning, the middle and the end of our praise, our joy and our love must be for Him alone who is Holy, Holy, Holy, three persons, one Lord God Almighty.

Consider how in the work of our salvation each one of these three glorious persons has severally manifested His own infinite holiness, His hatred of sin and His love of all kinds of goodness. God the Father, who made us and all the world, made us pure and without spot of sin and so declared how perfectly holy He is. And when we had sinned, He again declared Himself holy by passing that fearful sentence which turned us out of Paradise, out of God's presence. And now being minded in His unspeakable mercy to forgive us, He requires no less a sacrifice than His only-begotten Son, to reconcile Him to sinners and obtain them His blessing. Alas, my brethren! What have we done? To think lightly of any known sin and to think well of ourselves after we had knowingly sinned, while yet we had learned so much of the holiness of the eternal Father — that He has prepared hell for the impenitent and will not save even the penitent but by the blood of his only Son!

Think now of the word Holy, repeated the second time, and think withal of the holiness of the only begotten Son, our Lord Jesus Christ: how pure and undefiled He was, without blemish and without spot, and how His very enemies and murderers were compelled to cry out "I find no fault in this man" (Luke 23:4). Think why He took our nature upon Him at first. It was because of His tender love towards us, joined with His entire hatred of sin. He sought to save us, but He knew and felt that our sins were so very bad that the only way for us to be forgiven would be for Him to stoop from heaven to earth, become one of us and bear our sins in His own body on the tree. So holy is He, so unchangeably set against sin, that He will dismiss those who have not repented in time and who will appear before Him at the judgment seat. He will send them away once for all — His own redeemed He will send away, if impenitent — into everlasting fire. How then can we hope to be ever in His favor so long as we permit ourselves to be entangled in any known sin?

Think, once more, of the third person of the blessed and glorious Trinity. Think, Christians, of God the Holy Ghost, the good and gracious Spirit of the Father and the Son, how He condescended, as on Pentecost, to come down and abide in men's hearts for the very express purpose that we might be able to fight the Lord's battles manfully against sin and wickedness. Think how near, how close He is to you, dwelling in the silence and solitude of your very hearts, counting your body as His temple, your members as so many limbs of Christ's own body, hating sin entirely and making you feel, when you are tempted, that He really does hate it.

Think seriously, think earnestly of this. Is it not true that when evil comes in your way you feel a certain inward whisper, deep down in your own hearts, "Why will you do this? God sees it and entirely hates it." You perceive this and you call it, perhaps, the voice of conscience, and you know that it is a very serious thing. But will you now set your heart in earnest upon this certain truth that such inward whisperings, in you who are baptized, are indeed the voice of God, not at a distance but dwelling in your own soul and body? What a horror, then, what a sin and misery it must be to go on with anything amiss, in despite of that still small voice!

And remember this also. When we say that the Holy Ghost is dwelling in Christians' hearts we do not so mean it as if the Father and Son were away. For these three persons, as the text teaches, are one "Lord God Almighty." Their works are inseparable, so that where one is there, in presence and in power, are all three, as our Lord Himself gave us to understand when He was taking leave of His disciples before His death. "If a man love me he will keep my words: and my Father will love him and we" — that is the Father and the Son — "will come unto him and make our abode with him" (John 14:23). The Father and the Son will come by the Holy Ghost to every Christian who does not throw away the blessing, and will dwell within him so that his soul and body shall be night and day full of God, a true temple of the Holy and Glorious Trinity.

Do not turn away from this thought because you cannot understand how it should be so. Do not forget it because the wonderful presence is all out of sight. Your own soul is out of sight, but yet you know very well what must become of you if you forget and neglect your own soul. In like manner be careful, I beseech you, to worship and adore the living God — the Trinity in Unity — vouchsafing to abide in your hearts. And remember that when you let your will go after anything sinful you offend and affront not God the Holy Ghost only, but God the Father likewise and God the Son, for where the Holy Ghost is there are also the Father and the Son in all their glory, love and holiness. And so, when a Christian man sins wilfully — when he tells a lie, or looks on what is forbidden — it is as if he said to the Father who made him, "depart from me, for I desire not the knowledge of thy ways" (Job 21:14). It is as if he said to the Son who redeemed him, "I will not have you to reign over me: depart from me, for what have I to do with thee?"

If this is almost too shocking to think of, what must it be to live in the habit of saying such words, in heart, to the Most High God? And yet, in heart and in meaning, we do say such words every time that we consent to what He has forbidden.

This is indeed very terrible to think of. But on the other hand what joy and gladness is it when we reflect on what Holy Scripture tells us of the presence of the Blessed Trinity in all our endeavors to do good and obey our Savior! St. Paul says "I can do all things through Christ which strengtheneth me" (Phil. 4:13), and "Not I, but Christ liveth in me; and the life which I now live in the flesh I live by the faith of the Son of God, who loved me, and gave Himself for me" (Gal. 2:20). The apostle says not this of himself only but of everyone, even the simplest believer. The prayers and alms and other good deeds, the faith and patience of such a one, are not his own but Christ's. They belong not to the man himself but to the Holy, Blessed and Glorious Trinity which has abode in him ever since his baptism. They are therefore good and acceptable before God as being the works not of corrupt human nature, but of the Holy and good Spirit of the Father and the Son. The simplest action wrought by a Christian in Christ's name with a good mind is thus turned into something very precious and holy, and will in no wise lose its reward.

I do not, of course, mean that good Christian people will themselves know when they do things in this acceptable way and so as to have a blessing laid up for them in heaven. The better they are the more they will humble themselves, and of course so much the less will they know of their own goodness. Still, however, there will generally be in the bottom of their hearts a secret indescribable peace, a calm courageousness of spirit, a deep conviction of their Lord's unfailing mercy, which will carry them through this world far happier, on the whole, than they could be any other way. And by and by, in the other world, they will find how all things have worked together for their good. They will then perceive how their constant endeavors to be indeed holy here have prepared them for the constant solemn services, the praising God in His holiness hereafter. They rest not here, but according to their measure are trying day and night to be holy. Therefore to them it will be in comparison no strange thing to find themselves hereafter wholly taken up with such anthems as that in the text, "Holy, Holy, Holy, Lord God Almighty": wholly employed in gazing on God, their Creator, Redeemer and Sanctifier, and in receiving light from His light, holiness and righteousness from His adorable perfections.

So be it, O Lord, with us Thy unworthy servants, for His sake who died to purchase the blessing for us!

• 17 •

Christian Courage

··

Volume 8, Sermon 4
Preached in 1855, during the siege of Sebastopol.

FIRST SUNDAY AFTER TRINITY

*"Only be thou strong and very courageous, that thou mayest observe
to do according to all the law which Moses my servant commanded
thee: turn not from it to the right hand nor to the left, that thou
mayest prosper whithersoever thou goest."*

JOSHUA 1:7

Who would not wish, if he might, to be brave and valiant? To be able to set
about and continue his work and win his way through the world, undisturbed by those natural tormenting fears of death and pain and bodily suffering of which we all know so much? Who does not admire those who
show by their courage and calmness in dangerous and sharp trials that
they have got over these feelings, or at least know how to keep them in order? Who does not know at once what we mean when we speak of a brave
soldier or sailor? Who does not feel a certain swelling and lifting up of his
heart when he hears or reads of venturesome deeds boldly and steadily
done?

Indeed these feelings are so natural that the chief danger concerning
them is lest we should think too much of the mere bodily courage, not unlike that of a wild beast, which many seem to have from their birth. But,
my brethren, this is not true courage, else a lion or a bull or tiger, once
made angry, would be more admirable than the bravest man. True Chris-

tian courage is just this: to fear God and His son Jesus Christ so heartily, constantly and entirely, as to be above all other fear. None of us ever can be perfect in it so long as we are in this frail body and in this imperfect world, but the grace of God may and will do very great things for us in the way of training and educating us to more and more perfection in this great virtue, if we for our part will pray and strive in earnest. And the book of God is full of noble examples, glorious patterns for young persons especially who desire to "quit them like men and be strong" (1 Cor. 16:13).

The Church of God today directs our attention to one of them: to Joshua, the great leader and captain whom the Lord raised up in the place of Moses, to conduct His people into the land of Canaan and to guide them in their long and bloody wars till God had given them the possession of it. Our attention, my brethren, has been turned of late, more than may be quite good for all of us, to thoughts of war and conquest and the kind of praise which the world gives to valiant soldiers. It is well that we should mark and learn what manner of soldiership they practiced, on whom the Great King of heaven has set His mark as approved and faithful champions in His own great cause, dutiful and loyal warriors in his own noble story. Most seasonably, then, are we invited, in the example of holy Joshua, to learn what it is to be truly brave in God's sight, and how people may train themselves to it.

And take notice, my brethren, that this is he who is set before us as the type of our Lord in His office as captain of our salvation and chief of all Christian warriors. His very name, as you know, is the name of our Lord, Jesus. As their name is one, so their offices and callings are plainly alike: the one is a shadow of the other. Joshua led the people of God over Jordan to the promised land; Jesus Christ, our forerunner, takes us through baptism into the kingdom of heaven. Joshua led the Israelites in their warfare and subdued the seven nations under them; Christ, on our behalf, overthrows the enemies of our souls and casts the wicked spirits out of us, beating down and destroying the whole body of sin. Joshua, having conquered Canaan, divided the land to the twelve tribes for an inheritance; our Lord, having conquered sin and death, ascended up on high, leading captivity captive and received gifts for men, the great unspeakable gift, the Holy Ghost, in which all other gifts are included — Jesus Christ sent Him down upon His Church with all His good and gracious blessings, dividing to every man severally as He willeth. Thus, as I said, Christ fulfilled the figure of Joshua portioning out the holy land to the holy people.

But as Joshua was a type of Christ, so was he also a type and pattern of Christ's Church and of each member of it — of each one of us in our measure. For we too have, each one of us, passed through the water into the kingdom of heaven. We too have, each one, our warfare to carry on with the Canaanites, the enemies of our souls; we are to meet them in the name of our God and Savior, to fight against them all the days of our life, to follow upon them and overtake them and not turn again till we have destroyed them.

So far we see that our work is like unto Joshua's. Outwardly, indeed, and to the eye of sense, no two things could be more different; peaceful persons as we all are in this congregation, more than half of us women and children, having to get our bread and to do our part in the quiet offices of ordinary life, who would have dreamed of our having, each one of us, an office and calling like that of a great warrior? And yet so it is: the spiritual meaning of Scripture plainly teaches it. As Joshua then had need of courage, so hath each one of us; as the savage champions, the children of Anak such as Goliath in after times, set themselves against Joshua and the children of Israel, so the evil spirits and the world and our own corrupt habits set themselves against our souls, and therefore the word which was spoken to Joshua was afterwards repeated by the Holy Ghost to us Christians, even to the feeblest, even to the most gentle; "Quit you like men, be strong, be strong and of a good courage: I will never leave thee nor forsake thee" (1 Cor. 16:13; Josh 1:5-6).

Well, now we are come back again to the question which I put just now. What is true courage? What is being truly brave in God's sight, after the example of Joshua? We learn from God's own mouth that it consists not in merely being bold and fearless in war and other bodily perils, but "be thou strong," saith the Lord, "and very courageous, that thou mayest observe to do according to all the law which Moses my servant commanded thee: turn not from it to the right hand not to the left, that thou mayest prosper whithersoever thou goest." Joshua's valor was not only shown at the time of action by his not shrinking back from the enemy nor losing his presence of mind when he found himself in danger, but it was shown much more by his resolute and steadfast obedience to the law and will of God *at all times*, come what would of it — and such must be our courage also if we would please God as Joshua did and tread in the steps of Him of whom Joshua was but a shadow.

We must not be contented with a certain natural coolness or daring which may carry us with little or no fear through seasons of bodily danger. What we must practice is *moral* courage: courage to bear being laughed at and thought ill of for His sake who for us was buffeted and crowned with thorns; courage to make good resolutions beforehand and keep them when the time comes; courage to overcome your own inward weakness and dislike of trouble and hardship; courage to get up in the morning and set about your work at once; courage to persevere in that work if you know it to be your duty, however untoward and unprosperous soever it may seem; courage to part with bad company when your soul's good and faithfulness to God requires it, however pleasant the companion may be, and however much you may have depended on him in time past; courage to bear hardness in the way of self-denial, as the New Testament teaches and all the saints have practiced; courage to break off what you are about when a plain call of piety or charity interrupts it — your prayers, for instance, or your help needed by a poor or sick person; courage to speak unpleasant truths and to bear cross and angry looks when, being in any way trusted with people, you find that they need you to tell them of their faults.

In these and a thousand other like instances, one or other of them, we are called on to exercise Christian courage — moral courage and not mere fearlessness in danger — every day, yea every hour of our lives. And the time, the season to which we are come in the Church's way of dividing the year, may put us particularly in mind of this. For now we are come to the end of the days ordained for the remembrance of the great things done and suffered for us. Christmas, Lent, Holy Week, Easter, Ascension-tide, Whitsuntide are over. All things are, in a way, done for us; it only remains for each one to go in and possess the good land — and why do any of us linger and draw back? Why, but for want of this true courage? The healing waters are cold and we will not plunge into them, so we stand on the brink, shivering.

Is it not so, my brethren? Are there none among ourselves who, in this or in other years, have with some real attention marked the meaning of the Church's great days and so have come to know more than they did of the exceeding greatness of their own calling, and it has come strongly before their minds that they ought to make the venture which their Lord requires and offer themselves to Him for the rest of their lives by the sacrifice of Holy Communion, and they have drawn back for fear of growing weary, or from apprehension of what people might say, or from shyness, or from dislike of strictness or of trouble? Some fear, in short, other than the fear of God, has kept and is keeping them back from accepting His gracious call. And what can we say of them? Not less, surely than this: that they are not yet strong, nor of a good courage, to do all that the law of Christ their Savior commandeth them. Far from *that* they dare not even go on and take possession of the good land, even when the Lord hath brought them over the waters of Jordan. What is to become of them? Can they ever, continuing such, enter into the rest and portion of their Lord? Alas, they are wanting in the first requisite of a true soldier of Joshua; they are spiritual cowards; they want courage to enter on the good part and once for all become followers of Him who goeth on conquering and to conquer. But His word is "If any man will serve me, let him *follow* me, and where I am, there shall also my servant be" (John 12:26). "Let him *follow* me: otherwise he never can be where I am." O my brethren, consider this.

But you may think, perhaps, in your heart, "Well, I know I am too weak, too fearful, too worldly, but what must I do? I cannot change my heart and become brave out of cowardly at once." True, my brethren, you cannot change your own heart, but there is one at hand who can and will change it, if you will in earnest apply to Him. Would you know how to apply to Him? Look again to Joshua's example, and as you have learned from him what is that true Christian courage in which you are so wanting, so now learn how you may be trained to it and gradually become, by God's help, brave and energetic — *morally* brave.

See what Scripture tells us of Joshua's early training and how it evidently tended to make him strong and very courageous in his duties to God. First, when quite a young man, he was with Moses on the mount; Moses took Joshua up as his minister when he went up the first time to receive the tables of the Law. Thus he must have known more of the awefulness of God's presence than any one person except for Moses himself and, being thus filled with the fear of the Lord, there was small room in his heart for any other fear. And you too, brethren, you too have been with God in the mount, at least when He took you up in His arms and blessed you in baptism; you were then brought inconceivably near to your Savior and so you were again, if you have been confirmed, at the moment of your Confirmation when the Holy and powerful Spirit came down upon you for the very purpose of making you strong and courageous in fighting the battles of the Lord. Be very sure that, if you will remember these things in faith; if you will try to think of your baptism and confirmation as the dutiful Israelites thought of their deliverance from Egypt; if you will make the most of any special opportunities afforded you for seeing God with your mind's eye; if when He gives you a good and deep thought you will value it and attend to it and turn it over in your heart and pray that you may not let it go, then you will be so far like Joshua, remembering Moses in the mount and making much of the remembrance afterwards, all his life long.

Next we read in what place Joshua spent a time of trouble. Moses had to be much out, pleading with the rebellious people and looking after them, but "his servant Joshua, the son of Nun, a young man, departed not out of the tabernacle" (Exod. 33:11). In like manner whoever would fain be a happy warrior, a true soldier of Christ, let him every day be alone with his God in prayer, let him be very diligent in going to church and very reverential and attentive while he is there. Let him persevere in these two things — thoughtful prayer and reverential church-going — and see whether the Holy Comforter will not open the windows of heaven and give him a love that will make him strong and courageous.

And now if you would know whether you are really improving in God Almighty's school, learning this hard lesson of true Christian courage, here again the history of Joshua will help you — you may see whether or not you have his tokens. Joshua, for example, was very jealous for the honor of God and of Moses the messenger of God, and when he saw some who prophesied apart from Moses he was vexed and wanted Moses to stay them, and although in the particular instance he was mistaken yet it was an honest and dutiful feeling. When you, like him, begin in a certain way, wherever you are, to keep God's watch: to be hurt and mourn in secret for other men's sins — of course never forgetting your own — when it is a real pain to you to see irreverence in God's house or hear His name taken in vain, then you too are in a way to that excellent grace and gift of Christian fortitude, and there is good hope that the Holy Ghost is making you strong and very courageous to keep all Christ's law.

By and by this spirit will be tried. It may be your duty, as it was Joshua's, to speak out and reprove with your lips some evil in your friends or companions which sorely vexes your heart. Joshua, you know, being one of the twelve who were sent to spy out the land, joined with Caleb in reproving the false report which the others agreed to bring of it; he would not follow the multitude to do evil but, in faith and charity, pleaded the Lord's cause with them.

Which of us all does not feel how good and noble, how truly courageous it was in him? Who does not wish and pray in his heart that when he too shall come to be tried in like manner, God would grant him also to be strong and very courageous in standing out against the persuasions, the bad examples, the unholy taunts and jeerings of those who think themselves brave and high-spirited because they have not learned to fear God and keep His commandments?

You all feel this — I know you do — when you give the matter a thought. You all know and feel that it is much better to be valiant on God's side than against him. Well, lift up your heart and pray to God to settle and establish this good feeling in your souls. I speak unto you, especially, young men, because, as the beloved disciple says, you are strong: your time of life is the time of strength and courage and the word of God as yet abideth in you. You have not as yet, it may be hoped, driven away God's Spirit by deadly sin. Yet you, who by nature are bravest in earthly things, are in the things of God apt to be most weak and cowardly, shrinking from plain duties and plunging into mortal sins because you are afraid of being laughed at and have not the courage to make yourselves "particular." O let it be so no longer! Set out at once and follow your heavenly Joshua. He has brought you over Jordan; He is with you in the holy land. Follow Him in faith in all His warfare with the evil one; He will reward you with a goodly heritage and protect you with the miracles of His grace. Only be strong and endure unto the end: remember that as Joshua began so he ended: the last word of his which we read is "As for me and my house, we will serve the Lord" (Josh. 24:15).

He is Almighty who hath said, "I will never leave thee nor forsake thee" (Josh. 1:5; Heb. 13:5). So that if you are but on His side you may boldly say "The Lord is my Helper: I will not fear what flesh can do unto me" (Heb. 13:6). Fear God in earnest and you need fear none besides.

· 18 ·

The True Riches

....

Volume 8, Sermon 26

NINTH SUNDAY AFTER TRINITY

"If therefore ye have not been faithful in the unrighteous mammon, who will commit to your trust the true riches? And if ye have not been faithful in that which is another man's, who shall give you that which is your own?"

LUKE 16:11-12

Supposing any great rich man in any neighborhood were to give out publicly what he intended to do with his property, how eagerly would all persons who thought themselves at all concerned come to hear about it! If they had but a chance of receiving something of it — themselves, their friends or relations — no doubt their minds would run very much upon it beforehand; they would listen as earnestly as possible when he began to make his will known and they would be very diligent in fulfilling all the conditions which he required of them in order to the receiving of his bounty. I suppose we should, of course, most of us behave in this way, to make the most of any kind purpose which a wealthy neighbor might have towards us.

Now here in the parable of the unjust steward and in the remarks of our Savior upon it He, the great Lord of heaven and earth, gives us to know what He will do with His own. The owner not only of all gold and silver but of all the treasures of the eternal and glorious kingdom plainly tells us by what rule He intends one day to dispose of these treasures. If a man desire to be rich and great, now let him listen: now let him learn how to be rich and great forever.

"If therefore ye have not been faithful in the unrighteous mammon, who will commit to your trust the true riches? And if ye have not been faithful in that which is another man's, who shall give you that which is your own?" Here are two lessons which we must thoroughly learn and practice if we would have our part of that glorious inheritance. First, we must understand that the riches and good things are but shadows or tokens or types of the true, and next we must make up our minds to consider none of them as being properly our own. What we seem to have here is neither real in itself nor are we the real owners of it. So far as it is good it is but the shadow of something better, and we are only entrusted with it for a time, for a little while. We are God's stewards and shall soon be called to give an account to the great master of the family.

Whoever will always remember these two things — that what seems desirable to him in this life is but a figure or token of a real blessing in the next and that he has but the charge of it for a year or two during the owner's pleasure — such a person will be on his guard against every wrong use of worldly goods. He will neither depend upon them nor think he may please himself with them.

But let us repeat the first of these rules as it stands in our blessed Lord's own words. "If therefore ye have not been faithful in the unrighteous mammon, who will commit to your trust the true riches?" The unrighteous mammon simply means money, possessions, property, which is called *unrighteous* because it too generally tempts men to dishonesty and wickedness. The word "unrighteous" is a kind of bad mark set by the Almighty on the very wealth itself, to hinder persons from desiring it or taking any pleasure in it for its own sake. Because we are apt to be so fond of money, He plainly tells us that it is unrighteous: it has the stain of wickedness and dishonesty upon it and, as the apostle tells us, it is the root of all evil. It is good for nothing but to be well spent and got rid of.

And when is it well spent and got rid of? When we make friends of it in heaven. When we so spend it that the holy beings there may pray for us and wait for us and be ready to receive us into their blessed company. This is being faithful in that base and unrighteous thing, money, when we lay it out as He who trusted us with it will approve. The happy and glorious consequence will be that Christ will commit to our trust the true riches.

What are the true riches which our Lord teaches us thus to set against the dishonest riches of this world? We know not yet what they are; we have only some faint notion, but we know that the Scripture everywhere speaks of them and leads us to think very much of them. Thus in the Revelation the holy city, the heavenly Jerusalem, is thus described: "The city was pure gold, like unto clear glass: and the foundations of the wall of the city were garnished with all manner of precious stones: and the twelve gates were twelve pearls, and the street of the city was pure gold, as it were transparent glass" (Rev. 21:18-21). So St. Paul speaks again and again of "the riches of the glory of the inheritance of the saints" (Eph. 1:18) and we are given to understand that the Holy of Holies in the tabernacle and Solomon's temple, which were all inlaid with gold, were but images, shadows, patterns of things in heaven, shown to Moses in the Mount and to David by the Spirit of God. The gold and silver and jewels and other like things on earth are but pictures and tokens of the real treasures; *they* abide in heaven far out of sight and beyond thought; *they* are the true riches, the others are but riches of unrighteousness — that is, to the corrupt, carnal, unrighteous mind they seem to be riches, but not to the mind that is opened to the truth of God.

And it is the same with other earthly things: with praise and honor, with pleasure and delight, such as men give their hearts to here. The love and the honor which we so earnestly seek from one another, what is it but a pattern and shadow of the love and honor which God promises good Christians from His saints and angels in the Church made perfect? A happy family here is a type of heaven, where God our Father, the Church our mother and our holy and loving brethren and sisters who have gone before or are to come after, shall one day make up one blessed and glorious company with us, accounting nothing too good, too honorable for us if we have but kept the blessing which Christ gave us when He made us members of Himself.

Again, these things which we call pleasures on earth, and which so carry away our weak hearts, what are they to the heavenly joys, the pleasures which are at God's right hand for evermore? They are nothing to be compared with them, yet it would seem that by God's merciful condescension the one are made images and shadows of the other. There is the pure river of the water of life, the tree of life with its twelve manner of fruits, the voice of harpers harping with their harps, the new song chanted continually before the throne, the sun that no more goes down, the moon that never again withdraws itself. All that here seems bright and desirable has in heaven something to answer it, only infinitely brighter and more desirable than it. As a picture stands for the living man and the shadow for the substance, so what we admire and love here stands for something there to be truly admired and loved.

On the other hand the miseries also, the shameful and tormenting accidents which our life is beset with ever since Adam sinned, are to a considerate mind, understanding the Scriptures, so many tastes and samples of God's anger: faint tokens of the anguish prepared in the other world for them that hate Him. To be tormented with fire and brimstone; to have no rest day nor night; to have poison for drink; to be torn with wild beasts and with the teeth of serpents of the dust; to be chained hand and foot in outer darkness where is weeping and gnashing of teeth; to be turned with shame from the highest room to the lowest; to be driven out for ever from the presence of Christ, the care and love of His holy angels and the brotherly kindness of His saints: these are the accounts of the portion of the wicked after they shall have completed their wickedness, dying impenitent, and all these, dreadful as they are, we know are mere shadows and parables compared with the horrible and eternal reality.

This is how Christ would have us look at things. He would have us see them as they really are; he would have us despise both the good and evil of this world in comparison with that which is to come. He would have us firmly believe that nothing is true and real which passes away so very soon: that it is all but a shadow cast before, in the way which God knows best for us — a shadow of the true riches, the true glory, the true want, the true shame and reproach which are to come.

So much our Savior teaches by what He says of the true riches and the unrighteous mammon and He adds, moreover, that none of the things here in fact belong to us. Men call themselves owners: they say commonly *my* house, *my* land, *my* money, *my* children, *my* servants, but the truth is that these all belong to another. They cannot be our own since we are not our own. We are left awhile in the midst of these shadows in order that by them God may try us, whether we are meet to receive the true blessings which are the substance of these things, much in the same way as little children are taught this and that by "making believe" as they call it.

Again, God trusts us for a while here with a little portion of that which is not our own but His, in order that by and by we, having rightly and sufficiently proved and exercised ourselves in this little, may have not the same but a great deal more, and more perfect, given us for our own and for ever in heaven, even as people give their children a little something which they may call their property — a little garden, for instance — and tell them, "now let us see how well you can manage this; do your best and by and by you may have one for your very own."

Or we may liken our own case to that of servants when their master is out of sight: that is, of course, for the far greater part of their time. Like them we have the use and handling of our heavenly Master's goods, and He expects us to be very conscientious in preserving them and improving them. If we spend them as our own we break our Lord's trust and forfeit his favor. We had need make the most of any little pleasure they may give us, for it is all we shall ever get from them: they will soon be taken from us forever and will leave nothing but a bitter taste behind. If, on the other hand, we do our best with them conscientiously because they are His, He will give them back to us and far more than they are, infinitely higher in their kind, made perfect and eternal.

Though we and all we have must ever be in God's hand, yet in some secret and wonderful way the heavenly blessings shall be our own. What we have here is not at all our own: it is strictly and properly His, to be accounted for by us, but what we shall have there will be indeed our own, our portion forever, in some sense which we cannot yet at all imagine. For indeed the great God and wonder of all will himself vouchsafe to be ours in that day, and all that is His will be truly ours, according to our measure and fitness for such a blessing. All that is Christ's will truly be the property of each one of Christ's glorified members, though as yet we cannot say how, nor perhaps shall we ever be able to do so. This is what our Lord is doing with us when He trusts us with any kind of property, and what he does we know not now, but if we be worthy we shall know hereafter.

In the meantime, let us cast aside once and forever that most unworthy and unchristian way of saying or thinking: "I will do what I will with mine own." Too many think in this way of their worldly substance, be it more or less. Rich men think they are free to please themselves with their riches, poor men think the same of their bodily health, their time, skill and strength, which are in fact their riches on earth. We are all too apt to say "It is mine own: who has any right to challenge my doing what I will with it?"

But you and I, my brethren, if we would be good and happy, must entirely leave off all such words and thoughts. We have nothing of our own in this world — how should we since we ourselves are not our own, but bought with a price? And again how should we, since the things of this world are not real things but shadows only, for a time, of great and true and eternal blessings to come? Christ's merciful purpose in teaching us these things will be accomplished if we will begin this day and go on every day of our lives to use everything as being not our own but His, and if we will every night on our knees give an account to Him of our stewardship for that day, certain as we are that the time must soon come when we shall be no longer stewards.

19

Christian Forbearance

Volume 9, Sermon 13

SEVENTEENTH SUNDAY AFTER TRINITY

"Forbearing one another in love."

EPHESIANS 4:2

There is hardly a word more thought of at present, especially among us English people, than the word "toleration." Many — very many — there are who seem to think more of that than of anything else in their judgments of others. If a man be a *tolerant* or, as it is sometimes called, a *liberal* person, plenty of people may be found to praise and admire him without asking any further; if he be supposed illiberal or intolerant nothing will make up for it: he is condemned at once.

But these two hard and disagreeable words, "illiberal" and "intolerant," as well as the words which sound most contrary to them, the pleasant words "liberal" and "tolerant," do not at all mean the same things when they are used by different persons. Liberal and tolerant are like a good many other words: they have a good meaning and a bad one. For what, in fact, is the meaning of the word "tolerant"? It signifies just this: bearing with things and persons which are or seem to be wrong. Now there is a way of doing this which is wicked and ungodly, and there is a way of doing it which is merciful and dutiful and Christian. We bear with wrong things and bad people in a wicked ungodly way when we do it so as carelessly to encourage sin and unbelief and the things which God abhors. We bear

with wrong things in a dutiful Christian way when we try to keep ourselves calm for Christ's sake, putting down the risings of anger and discontent and turning them, as well as we can, into prayer. And of course if we
be so inwardly minded we shall be gentle and considerate in all our outward behavior, making the best of things and endeavoring to do always as
we would have others do to us, in little things and in great. This is true toleration: "forbearing one another in love," the duty which the Holy Ghost
by the apostle so earnestly urges on us all in the epistle for this week — "I
therefore, the prisoner of the Lord, beseech you, that ye walk worthy of
the vocation wherewith ye are called, with all lowliness and meekness,
with long-suffering, forbearing one another in love; endeavoring to keep
the unity of the spirit in the bond of peace" (Eph. 4:1-3).

Now upon this "forbearing one another," I would observe first of all
that it is very far from being, as some might imagine, a mere point of natural temper, a part of that ordinary good-nature which all, even the worst,
practice by themselves in some degree, more or less. To take things easily
because we do not care much about them has very little, surely, to do with
patience; to let people go wrong without concerning ourselves so as to
save ourselves trouble and annoyance is the very contrary of charity. It is
more like that unhappy man who, when God asked him for his brother,
replied "I know not, am I my brother's keeper?" (Gen. 4:9). Let no man
then deceive himself and imagine that because he just lets persons alone
he is practicing such forbearance as the apostle enjoins; nor let the eager
and fretful say "I cannot forbear, I cannot bear with vexations; another
man might, but it is not in my nature nor in my way." No, let our natures
and our ways be what they may, this forbearance is a thing which God requires of us all alike as a great point of Christian duty: without it there is
no walking worthy of the vocation wherewith we are called.

St. Paul gives us plainly to understand as much. His words are, "I, the
prisoner of the Lord, beseech you, that ye walk worthy of the vocation
wherewith ye are called, with all lowliness and meekness, with long-
suffering, forbearing one another." You see our bearing with one another
was a thing extremely near the apostle's heart. He writes as a father to his
children in Christ; he seems to say "Do not add affliction to my bonds —
let me have the comfort of hearing that you are called Christians, so you
behave yourselves Christianly, and most especially that you bear with one
another's infirmities." You know our Master and Savior hath charged us
all to be like Himself, meek and lowly of heart. Now there is no lowliness,

no meekness, if men will not be forbearing towards one another. It is all very well for a man to say "Yes, I know I am a miserable sinner; I depend on nothing but Christ; I try to cast myself humbly before Him." The apostle seems to say to such a one "Well is it if you do so — it is a sure hope and we can have no other. But mind, you are but deceiving yourself in your notion of humility and lowliness towards our Lord unless you be careful also to bear and deal gently with your brethren." If you let yourself be scornful or affronted towards them, it shows you to be neither meek nor lowly.

And there is another thing, so the apostle seems to go on. Not forbearing, not bearing with one another, is as contrary to the outward peace and unity of the Church as it is to inward meekness and lowliness. Therefore, having said "forbearing one another," he goes on to say "endeavoring to keep the unity of the Spirit in the bond of peace. There is one Body and one Spirit, even as ye are called in one hope of your calling; one Lord, one faith, one Baptism, one God and Father of all, who is above all, and through all, and in you all" (Eph. 4:3-6). Thus the Holy Spirit gives us to understand that if we refuse to consider one another and make allowances we are in fact denying a great doctrine of the Christian faith, "The Holy Catholic Church, the communion of saints." And so all experience has shown and is showing every day; there would never have been heresy or schism if Christians would have been careful to bear with one another in love. But because they are discontented and fretful and will not make the best of things they are tempted, and tempt others, to separate themselves, and divisions take place in the Body, the members refusing to have the same care of one another.

There must be mutual forbearance, then, among Christians as Christians. And mark what the apostle adds further: we must forbear one another *in love*. Each is to spare his brother and enter into his feelings and make the best of him and not the worst for this simple reason: because he loves him. Not from natural sweetness only, and from what people call good-nature, nor yet because it is the best way to win people's hearts and to do the most good that we can in the world. These things are well enough as far as they go, but they do not come up to the heavenly wisdom which the Holy Spirit is teaching us when He says "forbearing one another in love." Love, Christian love, must be at the heart, otherwise the lesson of forbearance will be too hard for us. We shall never be able to learn it perfectly.

I do not mean that it will be hard to *understand*: everyone knows at once what is meant when we say "Bear with such and such a person. He is very provoking, but bear with him — bear with him for Jesus Christ's sake." We know and feel the meaning of this and the difficulty is not to understand but to practice it. Some can command themselves and be forbearing when they are tried in great things, but the ordinary temptations of life are too much for them; they would forgive one who had done them a serious wrong, but they allow themselves to be out of temper every day and every hour when they are crossed in little things. Others can bear with opponents and endure contradiction well enough on most subjects, but there are some one or two matters or pursuits on which they have set their hearts, and when anything happens in respect of these they are carried away; they lose their tempers and quite forget the law of love. Others can be kind and patient as long as they see any chance of the offending party's repentance, but if they come to despair of that they grow reckless; having in their own minds given him up, they care not how they deal with him, and, being given up, he is almost sure to grow worse and worse and be entirely lost.

Anyone, in short, who will consider for a moment, will feel that one way or another it is a very hard thing which the blessed Savior requires of us all when he says "Bear with one another": endure the folly of this man, the ignorance of that, the restless unstable ways of the other. Such a one is rude to those to whom he most owes respect; such another has mean deceitful ways and you cannot trust a word he says; a third is even base and profligate and it is your duty to keep him at a distance; yet in some sense you must bear with them all. So Holy Scripture teaches. You are not entirely to give up any one of them. You must bear with them in deed and in word as long as charity to them and others allows, and when you are forced entirely to separate from them you must still bear with them in thought, still pray for them, still endeavor to love them.

Will any man say that this is too high and too hard — that it is beyond nature and that no man can bring himself to it? The Bible will tell him that what he says is most true: steadily to bear with one another is indeed beyond nature. No man can bring himself to it. But it is not beyond grace, and the Spirit of God both can and will bring every man to it who heartily strives and prays for it. We are quite sure of this; it is our wisdom, then, and our duty, not to pass over the words of Holy Scripture as if they could not mean what they say because it seems to us impossible, but simply to set ourselves to obey them in the next instance in which we are tried. For example, when you are gone out of church, watch for the time when something shall happen to provoke and disturb you. It is sure to happen before long and when it does happen, be it small or great, remember this word "forbear" and force yourself to be gentle, force yourself to consider; even when you cannot help being angry, still force yourself to consider what will be most for the good of the provoking person. Perhaps some very sharp saying, some very cutting word, may come into your head, and you may feel as if it would be a great relief to utter it; yet conscience will tell you it will be provoking to the other and will only tend to make matters worse. You will leave it unsaid, then, and so far you will fulfil the law of Christ.

And this may happen many times a day and for many days together. The person who so tries you may be in continual intercourse with you, it may be all your life long. "What a weariness!" (Mal. 1:13). But never mind. It must not, it cannot be, too sore a trial for you if you will but sincerely use the helps which God has given. You will be able to bear with others if you will but earnestly remember how you have been borne with, and by whom. What are the histories of Holy Scripture, what the recollections of our lives, but a continual course of miraculous forbearance for love's sake? The Lord came walking in Paradise presently after Adam had sinned, "and Adam and his wife hid themselves from the presence of the Lord God amongst the trees of the garden" (Gen. 3:8). The Lord might have passed them by, and then what would have become of them and of us all? But He was forbearing; He called unto him and gave him and all of us another chance: a chance to be saved by penitence and faith in Christ when we could no longer be saved by innocence.

Think again of the history of the Jews — no end to their disobedience and rebellions. As fast as ever He gave them a commandment and showed them a favor they seemed to take pride and pleasure in slighting the favor and breaking the commandment, yet He bore with them those forty years in the wilderness, and all the time of the judges and the kings, and through the captivity, and after their return, quite down to the rejection of our Savior. And, O my brethren, think of our Lord upon earth, what contradictions of sinners He endured against Himself the whole time that He was among us: how he bore with Herod persecuting Him, and with His own townsmen scorning and trying to cast Him down headlong, and with the Pharisees plotting to bring false charges against Him and sending spies to try Him with hypocritical questionings and flatteries, and with His disciples' great inconsideration and hardness of heart, and with the selfish in-solent ways of those who followed Him not for the miracles but the loaves, and with the ingratitude of those whom He healed, and with the fickleness of the men of Jerusalem, and with the treachery of Judas, and with the mockery, the cruelty, the bitter reproach of the Cross. Remember how He bore with all this, He who, as the wise man says, might have destroyed all his enemies with "one rough word" (Wisd. 12:9). Think of Him, for in-stance, quietly remonstrating with Judas, then in the very act of betraying Him; "Judas, betrayest thou the Son of Man with a kiss?" (Luke 22:48). Think of this, and let the thought help you to be forbearing the next time you are ill-used. Whatever the ill usage be, it can be nothing in compari-son of what He had to endure. As therefore you know you ought to bear pain for the sake of His tortures on the Cross, so pray and labor that you may bear ill usage, insolence, disrespect, whatever shocks you in the be-havior of others, for the sake of His betrayal, his chains, cruel mockings and scourging.

Does it yet seem hard to you? Then remember — remember and never forget this one thing more — how very sadly, time after time, you yourself, yea every one of us in his own proper person, has tried our Lord's gracious forbearance, and still He has gone on bearing with us. He hath said to His angels of punishment, again and again, "It is enough, stay now thine hand" (2 Sam. 24:16), and here we still are, still on our trial, not yet in the place of torment, not yet cast into hell. More than that, we are still in His Church. He permits us to hear and read His Gospel, to pray to Him, to prepare our-selves by true repentance and earnest faith, and so to draw near and re-ceive His own Body and Blood in the Holy Sacrament of the Eucharist. He puts it within our reach, and along with it all the helps and instructions we could need to make us worthy partakers of it. It may be that He has from time to time chastened us; very sore and severe his chastisements may have seemed to us at the time. Want, anguish, disappointment, reproach, bereavement, sickness, desolation of spirit — at the time His hand seemed heavy upon us indeed, but now, if we have at all made the right use of His warnings, if we have heard His voice and not hardened our hearts, now we see and thankfully acknowledge the meaning of it all. Now we feel and own that in His severest dispensations He was chastening us in measure because he knew it would be our ruin if He left us wholly unpunished. When we were judged, we were "chastened in the Lord, that we should not be condemned with the world" (1 Cor. 11:32).

Thus it has been with Him and how, meanwhile, has it been with each of us? Our own consciences will answer, if we ask them sincerely; they will say to each one, "Little indeed, O man, is the good fruit which thou hast borne, overwhelming the heap of sins, errors and ignorances wherewith thou hast requited thy Savior's fatherly forbearance, and still He has gone on, all perfection as He is, and of purer eyes than to behold iniquity, still he goes on bearing with thee. And why? Just because he loves thee. He loveth thee yet with that everlasting love which caused Him to become man and die for thee: therefore with these cords of loving-kindness hath He drawn and is yet drawing thee. Only be thou willingly drawn. Refuse not to love Him who loveth thee so tenderly." And that thou mayest learn to love Him better and better, practice thyself in dealing gently for His sake with all who in any way misuse, molest or annoy thee, as the apostle describes his Lord's people in another verse, "Forbearing one another, and forgiving one another, if any man have a quarrel against any: even as Christ forgave you, so also do ye" (Col. 3:13).

20

The Law of Liberty

Volume 9, Sermon 31

TWENTY-SECOND SUNDAY AFTER TRINITY

"So speak ye, and so do, as they that shall be judged by the law of liberty."

JAMES 2:12

We all of us naturally think a good deal of freedom, liberty, having our own way, and yet I suppose that we all at the bottom of our hearts have a certain respect and regard for law and order and walking by certain rules. Thus you may observe that the same children who are most free and joyous in their play are also (if they are at all well trained) very often the most exact and orderly in their work and lessons. Thus also high-spirited youths who had seemed as if they could in no wise be kept in any kind of dutifulness or order at home are often found, if they become soldiers or sailors, careful and obedient enough in the discipline they are called on to learn.

Why is this but because, as I said, they have in them both these two instincts: a natural love of freedom and independence, and also a natural love of regularity and order? They hate to do things against their own will, and yet they like to be told what to do. How can these two minds, seeming so contrary, ever be brought into one? How can a young man longing to be free ever submit himself in good earnest, wholly and entirely to the will of another, even though that other be his Savior? We like our liberty, and we like the law; how are we to keep both in perfection? Simply, if we hold fast by the Gospel which we have received, for the Gospel is a law of liberty; those who love order will find in it order and rule and those who love their own way will find in the same Gospel perfect freedom.

I must try and make this a little plainer. In the first place, all men know that the Holy Gospel of Jesus Christ is a law, and a perfect law; it binds us one and all to our several duties, it draws a line and points to that line and says to each one of us "this is the way, walk ye in it, when ye turn to the right hand and when ye turn to the left" (Isa. 30:21) — and this not now and then at certain times when we are inclined to attend to it, but at all times, at every moment of our life. It is a law for boys and girls, a law for young men and young women, a law for the middle-aged, a law for the old and the dying. It provides for all times and also for all sorts of persons. It is a sufficient rule both in health and in sickness, in riches and poverty, in prosperity and adversity, for beginners, for persevering and steady persons, for those who have fallen and desire to be true penitents. For all these and for all others the Gospel is a law and a rule: a perfect law, a commandment holy and just and good. How should it be otherwise, seeing that it is the very same with the commandments spoken by the Most High God from Mount Sinai, and with the blessings uttered by our Lord and Savior to His disciples and the multitude on another mountain? The Gospel is the new law, the law of Christ, the most strict and exact of all laws, and yet it is called the law of liberty: it makes and keeps us perfectly free.

Mark, my brethren, that here is a rule more particular, more interfering with every part of our behavior, than any other could possibly be. It never for a moment leaves us alone; its eye is always upon us, searching and judging; whatever we think, speak or do it lays its strong hand upon us, on all the limbs of our body, all the powers of our soul, to move, stay, direct them at its will, in great matters and in small. And yet it leaves us entirely free. God's service (so saith the collect) is perfect freedom. We are sure it is so, for our Lord Himself hath told us so: "If ye continue in my word, then are ye my disciples indeed; and ye shall know the truth, and the truth shall make you free" (John 8:31-32).

Now how is this, that the strictest of all laws should be the only one which leaves them free who obey it? First, because it delivers us from a fearful bondage: the bondage and slavery of sin in which we were born, that bondage which St. Paul describes when he says "The good that I would I do not: but the evil which I would not, that I do." "I am carnal, sold (i.e. sold for a slave) under sin" (Rom. 7:19, 14). For as you all well know, such is our natural condition since the fall of Adam — that no man, left to himself, could escape being under the dominion of sin. Whatever good thoughts and feelings he might have he could never bring them to good effect; they would be at best only as the strugglings of one bound in heavy chains and quite unable to shake them off. This is the slavery in which we are born, and there is a worse slavery which we bring on ourselves by indulging our own evil passions, going on in the ways of lust, of malice, of dishonesty, of profaneness, in spite of the knowledge of God and His grace given us before we could know. There is the slavery of bad and corrupt habits, whereby men seem even forced to swear and blaspheme, to lie and deceive, to seduce others and dishonor their own bodies, in short to do all the works of the devil; a bondage such as that wicked Ahab's of whom it is written that he "sold himself to do evil in the sight of the Lord" (1 Kings 21:25).

Every child of Adam is naturally *sold under sin,* but the wilful habitual sinner has *sold himself:* he has doubly riveted and fastened his own chains. And yet ever for such a one, and much more for the ignorant heathen and for the little child who is only born in sin but never yet committed any, there is deliverance, sure deliverance, if they do not put it away from them. The blessed Gospel is sent down from heaven to be to each of them a law of liberty: to be a law which makes those who receive it free and able to practice it, which otherwise they could not be. And so it is unlike all other laws, for they tell you what is right or wrong for you to do but do not furnish you with power to hold to the right and keep from the wrong. The law of the land bids you pay your debts, but it does not provide you with money to do so. The law of Moses said "Thou shalt not commit adultery" (Exod. 20:14), but it was not accompanied with any promise or appointed means whereby people might obtain grace to subdue those evil passions which carry them away to such sins. But Christ's law, which is His Gospel, our perfect law of liberty, not only teaches us exactly to know what is sin and how we should overcome it, but also it gives us strength and power, if we will, to overcome it indeed. There is as much difference between the two as if a tired person should ask his way of two persons on the road, and one of them should only just point out the way and the other lift him and bear him safely along it. So the apostle teaches, saying, "The law made nothing perfect, but the bringing in of a better hope" — the Gospel of Christ — "did; by the which we draw nigh unto God" (Heb. 7:19) — not only learn about Him but draw nigh unto Him.

The law of Christ works this for us by uniting us to Him in Holy Baptism, whereby we receive His good Spirit and are put in a way to overcome our sins, if we will. And again, if we have fallen into grievous sin of our own, and are lying as it were on the ground like the wounded traveler whom the good Samaritan saw, and are in no wise able to lift up ourselves, then Christ's law, the blessed Gospel, comes to us not only with its gracious promises but with the gift also of penitential grace, the benefit of absolution to seal our pardon, and the strengthening and refreshing of Christ's Body and Blood to undo the accursed work of sin and make us again, please God, as free as at the moment of our Baptism. Christ's law is a law of liberty because, while it gives us a full account of our duty, it brings us also into communion with Him through whom alone we have grace and power to perform it.

And there seems to be another reason why the Gospel and law of Christ is called by this especial name — a law of liberty. For thus it is, my brethren. When a man gives himself quite entirely up to our gracious Savior it not only frees him altogether from all the sad slavery of sin, but it puts him also in a new and most blessed condition: not a better kind of slavery, as if one should change an unkind master for a kind one, all the while continuing a slave, but a free and very glorious service, much like that wherewith the angels in heaven do all their Lord's will. They cannot swerve a hair's breadth from it, either to the right hand or the left; they cannot but "fulfil His commandment and hearken unto the voice of His words" (Ps. 103:20), yet they are not slaves, for they do it all freely and willingly, it is their happiness and glory to do it. Just so is it with regenerate souls on earth; their freedom grows in proportion with their holiness. By earnest prayers and endeavors and above all by devout Communions, their hearts and wills are more and more sanctified, more and more one and the same with the heart and mind of Jesus Christ and the will of Almighty God. Angels and glorified saints are quite free because their will is quite one with God's will; we on earth are growing more and more in this true Christian liberty as the good Spirit trains us more perfectly in conforming our wills to the will of our heavenly Father.

Where among moral men, should you think, is more entire and happy freedom than in some loving and wisely ordered family, when father and mother and sons and daughters are all so thoroughly and affectionately agreed on all matters of consequence that the father's will is the will of all the rest? And this is but a faint type and image of the saints in heaven agreeing in will with their Lord and therefore being in perfect freedom. And as the younger children in such a happy family would learn that perfect agreement with their parents by submitting their own wills to them in everything while they were themselves yet children, so the saints only attained the glorious liberty of the children which they now enjoy without measure by giving up their own wills unreservedly to His will when they were here on trial.

This being so — our Gospel freedom being to have the same will as Almighty God — we may understand that in proportion as the Gospel does its work on our souls, we shall need less of positive command to do right and shall become more able and willing to act by the Spirit without waiting for the letter of a command. We shall not be so very particular in demanding to be told where in Holy Scripture such a thing is enjoined or forbidden: rather we shall take the least hint, if it be real, of what He would have us do, and try to act on it as the best chance of pleasing Him.

For instance, there is no precept in Scripture that I know of directly ordaining in so many words that Christians should forever keep Sunday as the holiest day of the week instead of Saturday, yet all sincere and reasonable Christians do so because, looking freely and fairly at the great things done for us on that day, and at the conduct of the first Christians concerning it, we cannot doubt that it was His will so to set it apart. Again, I cannot remember any text distinctly ordering all Christians to say their prayers every morning and evening, yet we all know very well that whoever wilfully neglected that service we should hardly call a Christian at all, because in that case the will of God, though not expressly written down, is so plain that no good Christian has ever doubted it. And I make no question that as people go on, and grow better and better Christians by daily endeavor, there are more and more things not expressly mentioned in the Bible which they come to perceive to be sacred duties and, doing them freely without stopping for a command, they grow as St. Paul says, more "perfect and complete in all the will of God" (Col. 4:12).

It is so, you know, in all acts and trades and works. As people come to know and understand themselves better they may be left more to themselves — that is, they may have greater liberty. That is the difference between a skilled workman, be he carpenter, mason, smith, or whatever else one may think of, and another who is unskilled. The one wants to be told every turn of the work beforehand and to be watched every moment and the other may be left in great measure to himself — left at liberty. St. Peter, for instance, in the Gospel for this day showed himself to be a beginner, and not quite acquainted yet with the spirit of Christianity, when he asked the Lord that question, "How oft shall my brother sin against me, and I forgive him? till seven times?" (Matt. 18:21). He seems to have made two mistakes which he could not have made had he known more of the perfect freedom of Christ's people under the Gospel. First, he may have imagined that *entire* unlimited forgiveness, quite passing over *any* number, ever so great, of transgressions, was out of the question for any one. He speaks as if of course there must be *some* special number of offenses after which none need be forgiven. This is one mistake; he did not know that the Holy Spirit given to the members of Christ would so entirely free them from all tendency to malice. And he made also this second mistake, that he imagined that one ought to *know* that exact number of times, like a child who is set a certain number of words to spell. How our Lord corrected him you know: "I say not unto thee, until seven times: but until seventy times seven" (Matt. 18:22): and you may partly judge what kind of words he would say to any of us, falling so often as we do into the very same kind of fault as St. Peter's.

We show ourselves every way beginners in religion, and far more inexcusable than St. Peter in that inquiry, when *we* are for narrowing our duty, as he proposed, within exact limits, as in this matter of forgiveness. Notwithstanding our Lord's words I fear nothing is more usual than for persons who have been, or think themselves, much ill-used, to say in their hearts "I will endure so much, but such and such behavior I never can and never will forgive." Our Lord made no such reserve. He died for *all* our sins. He makes not exceptions but forgives *all* when truly repented of. If we truly believe and consider this, we shall leave out no one but forgive all from the heart, and so far make known our forgiveness that the person who has wronged us may always be sure that on his truly repenting all will be blotted out.

So again in respect of the outward service of God — prayer, churchgoing, Holy Communion — there is a constant temptation to say "how often *must* I go, how many services may I miss and not sin grievously?" We are in danger of inquiring, on purpose, what is the least measure of worship and sacrifice which our God will be satisfied with. How does this agree with true love, with that feeling which would make us glad to have as much of our Lord's company as ever we can? One more: in respect of avoiding dangerous liberties, keeping far away from the sinful lusts of the flesh, many walk as if the right question for a Christian man or woman to ask were "How near may I go to the edge of mischief?" Nay, worse, "what lengths may I go in sin and yet not sin mortally?" It is as if one should say "How much may I burn myself and yet not be burned to death?"

In these and other ways men are apt to show too plainly that whatever professions they make, their hearts are not really in God's service. How is so great an evil to be mended? There is but one way. All would be right if we would seriously try to walk by love: true love of Him who loved us and washed us from our sins in His own blood. True love would set us upon earnestly seeking what would please the beloved, and courageously doing it. Would that you and I may do so for the rest of our lives, for there is no other way to heaven. "If ye love me, keep my commandments" (John 14:15) is the very law of liberty, by which we shall be judged.

· 21 ·

Entire Self-surrender and Humility, Lessons of the Incarnation

· ·

Volume 10, Sermon 20

THE ANNUNCIATION

"Hail, thou that art highly favored: the Lord is with thee: blessed are thou among women."

LUKE 1:28

Whether this day is much thought of or not, it is surely a very great day with all who believe the Gospel and the Creed: with all who believe in Jesus Christ, the only-begotten Son of God, and that He was conceived by the Holy Ghost of the Virgin Mary and was made Man. For this is the day which the Church keeps in yearly remembrance of that great thing, the greatest thing which ever happened to the children of men: how He became Incarnate and took our nature upon Him. For so it was that on this day He, the second person in the eternal Trinity, having been God always, made Himself to be man of that most blessed woman whom we honor by the name of the Virgin Mary. "Before the mountains were brought forth, or ever the earth and the world were made" He had been "God from everlasting, and world without end" (Ps. 90:2). From everlasting He had been with the Father, begotten of Him yet one with Him; one in Nature, but not the same person; the same God, yet not Himself the Father; God, begotten of God the Father; light flowing out from the source and fountain of light.

Thus had the Son been, with the Father and the Holy Ghost from all eternity, but He was never man until now. There was no beginning of His divine nature, but His human nature began on this day when He took to Himself that soul and body which the Holy Ghost, in some mysterious way, prepared for Him in the Virgin's womb. Then did the Son of God begin to be what He was not before — the Son of Man. Just then He began to be man, but never, never will He cease to be so. This is our hope and joy and crown of rejoicing: that God Himself hath vouchsafed to be of our bone and of our flesh and will be so to all eternity. So that however mean and worthless a frail child of Adam may be in himself, in this he is exalted above the angels: that he is verily and indeed and not in a way of speaking only akin to the second person in the most Holy Trinity. The poorest beggar on earth — nay, which is more wonderful, the foulest and most reprobate sinner upon the earth — is cousin, within so many degrees, to Him who sitteth on the right hand of the Father, and whom all the angels worship.

God is become Man for ever. One would think there could be no greater wonder, no surer token of exceeding love. But behold a wonder and a love yet more wonderful and loving. He is become Man that He may die for us. He could not die, His spirit could not be parted from His body, unless He had taken to Him a spirit and a body both. His wonderful and gracious Incarnation was in order to His yet more wonderful and gracious Passion. God prepared for Him a body, and in that body He came among us that He might do God's will therein: *that* will of the Father which made it requisite that He should die and suffer for us. Thus Lady-Day prepares the way for Good Friday, and in the collect for this feast we make mention, as it were, of both together; "Pour Thy grace into our hearts, that, as we have known the Incarnation of Thy Son by the message of an Angel, so by His Cross and Passion we may be brought to the glory of His Resurrection." And it is well that the day should sometimes come, as it does this year, on what is called Passion Sunday, on the fifth Sunday in Lent, at which time the Church sets herself to the more especial remembrance of the sufferings of Jesus Christ.

In a very few days we shall see Him before our eyes in a manner visibly set forth — crucified, as it were, among ourselves. We shall not think of *that* rightly unless we have used ourselves to think a good deal of that which happened today. We shall never thank our Redeemer as we ought if we bear not in mind how, from the beginning, He counted all the cost of redeeming us; how He had present to His divine Soul, even all His life long, all the pains, miseries and indignities which He afterwards permitted actually to come upon Him.

Little children, we know, are born into the world in much ignorance. They come crying among us, but it is not because they can weigh and measure beforehand the affliction and anguish they are to endure. But Christ *did* know it all beforehand: knew not only all the throbs which His cruel pains would bring upon Him, all the agony which would tear Him in pieces in the garden and on the Cross, but knew likewise how unworthily the greater part of us would receive His unspeakable mercy, how many, notwithstanding it all, would cast themselves away for ever, crucifying Him afresh, and accounting His blood unholy. For all do so who, having been partakers of Christ, live and die in grievous unrepented sin. Wherefore, my brethren, when in the Holy Week and more especially on Good Friday we are trying to lift up our minds and our hearts to the Cross, it is well that we should bear in mind the mystery of this day also, and how at His Incarnation the Most High God devoted Himself beforehand to die on the Cross.

And there is another way in which the history of the Incarnation may help us. It sets before us the example of her of whom He was incarnate, and so gives us to understand what manner of men we should strive and pray to be, that His Incarnation and death may bring us the blessing He intended. The Son of God made man and sacrificing Himself for us is indeed the only hope of each one of the children of Adam: to each one of us, if we cast Him not away, an eternal and infinite blessing. Yet it may be truly said that some are more blessed in Him than others are and surely, then, *she* is most blessed of all who from the beginning was made nearest of all to Him: His Mother, of whose substance He took that pure body, which on the Cross was to be our atonement, and in the Holy Communion our life. His Mother, who bore Him in the womb and in her arms, is by divine appointment called by the special title of Blessed, and shall be so to all generations. See then how He gifted her whom He would most highly bless, and judge what virtues we ought to practice: we to whom He has made Himself so very near by what He took of her. If His Incarnation and death are to save us at last, we must not surely be altogether unlike her, to whom in a certain sense that salvation first came.

Observe how St. Paul describes the condition of a Christian person. He says that Christ is spiritually formed in such an one, as He was really and bodily formed in His Mother's womb, and that when such an one falls away the minister of Christ has in a manner to travail in birth with him again until the likeness of Christ, given in Baptism but marred and damaged by sin, be formed anew in him. And our Lord Himself cheered His faithful disciples by proclaiming that whosoever would do His Father's will was not only His brother or sister, but even His mother. What is that likeness of our Lord which, being formed in the heart and conscience, will entitle one who is naturally a sinful creature to that highest and purest privilege of being Mother of Christ?

Firstly, such likeness of Christ must be the work of the Holy Ghost within, as the true and real body of Christ was formed by the same Spirit in the Virgin's womb. Secondly, mark well the condition upon which the holy maiden received the great promise; "Behold the handmaid of the Lord: be it unto me according to thy word" (Luke 1:38). She believed God's messenger at once and meekly gave herself up to God, rejoicing that all should be according to His gracious will although, as it may seem, she neither as yet understood the fulness of the blessing, nor could she well help feeling that severe earthly trials would come with it. So must we, beloved brethren, if all generations are to call us blessed by virtue of our near union with Jesus Christ. We too must learn the spirit of obedience; we must count ourselves His servants and His handmaidens; we must say with all our hearts, "Be it unto me according to Thy word."

As this was the condition of that most holy woman, the chief of saints, becoming the Mother of Christ, so it must be when any by Baptism receive the Lord for the first time. They must, if they be of age, promise to keep God's holy will and commandments. They must give themselves up to be Christ's soldiers and servants, His slaves, His absolute property. And so no less when that first vow has been (as alas! by too many) unhappily broken and God's image is again defaced in the heart and Christ has again to be formed there by entire repentance and amendment. Then, as at first coming to Christ, the foundation must be laid in a penitent and *obedient* heart. A person may be greatly vexed at his sin, vexed that he should have so forgotten himself, angry with his own foolish heart for so leading him astray, afraid what may come of it and ready even in some ways to punish himself for it; and yet it may not be true repentance because he may be wanting in the desire and purpose of heart to do henceforth the *whole* will of his Savior. Thus a man may be displeased with himself for carnal sins or sins of intemperance, and may really leave them off, but his sins of pride and anger may remain unconfessed and uncorrected. Then Christ, the image of his Savior within him, will not be formed again after sin has defaced it. What is wanted is that such a person should give himself *wholly* back again to his God, even as his parents gave him at his Baptism, or as the loving penitent threw herself at Christ's feet and in token of her wish to keep nothing back from Him washed them with her tears, wiped them with her hair, and anointed them with that costly ointment.

Great indeed was the difference between that sainted penitent and her who was made, as on this day, the Mother of God, and greater still the difference between the Blessed Virgin and the ordinary sort of repenting sinners among Christians. Yet still so rich and full is His mercy that we may help ourselves much in our weak endeavors by considering how it was with her in that moment of most heavenly exaltation.

One thing we may learn of her is deep reverence: a trembling, aweful sense of the presence and power of God. For we read that when the Virgin saw the glorious angel Gabriel she was troubled at his presence. The Virgin was troubled at the presence of the angel. We know that angels are present with us; why are we so careless of their presence? Yet she was pure and holy beyond what we can imagine or express and we, alas, how many things are we continually doing quite unfit for heavenly spirits to behold! If she was troubled at the greatness and wonderful nature of what he said concerning herself, what thoughts ought not we to have of God's high purposes towards us when we are told, each one of us, that He hath made us members of His Son, His own children, inheritors of His kingdom! And so much the more, as she in her humility could not well make out what manner of saying it should be, it seemed so very strange to her that *she* should be highly favored, that the Lord should be with *her* especially, blessing her above other women. One may almost suppose that she doubted whether it might not be an evil spirit, Satan transforming himself into an angel of light.

But we can have no doubt of the kind. We know for certain, from our mother the Church, whom we are made members of and what a glorious heritage He has prepared for us. We cannot doubt it; we can only cast ourselves down in awe and dread to think where God placed us, where we might have been, and where alas! we are now. Think of it again and again. We are members of Christ. He came by His Spirit in Baptism to dwell in our souls and bodies. How can we ever forget it for a single waking moment? Do you suppose that holy Mary ever forgot her Son Jesus, and how near He had brought her to God? How then can we forget our calling, our nearness to Christ, the glory of our promised inheritance?

Observe again, how simple, plain and holy is the course of the highly favored Virgin's life after she had this more than heavenly blessing. The next thing we read of her is that she goes to wait on her cousin Elizabeth, now within three months of her delivery. She minds not the long journey over the mountains; she does not say to herself, "I am to be the Mother of God's Son, Elizabeth only of His prophet; she ought rather, if she could, to wait upon me," but with all humility and charity she hastens to wait on her aged kinswoman in her travail.

And then when the holy Elizabeth, full of the Holy Ghost, congratulates her in the heavenly hymn "Blessed art thou among women, and blessed is the fruit of thy womb," Mary's answer is that other hymn, so well known among Christians, in which she seems in a manner to put away all glory from herself and to return it all to God her Savior, who by His inconceivable mercy and favor towards her had both fulfilled the prophecies to Abraham and his seed and had also shown to angels and men for ever that His will is to regard lowliness, to put down the rich, the mighty and the proud, and to exalt the poor, the meek and the humble. Here then we see another great point in which the blessed Virgin's example may help us to try our penitence. We may be sure it is insincere and unsatisfactory so far as it permits us to indulge in any proud or self-pleasing thoughts. Behold, the Mother of Jesus Christ ventures not to take anything to herself, but ascribes all the glory to God and His free graciousness. Shall we who but yesterday, perhaps, were in the pit of deadly sin, secretly praise ourselves in our hearts, perhaps even while we are on our knees before Him? O, make haste and put away such thoughts. Humble yourselves exceedingly when you find, as too often many have found, that in your very prayers, your morning and evening prayers, your thoughts go wandering about what you have done well and how highly such and such a person may be thinking of you. Be greatly ashamed of this. Humble yourselves for it before God and His holy angels. For what can be more foolish, more affronting to the all-seeing eye, than a sinner on his knees professing to be penitent, and asking pardon for many and great sins, yet inwardly praising himself, at least by comparison with others?

Finally, you know that in a very few days we shall keep the solemn time when the Mother was parted from the Son — the blessed Mary had to give up her Son Jesus. The sword passed through her soul, but there was no impatience, not a murmuring thought. Remember this when next your good Lord shall try you, whether it be in your own body or in the sickness and grief of those dear to you. Remember that Christ spared not His own body, nor His Mother's grief. Say to yourselves, "If the Mother of our Lord parted so meekly with her heavenly Son, why should I think so much of the trouble of now and then giving up some earthly good for His sake?"

Thus may the worst of sinners in their penitence follow the example of Christ's Mother in her high exaltation and secure to themselves, by His mercy, a place under her feet in heaven. May we all be of the number, by His gracious and undeserved favor!

22

The Name of God Put on Us in Our Baptism

Village Sermons on the Baptismal Service, Sermon 26

> *"The Name of the Lord is a strong tower: the righteous runneth into it and is safe."*
>
> PROVERBS 18:10

There are two names which come into the actual administration of the sacrament of Baptism: the Name of God and the name of the child. And the wonder and mystery is that these two names are in a manner made one. The child is so united to God Almighty that from thenceforth the Name of God is in a manner the child's name. Of the child's own name — that which is commonly called his Christian name — we said something in our last catechizing. Now let us go on to the other, the Most Holy Name, that Name which by an ordinance for ever is annexed to the sacrament of Baptism so that without it there can be no Baptism: the Name of the most Holy Trinity, the Father, the Son and the Holy Ghost. For such is the foundation law of the kingdom of heaven, enacted by the great king at the moment when He was just about to take Him His great power and reign. He met His disciples by special appointment in Galilee, on the same mountain, probably, where he had spoken in the hearing of the same apostles His eight Beatitudes and the rest of his divine sermon, which mountain may in some respects appear to hold the same kind of place among Christians as the mountain of Sinai among God's ancient people.

Consider Him with His apostles on the mountain in Galilee, and mark what His words are. It is the king meeting His chosen officers and giving them their instructions for nearly the last time as to how they should order the kingdom in His absence. And this is the proclamation He makes: "All power is given unto me in heaven and in earth: go ye therefore and teach all nations, baptizing them in the Name of the Father, and of the Son, and of the Holy Ghost" (Matt. 28:18-19). These are the words or form of Baptism, settled for all by Him who baptizes all. For however many and various are the persons baptized and the circumstances under which they are baptized, the real Baptizer is always one, as the forerunner said, "This is He which baptizeth with the Holy Ghost" (John 1:33), and the words used by the priest are always the same: "In the Name of the Father, and of the Son, and of the Holy Ghost."

On this sacred and mysterious Name I have first of all to observe that here is the most express acknowledgment of the faith of the Holy Trinity, ordained by our Lord Himself at the very entrance into His kingdom. No one can be a disciple of His — no one can be a Christian — without this solemn acknowledgment: that the God to whom He belongs is both One and Three: One, for it says "I baptize thee in the *Name* of the Father and of the Son and of the Holy Ghost" — not "in the Names" but "in the *Name*." There seem to be three Names, but in reality it is one Name, because the three Persons severally named are One God, and this God is our God for ever and ever. He is Three also, and therefore the three personal Names are added, the Father, the Son and the Holy Ghost; the Father, the one fountain of all good from whom in eternal unspeakable ways the other two divine persons have their being; the Son or Word of God begotten from everlasting of the Father; and the Holy Ghost proceeding from the Father and sent out by the Son or, as we acknowledge in our Communion service, "proceeding from the Father and the Son." In the one divine Name of these three Persons our Lord hath commanded us one and all to be baptized. He will have us love, trust and serve them all alike, they being so inseparable that whatever obedience, love and honor is paid to one is paid to all, although with respect to that one of them who vouchsafed to be made man for us we must have special feelings turned towards Him as He is man, doing and suffering so much for us — feelings which we cannot have as concerning those who were never incarnate. However, it is quite plain that our Lord has here put the faith and Name of the Father, the Son and the Holy Ghost at the very door of His house and kingdom, so that no one can enter in without taking that Name and that faith upon him.

Now by this we may understand, secondly, that our Lord expects each one of us to keep up and practice the same faith continually, even as the priest inquired of us when we were brought to the font, "Wilt thou be baptized in this faith?" and we answered by our godfathers and godmothers, "That is my desire." We desired to be baptized into the faith of the Father, the Son and the Holy Ghost and He graciously granted our desire. You see then how we are bound in all duty and thankfulness to go on living in that faith. What is "living *in the faith*" of such and such a doctrine? It is turning our minds to it, recollecting it continually, making very much of it in our thoughts and in all our behavior. You would not say a man lived in the faith of Christ if he never thought of Christ, never made any difference in his doings for Christ's sake and in order to please Him. So neither ought you to consider yourself as living in the faith of the Holy Trinity, unless you very often think of the Trinity and lift up your heart in prayer and praise, in love and worship, to the divine Three in One.

Are you accustomed to do so, my brethren? Do you carefully use the opportunities which the Church in her wisdom and charity gives you of acknowledging the "Holy, Blessed and Glorious Trinity, Three Persons and One God," giving glory to the Father, the Son and the Holy Ghost? You know how often she invites you to do so at the end of every psalm and canticle. Do you always endeavor to answer her invitation with all reverence and earnestness of heart? There is fear of our not doing so, and if we do not it cannot but prove a serious harm to us, for the very reason that the opportunity occurs so often. In truth, if you have not hitherto taken *special* care on this point there must have been more or less inattention and irreverence though you were far, perhaps, from meaning it, and it may have been silently hurting others as well as yourself. Let me beseech you then, brethren, henceforth always to pay special regard to the most Holy Trinity, the three Persons in one God, making some act of reverence, if not in body yet at least in mind, as often as you read, hear or speak of them. Those divine Three are ever present in all their love, wisdom and power. Whenever and however they are mentioned the mention of them is their own providential way of putting you in mind of their presence. Can you do less than notice and acknowledge it?

Certainly you cannot do less if you at all believe what I am next going to point out to you as the undoubted teaching of Holy Scripture concerning our portion in that Holy Name: that we are baptized not only *in* it but *into* it. We have the Name of the Most High God, Father, Son and Holy Ghost, so put upon us as that we shall be rightly called by it; it becomes in a manner *our name*. We are called by the divine Name as being made partakers of the divine nature. So St. Peter tells us, referring particularly to the regenerating grace of the Holy Ghost making us members of Christ, who is God, in the moment of our Baptism. But let us consider how the three sacred Names, the Names of the Father, the Son and the Holy Ghost, are each severally *our* Names — how we are in a manner called by each of them.

First, we are called from God the Father, of whom the whole family in heaven and earth is named. Being admitted into His family we take our names from Him as His children, for all children have their being and their name from their father. In Baptism we are regularly adopted to be His children, and His Name is thenceforth called upon us and the angels looking upon us think of Him and of the love which He hath towards us, just as we, meeting with any child whom a great rich person had adopted, should naturally think of that person and of the love which he had shown to that child. Can we then help saying to ourselves, "He is our Father; where is His honor? I am His child, His adopted child; how can I ever reverence and love Him enough?" Such as these ought to be our thoughts of God the Father, seeing we are called by His Name.

And then as to the second person, God the Son, we are baptized into His Name, as you all know without my telling you, in that we are by that holy Sacrament made members of Him, bone of His bone and flesh of His flesh, and as truly united to Him as a wife is joined to her husband in the holy and mysterious ordinance of matrimony. And therefore as the wife from thenceforth takes the husband's name, giving up her own, so the baptized person is thenceforth called a Christian after the Name of Jesus Christ, and of his own earthly names and connections he ought to think little in comparison, as they are indeed nothing to compare with the honor and blessing of becoming a member of Christ.

Has it been so with us, brethren? Is it so even now? We know that we are members of Christ; those who know least of their catechism can hardly be ignorant of *that* — how often in the day are we used to remember it? When we are tempted to sinful or doubtful liberties, either in thought, in word or in deed, do we regularly check ourselves with remembering, "Nay these members of mine, this heart, this tongue, these hands, this whole body and soul, are the heart, tongue and hands, the body and soul of Christ Jesus: shall I take the members of Christ Jesus and make them the members of an harlot? Shall I tell lies with the tongue of Christ, steal with the hand of Christ? God forbid." And on the other hand, do we encourage ourselves in every good word and work with the sure and certain hope, "it is not I, but the grace of Christ which is in me? I may hope for a blessing since it is not I, poor frail unworthy being, but Christ that dwelleth in me — He doeth the works?" Do we say to ourselves, "Come, let us be up and doing; let no good opportunity pass away. We have our Lord's eyes to see with, our Lord's hand to work with, the tongue of Christ to utter our words, the mind of Christ to order our thoughts. We are inexcusable if we bear no good fruit. Whoever else may be slothful, we may not." If we are really members of Christ, this is how we ought to quicken ourselves and not let our time and all our blessed opportunities pass away as in an idle dream. And this because we are baptized into God the Son, into the Name of Christ.

But, thirdly, we are also baptized into the Name of the Holy Ghost. We are the children of the Father, being members of the Son, and how are we members of the Son? By the work of the Holy Ghost. Therefore we are called regenerate, sanctified, spiritual persons — the Name of the Holy Spirit is put upon us, no less than the Name of the Father and of the Son. That blessed Comforter, uniting us to Christ, has also united us to Himself and to the Father. It is a three-fold cord: who may break it? Who shall separate us from the love of the Holy, Blessed and Glorious Trinity? From the God who made us His own, before we could think or know anything?

Here then is the saying of Solomon wonderfully accomplished, "The Name of the Lord is a strong tower; the righteous runneth unto it and is safe." We are here in an evil and trying world, encompassed with many and great dangers. Storms are in the air and may come down upon us any moment — whither shall we fly for shelter? To our earthly homes and friends? Alas, they are under the same sky as ourselves; they are subject to the same tempests; they, no less than we, may this very hour be swept away suddenly and without warning. Shall we set to work and build ourselves up a shelter, a tower, as some did of old time, whose top might reach unto heaven, a great Babylon of our own contrivance, in which we may have our own way undisturbed? We know beforehand it will all be in vain: the experience of near six thousand years has told us, and the most simple among us knows it as well and as certainly as he knows his own existence, that all such devices are in vain.

And so, when we have looked far and wide, when we have thought and dreamed all things over, we shall find but this one refuge, this one hope and shelter: the Lord God Almighty, who hath taken us to Himself, putting His own Name upon us in our Baptism. To Him let us hasten, as children run to their parents. Why should we seek any other refuge? His own saving Almighty Name, the Name of the Most Holy Trinity is ours, if we will use it, for a sure defense and strong weapon against all that our enemies can do to hurt us. To flee away to any other, neglecting this, is in reality setting up the evil one against God; it is the sin of witchcraft, so called in the Scriptures; it is trusting in names and divinations and charms. But may our trust always be in that worthy Name of the Most Holy Trinity, which we carry about us ever since our Baptism! Whatever else we use, and thankfully use, to help and comfort us for a while on the way, let us never trust in anything but in this one Holy Name, this glorious and fearful Name, the Lord our God, the Father, the Son and the Holy Ghost. Into this tower we will run, and there by His mercy we shall be safe. Only let us remember to what manner of persons this is promised. The righteous runneth into this stronghold and is safe: that is they who by sincere obedience or true repentance have kept or recovered that righteousness of Christ which He bestowed on them in their Baptism. But if you turn back to your own wickedness, to the evil works which were your own by nature, the Holy Name which should have been your salvation will turn in the end to your more dismal ruin. Preserve us, O Lord, from that worst of sin and misery.

23

The Holy Eucharist the Crown and Center of Christian Worship

Volume 11, Sermon 23
Preached before the consecration
of the new parish church at Hursley

> *"Blessed are they that do His commandments, that they may have right to the tree of life, and may enter in through the gates into the city."*

REVELATION 22:14

Here the Holy Spirit sets before us a picture. We may conceive in our minds a number of travelers approaching to the gates of the holy city, the new Jerusalem, and waiting till the gates be quite opened and they may see whether they shall be allowed to enter in. We seem to behold the city all bright and glorious, all gold and precious stones, only far brighter and more precious than anything we see on earth. The gates are so far open that those who are near enough may look in and see growing in the streets the tree of life, the immortal, never failing tree, growing by the side of the water of life, ever fresh with leaves, ever loaded with fruit, the leaves of the tree being for the healing of the nations and the fruit such that if a man put forth his hand and take thereof in due season, he shall live for ever. And no man may enter in, nor taste of this tree, but they who in earnest keep the commandments of God.

In all this, you presently see, the holy writer would have us bear in mind the account of our first father Adam, and of the Paradise from which he was driven. We seem to behold him waiting, as it were, outside the

192

gates through which he had passed in the day of his sin, anxiously looking and longing for the time when for His sake who is the true seed of the woman, he and those who had fallen through him may be admitted again to his first blessed privileges: when the angel who keeps guard at the gate will let him enter in once more and not lift up the flaming sword to repel him: when, being let in, he may go straight to the tree of life and put forth his hand and take of that tree and eat and live for ever.

This condition, which was in a manner Adam's condition just after the fall, is also in a very true sense a type of that in which we are all now living. For we are yet outside the gates of heaven. The best account that can be given of the most perfect man on earth is that he is waiting beside those gates. By and by, when our Lord shall come, the gates will be thrown wide open and then it will be seen whether we shall be admitted or not. If we are admitted we know not yet what we shall be, but thus much we know: that we shall have access to the tree of life, to the Cross of Christ and to Him that hung thereon and became the fruit of that tree for our sake. We now see Him "through a glass darkly; then" we shall behold him openly, "face to face" (1 Cor. 13:12). Now we feed on Him sacramentally, then we shall partake of Him by some far higher communion beyond what can be now imagined. And all will depend on our keeping and doing His commandments.

This is our condition in respect of heaven. It is also too much like the condition of most of us in respect of the highest Church privileges. For the Church of God is our glorious city, our heavenly Jerusalem, our Paradise, our heaven on earth. In one sense we are not waiting outside the gates of it, since we were all admitted there by Holy Baptism. But in another sense too many of us are still without in that they go not in to partake of the tree of life, the Body of Christ offered to them in Holy Communion. All would be set right if they would in earnest apply themselves to the keeping of the commandments. Blessed are they that do so, for here is God's own word saying that they and they only "have right to the tree of life, and may enter in through the" inner "gates into" the most glorious part of "the city."

Now as the vision of St. John in the book of Revelation represented all this to his inward eye, so the very frame and arrangement of a Christian church represents it to our outward eyes if we will but attentively consider it. For the church, the holy building where the Lord has come and vouchsafes to dwell, is as it were a paradise, a heaven upon earth. And the sacrament of the Holy Communion is the tree of life in the midst of that garden, seeing that in it we partake of Christ who is our life. The gates whereby sinners are admitted to this and all other divine privileges are first Holy Baptism, and afterwards our Lord's absolution: Baptism making them in the first place members of Him, and our Savior's absolution afterwards restoring that communion and fellowship when it had been interrupted by sin.

Whereas, therefore, on going into a church, we see presently that one portion of it is in a manner parted off from the rest: the portion, namely, which we call the chancel, as if there were something especially sacred about it. This signifies that the Holy Communion is the highest act of Christian religion on earth, and the presence of our Lord therein nearer and more gracious than His presence in any other way. Again, whereas Holy Baptism is as it were the wicket of entrance, the strait gate and the narrow way for admitting people into God's house, we ordinarily see the font or place of Baptism very near us at the first coming under the shadow of a church. And again, the place where the priest stands to give us our Lord's absolution after we have confessed our sins is commonly by the entrance of the chancel, to signify that in no other way but only upon the voice of our Redeemer and Judge saying to us "Thy sins be forgiven thee" (Matt. 9:2) can we be warranted in drawing near to partake of His aweful sacrifice.

We make ourselves clean and put on decent apparel to signify the marriage garment of Christian righteousness, without which whosoever cometh in is sure to be "cast into outer darkness, where is weeping and gnashing of teeth" (Matt. 8:12). We men uncover our heads to testify our deep reverence for our heavenly Lord and King into whose especial presence we are coming. But the women keep their heads covered in token of decency, modesty and submission. All, when they pray, are turned towards the chancel, for the same reason that they finish their prayers with saying "through Jesus Christ our Lord": namely that they may remind themselves continually that their prayers are nothing without faith in His aweful and merciful sacrifice. All stand up when they say the Creed, signifying that they hope to stand steadfast in that faith and continue Christ's true soldiers, and all at the same time look towards the altar, because the very chief point of that faith is to believe on Christ crucified, and He has ordained the sacrament of the Lord's Supper to be a continual remembrance of that sacrifice. One might keep on a long while explaining in like manner other parts and other circumstances of divine service, and one should find concerning one and all of them that they agree in pointing out to us the Holy Communion as the very greatest and holiest of all things that are done in the church. The very outward look and sound of things, all that we see and hear around us, seems to say that without attendance on the holy altar all is incomplete, and that if we do but rightly attend there all else is sure to go right.

The tree of life, planted within the city, is that one blessing which comprehends all others and for the sake of which chiefly we are invited to enter in at all. Blessed are they that have a right to it; they, and they only, may enter in through the gates of that eternal city of which these our visible churches are no more than signs and tokens. Blessed are they that come worthily to the holy altar; they, and they only, have the full promise of eternal life. Any person who entered into that first Paradise which the Lord planted for Adam in Eden would no doubt first be caught by the tree of life in the midst of the garden. We may suppose, by what is written in Genesis, that all eyes would be drawn towards that one tree; all the rest, how fair and noble soever, would seem to be gathered around it and to wait upon it. Not otherwise, on entering into a church, is the eye and heart of a believer drawn towards that one place where He who is the fruit of the true Tree of Life gives us His Body to be our meat indeed, and His Blood to be our drink indeed. The whole church looks, as it were, towards the chancel and the altar table: not for any holiness that naturally is in that place more than the rest, but for His sake who vouchsafes to be there with us continually, offering the remembrance of His most precious death and feeding us with what He offers.

My brethren, attend to this, I beseech you. The whole church looks to the altar, and shall not we, the worshipers, do the same? Observe what the Holy Ghost tells us of the rules and orders of the Christian paradise. "Blessed are they that do His commandments; *they* have a right to the Tree of Life; *they* may enter in through the gates." Does it not plainly appear that entering into the city through the gates is only in order to the tree of life? That it is vain and dangerous for any man to depend upon his Baptism, his faith, his good character, or anything else as a mark of his being within the city, while he wilfully neglects this sacrament? Surely there can be no doubt of it. Partaking of Christ must be all in all to a Christian. And how can you partake of Him if you slight and pass over that way of doing so which He specially ordained?

It is very true that not all persons calling themselves Christians have a right to this tree of life. Too many, alas! are leading such lives that even if they were heathen and unbaptized we could not ask them so much as to receive Baptism without first making a great change in their goings on. They are not fit as yet to enter through the gates; neither then, being in the city, are they fit to eat of the tree of life. It would be mere profaneness; it would do them more harm than good. I speak not to such but to all others, whether innocents or penitents. I say, "Come near, eat and live, your Savior invites you to eat bread with Him": "O taste and see how gracious the Lord is," "Come eat of His bread, and drink of the wine which He hath mingled," "Come, buy wine and milk without money and without price" (Ps. 34:8; Prov. 9:5; Isa. 55:1).

Some of us, I fear, are apt to regard these many gracious invitations of our Lord as if they related to something over and above the common way of salvation — to a sort of spiritual enjoyment, not at all to the very substance and necessary being of a Christian's life. Some of us are used to look on this sacrament as a kind of thing which does many a great deal of good but which they themselves may very well do without. I would they would consider it seriously over again. Christ says "You *may* come": none of you can deny *that*. But you think He does not say "You *must* come." But surely, where there is true love and dutifulness, there is no difference between *may* and *must*. If a father say to his son, "Now you may come near, my child, and receive my blessing," and the child were to disregard it, saying in his heart, "He does not say 'You *must* come'" could you look upon such a one as on a good and obedient child? Nay, good Christians, you may be quite sure that if Christ says "You *may* come" then you *must* and *ought* to come; for love and gratitude's sake, and for your soul's good, you *ought* to come, though it be a great undertaking and though there be more or less of doubt and danger and jeopardy in it.

For love's sake you ought to come, and for fear's sake also: for how can you live without it? As you cannot live the life of this world without constant supplies of meat and drink, so neither can you live the spiritual and heavenly life without constant supplies of the Body and Blood of Christ. You have heard His words over and over; many of your children know them by heart. I will now say them to you once again: "Except ye eat the flesh of the Son of Man, and drink His blood, ye have no life in you" (John 6:53). Are you not afraid when you hear this, as many as have hitherto neglected Holy Communion? Is it not alarming when you consider how fast the time is passing, and as yet you have only had good imaginations and half purposes to come; as yet the holy meal is untasted of by you; as yet you will not come to Christ that you may have life.

I have no doubt there are many among those who are not yet communicants who really intend and wish to become so ere long. They hear these warnings from time to time; they see their neighbors draw near while they turn their backs; they feel — they cannot but feel — that the days, months, years are passing faster and faster away and they have not yet come to Christ that they might have life. Their parents brought them when they were children but they have never yet come of their own accord. I make no question but there are many who feel this and really intend to begin, or to renew the good custom if left off, some time or other. I say to them all, why not begin now? Why not take occasion, from the solemn opening of this new church of ours, to set in order the things that are wanting, and thoroughly prepare to meet your God? It is something out of the common; depend upon it, our merciful God intends it in His fatherly providence as one call more upon you to consider your ways. The Bishop's coming, were that all, is a great thing: for the Bishop stands, as you know, in the place of our Lord and Savior — his coming is a true token of our Lord's coming, his presence in Holy Communion a token of our Lord's most sure and certain presence with us.

Again, when you enter our new church, you will see with your eyes many things which will draw your hearts towards Holy Communion. All, you will perceive, points eastward, because there God's altar is set. The chancel is fitted up more carefully and beautifully than the other parts of the church, because there especially Christ comes to give us Himself. These very words on which I have been speaking to you are engraven on the step which leads from the body of the church to the chancel — I mean the words, "Blessed are they that do His commandments, that they may have right to the tree of life, and may enter in through the gates into the city." These things, and whatever else we may see and hear which may put us in mind of the greatness of Christ's last sacrament, I would we might all take as so many calls from Him who we trust will be there. They are calls uttered to every one of us. To those who are yet in their sins, they say "Behold here what I suffered for you, see here the remembrance of my Cross: can you have the heart to go on, rejecting me and ruining yourselves for ever?" To those who are trying in earnest to repent, Christ will speak from our chancel and say, "Blessed are they that mourn, for they shall be comforted" (Matt. 5:4). To those who have kept their hearts pure, or are trying in earnest to purify them, He will say, "Blessed are the pure in heart for they shall see God" (Matt. 5:8), and to all, both bad and good, who seek Him, earnestly desiring to be made better than they are, He will say, "Blessed are they that do hunger and thirst after righteousness: for they shall be filled" (Matt. 5:6).

One call especially Christ utters to us all *today,* which I am sure we must all feel in our hearts to be a very grave and serious call indeed: I mean the notice which you just now heard that in the new church it is hoped by God's blessing to celebrate the Holy Communion every week. I have thought it right to give this notice but I could wish to do it in much fear and trembling, for it is a very great undertaking, surely, and requires on the part of those who make use of it more earnest care of their souls than ever. To those who truly endeavor to prepare themselves it will, I trust, be a real step towards heaven. But we must all beware of growing weary in well doing: we must all watch and pray more earnestly than ever against that most frightful danger, which frequent Communion of course brings with it, of feeding ourselves without fear.

And let us all pray for one another, that our weak endeavors to serve and honor our Lord most especially in His Holy Communion may be accepted in Him who is all and in all, our many and most grievous sins pardoned, and our few remaining days so ordered that our very prayers and churches and Sacraments may not hereafter rise in judgment against us and condemn us.

• 24 •

The Church Apostolic

Volume 6, Sermon 18

"Stand thou here by me, and I will speak unto thee all the command-ments."

DEUTERONOMY 5:31

This verse is a figure of what should be God's way of dealing with us in the Christian Church. He was to be the one teacher and governor in it, yet He was to teach and govern by certain whom He would choose. Accordingly we find that as the first word in the Creed concerning the Church is "One" and the second "Catholic," so the third word is "Apostolic."

It is One because our Savior is One, Catholic, because He is the Savior of all men. Why, and in what respects, is it Apostolic? The meaning of the word is, as you know, something belonging to the Apostles. And who are the Apostles? Messengers of Christ: persons sent by Him with a special commission to say and do certain things in His name. And the things they were appointed to do are the very things by which we are, one by one, united to Christ and kept in union and communion with Him, so that if one would be reasonably sure of belonging to Christ and being in a rea-sonable way to be saved by Him, he must have a reasonable hope that he is in that company and brotherhood which began in the holy Apostles on the day of Pentecost and that he continues, as did those first Christians, in the Apostles' fellowship.

And of this, by God's special mercy, we may be reasonably sure, each one for himself. We are not to doubt, but earnestly to believe it. For, first of all, we know quite for certain who the Apostles were, how and when appointed, and with what message, on what errand, Christ sent them. That there might be no doubt, their names are set down in three out of the four Gospels and in the Acts of the Apostles. They were ordained by our Lord Himself under the title of Apostles, after a night spent in prayer, and had a solemn charge given to them. They were in such constant attendance on Him that there could be no mistaking who they were; all that had knowledge of Jesus Himself might take knowledge of them, that they had been with Jesus. They were twelve in number to answer to the twelve tribes of Israel, whereby we may understand that in them was gathered up, as it were, the whole people of God, His new Israel, to be entrusted with His new law. They were to be sort of twelve patriarchs, like the twelve sons of Jacob, through whom the special blessings of God were to be conveyed to His spiritual children through all ages and in all lands.

Nothing could be plainer than that they are God's messengers, nothing greater or more solemn than their message. It was, in a word, to be as Christ in the world. So it was delivered to them the very first time they saw our Lord after His Resurrection. "As my Father hath sent me, even so I send you" (John 20:21). His Father had sent Him to be Prophet, Priest and King over his people, and now He sends His Apostles in like manner. They too were in their measure to do the work of prophets, priests and kings in the Church. They were to be prophets because the Holy Ghost should come and guide them into all truth. They were to be priests because He said to them "Do all this in remembrance of me" (Luke 22:19) — that is, "Make the bread and wine Christ's Body and Blood as I have now done, and offer it to the Father in union with the perpetual memorial of my death, which I shall be offering to Him in heaven." They were to be kings — lawgivers and judges in the Church — because He said "I appoint unto you a kingdom, as my Father hath appointed unto me" (Luke 22:29) and "When the Son of Man shall sit in the throne of His glory, ye also shall sit upon twelve thrones, judging the twelve tribes of Israel" (Matt. 19:28), and "I will give unto thee the keys of the kingdom of heaven, and whatsoever thou shalt bind on earth shall be bound in heaven, and whatsoever thou shalt loose on earth shall be loosed in heaven" (Matt. 16:19), and "Whose soever sins ye remit, they are remitted unto them, and whose soever sins ye retain, they are retained" (John 20:23). And once for all He gave the word to St. Peter, and through him to all the rest, "Feed my sheep," and "Feed my lambs" (John 21:15-17).

Thus you see the whole Church and all matters relating to it were entrusted to the Apostles, and that all the rest might obey them it was said "He that heareth you heareth me, and he that despiseth you despiseth me" (Luke 10:16) or as St. John said long afterwards, "we are of God: he that knoweth God heareth us; he that is not of God heareth not us" (1 John 4:6). The Apostles therefore were kings to rule the Church, as well as priests to offer up its spiritual sacrifices and prophets to teach its doctrines.

It is true that in a certain sense all Christians are kings and priests and all the Lord's people are prophets. St. Peter says, He hath made us "a royal priesthood, an holy nation, a peculiar people" (1 Pet. 2:9) and St. John says He hath "loved us, and washed us from our sins in His own blood, and hath made us kings and priests unto God and His Father" (Rev. 1:5-6), and Isaiah says "all thy children shall be taught of the Lord" (Isa. 54:13).

Yes, brethren, we are all kings and priests because we are all members of Him who is the true King and Priest. We are kings to rule over our own wild passions and fancies; we are priests to offer ourselves, our souls and bodies, a living sacrifice to God, and to join in offering the Church's perpetual sacrifice which is her Lord's Body and Blood. But this hinders not but that there should be among us an especial order of men whose business it is to govern the Church in His name and to offer up to His Father His appointed memorials: to bless us and to intercede for us. The Jewish people were called by the Lord on Mount Sinai, "a kingdom of priests and a holy nation" (Exod. 19:6), yet they had special kings, as David, and priests, as Aaron, on whose office no one might intrude. As St. Paul, speaking of the priest's office, says to the Hebrews, "No man taketh this honor unto himself, but he that is called of God, as was Aaron" (Heb. 5:4). And we know what fearful things happened to Korah and his company, who set themselves up as if they might be priests as well as Aaron. The fire came out from the Lord and consumed them, and as for those who took part with them the earth opened her mouth and swallowed them up. Yet the word which they spoke was in itself true: "All the congregation are holy, every one of them, and the Lord is among them" (Num. 16:3). But they would not receive what God had so plainly taught them, that His will nevertheless was to have certain special priests among them, Aaron and his family, who alone might offer incense. The whole Church, both Jewish and Christian, were to be priests, yet the outward work of priests was always to be done by persons especially ordained for it. Much in the same way as the whole of a man sees and hears things, but sees them only with his eyes and hears them only with his ears, so the whole Church sacrifices and blesses, but it is only through her priests; the whole Church confirms and ordains, but it is only through her Bishops.

I say through her Bishops, for this is the way in which the present Church may be truly called Apostolic; this is how it has fellowship with the Apostles, though the last of them has now been dead more than seventeen hundred and fifty years. The Bishops stand in their place. For example, before St. Paul died, he laid his hands on Timothy to make him Bishop of Ephesus, and on Titus to make him Bishop of Crete, and so in other places he and other Apostles did the like. And these persons, so made Bishops, stood in the place of the Apostles and had power to do what they did: to confirm, ordain priests, consecrate other Bishops, govern the churches, be judges in all Church matters. And they, before they died, laid hands upon others to be Bishops when they should be gone, and they upon others quite down to our time, and so the providence of God has kept up a constant chain or succession of Bishops, of persons coming in the place of the Apostles ever since St. Peter's time and St. Paul's, just as the same providence has kept up the succession of the plants and animals after their kind from the day in which they were first created, and just as it kept up the chain or succession of Jewish priests in the family of Aaron. Only that succession was kept up in the way of natural birth, and this by the laying on of hands. No man might be a priest from among the Jews unless he could make out his descent from Aaron; no man may be a priest or Bishop among Christians unless he can show that he was ordained by one who, by laying on of hands, had inherited from the Holy Apostles authority to ordain.

Thus each new generation of Christians may be called in some sense the spiritual parents of the next generation as Aaron was the natural parent of all the Jewish priests. Where such Bishops are, maintaining entire Christ's holy Creed, there is Christ's Church and there is Christ Himself: and well is it for those who, by God's great and distinguishing mercy, are members, perhaps hardly knowing it themselves, of such a Body as this. They must not doubt but earnestly believe that theirs is a portion of the One Holy Church Universal, and if they do not put themselves out by their sins, assuredly they are very members ingrafted into the mystical Body of Christ, which is the blessed company of God's faithful people, and are also heirs through hope of His everlasting kingdom, by the merits of the most precious death and Passion of His dear Son.

Now this, my brethren, is the privilege of each one of us. For the Church of England, that portion of the Church to which we, by God's mercy, belong, is as surely as any in the world tied to the Apostles by the Bishops. We in this village, for instance, have our Bishop, the Bishop of Winchester, and we can trace up each link in the chain of his succession quite back to the time of the Apostles, just as certainly as we can trace the natural descent of our Queen Victoria from the old kings and queens of England. We have a Bishop, and in many ways the good providence of God is from time to time showing us how we are tied to him, and through him to the Apostles and Christ Himself. Most of you may remember his coming here when this Church was newly built and fitted up, to bless and consecrate it in the name of Jesus Christ. Why? Because it was always held right in the Church that places as well as persons, churches as well as clergymen, should not be set apart to God's special service without a solemn dedication and blessing from one of those who are as God's high priests among men. The Bishop's blessing on that day was the sign and token of Jesus Christ coming to dwell in His temple.

Again, we remember more than once the Bishop coming here to confirm; we remember, the greater part of us, each one his own confirmation. Now, what a recollection is that, would we but in earnest apply our minds to it and think of it as it really was! We saw indeed but the venerable presence of an earthly father and high priest; we felt but his hand overshadowing us when we were on our knees before him. But faith, my brethren, true Christian faith, if it was then living and working in our hearts, caused us to see with our mind's eye something far greater and more blessed: Jesus Christ invisibly present, for to our Bishop as well as to all our Bishops His promise was given "I am with you always even unto the end of the world" (Matt. 28:20). He was present therefore with the Bishop confirming us as He had been with the priest or deacon taking us up in his arms at our christening. With the eye of faith, if we were not faithless but believing, we then saw approaching to us, as we knelt, the great shepherd and Bishop of our souls; His own divine, blessed, loving right hand we felt laid upon our head, and it was strength and comfort and effectual help to us, and has been ever since, in our hard fight against the world, the flesh and the devil.

Thus I am sure it has been, in a greater or lesser degree, with all among us who came to be confirmed in faith. They were aware of their Savior drawing very near them, and whether we knew it or not, my brethren, be sure of it, there He was, for it is His promise to His One Catholic and Apostolic Church to be with His Apostles and their successors when they bless in His name. And this very year we may expect him. In a few months time, please God, the Bishop will be here, and his and our unseen Master will be with him, to the blessing, strengthening and refreshing of those who shall kneel before him with devout and dutiful hearts, and to the shame, condemnation and great loss of the careless, irreverent and unbelieving. And surely our hearts — the hearts, I mean, of those who have already been confirmed — must be very hard and cold if we are not moved by the thought of Jesus Christ so coming among us, to serious consideration how it was with us when we knelt before Him to be blessed and how it has been with us ever since.

But we need not wait for such rare occasions as a church consecration or a confirmation to be put in mind how great a thing it is for us that this our Holy Church is Apostolic. For in truth we are, if we would consider, put in mind of it whenever we come in the way of a clergyman, an ordained minister of Christ. Every clergyman as such, every priest or deacon saying prayers, or preaching in church, or visiting the sick, or administering either of the Sacraments, or privately reproving or comforting or instructing any in Christ's name, he too is a living and moving token of our Lord's Presence. For from some one of the Bishops, the Apostles' successors, he received a call to do these things and by virtue of our Lord's promise to His Apostles he goes about doing them and his doings are indeed a most serious concern, both to himself and others, for the Lord who is with him is both to him and his flock either a savor of death unto death or else a savor of life unto life. Where Christ takes part, the matter cannot be indifferent nor safely put by as of small consequence. God give us grace to consider well both what we say and do and how we say it and do it, that His coming among us by His ministers continually may be for joy and not for grief.

Depend upon it, the presence of Christ's clergy is one of our chiefest spiritual blessings: not outwardly only, not for peace and order only, but inwardly and spiritually a true token to faithful men of our exceeding nearness to Christ. Surely we have need to go about, as the Israelites ought to have done in the desert, in fear and trembling, in awe and veneration, feeling that the glory of God is all around us and might break out at any moment. Christ risen and especially present among His ministers, how can we remember Him but with fear and great joy? And if we are used to such thoughts in our dealings with the minsters of Christ, it will help us to be very dutiful in the other parts of our behavior. And He will graciously fulfil in us what He promised to His ancient elect people when they were on their way in the wilderness: "My presence shall go with thee and I will give thee rest" (Exod. 33:14).

Index of Scripture References

References in bold type refer to the primary texts of sermons.

206